D0208070

WIKIPEDIA

The herald does not exclude from the platform even the man who earns his daily bread by working at a trade; nay, these men he most heartily welcomes, and for this reason he repeats again and again the invitation, 'Who wishes to address the assembly?'

Aeschines of Athens

My plan is to do something never before attempted. Our Encyclopedia will be not only the best work of its kind, but the greatest collaborative intellectual enterprise in the history of man, a synthesis of the French genius, the monument of our century.

Diderot to the printer, Le Breton

The online encyclopaedia was a simple brilliant idea, the latest flowering of the Enlightenment ideal of the collective pursuit of truth. By pooling our collective knowledge, gradually weeding out the mistakes and the myths, we would arrive at a 'repository of knowledge to rival the ancient library of Alexandria', a fantastic, free experiment in intellectual democracy.

Ben MacIntyre, The Times

Is it an encyclopaedia? Yeah, it's an encyclopaedia. Is it very accurate? I wouldn't bet my bottom dollar on anything in there. Do I use it? I use it all the time. I use it constantly, and sometimes I find stuff on there that's very funny. But I try to check it. I'm not making any investments on the basis of what I find on Wikipedia. No way, man. I'm calling my broker! I pay that guy.

Marshall Poe

Wikipedia

A New Community of Practice?

DAN O'SULLIVAN

ASHGATE

Published by
Ashgate Publishing Limited
Wey Court East
Union Road
Farnham
Surrey, GU9 7PT
England

Ashgate Publishing Company
Suite 420
101 Cherry Street
Burlington
VT 05401-4405
USA

www.ashgate.com

British Library Cataloguing in Publication Data
O'Sullivan, Dan.
   Wikipedia : a new community of practice?.
   1. Wikipedia. 2. Electronic encyclopedias--History. 3. User-
   generated content.
   I. Title
   030.2'85-dc22

Library of Congress Cataloging-in-Publication Data
O'Sullivan, Dan.
   Wikipedia : a new community of practice? / by Dan O'Sullivan.
      p. cm.
   Includes index.
   ISBN 978-0-7546-7433-7
   1. Wikipedia. 2. Communities of practice--Case studies. 3. Communication in learning
and scholarship. I. Title.

   AE100.O88 2009
   030--dc22

2009017572

ISBN 9780754674337 (hbk)
ISBN 9780754691938 (ebk)

Mixed Sources
Product group from well-managed
forests and other controlled sources
www.fsc.org Cert no. SA-COC-1565
FSC © 1996 Forest Stewardship Council

Printed and bound in Great Britain by
MPG Books Group, UK

Contents

PART III   USING WIKIPEDIA

Preface

These days we look to Wikipedia for the truth. A neat illustration of this occurred not long before I sent up the manuscript of this book to the publishers. Apparently Gordon Brown had claimed in a speech that he had much in common with the artist Titian, who did his best work in his dotage and reached the age of 90. A few days later, at 12.34 p.m. on 12 February 2009, someone at Conservative Central Office altered the Wikipedia article on Titian so as to reduce his age at death. This allowed David Cameron to go on the offensive at prime minister's question time the same day. 'The prime minister never gets his facts right,' said Cameron. 'You told us the other day you were like Titian aged 90. The fact is Titian died at 86.'

Two simple, yet potentially significant, propositions lie behind the themes of this book. The first, which I suppose as a historian I have always had in the back of my mind, is that the new – novel institutions, original ideas – usually turns out to be a lot older than we thought. The second, to which I have more recently come, is that, in cultural matters at least, working with one's peers can get one further than trying to go it alone. I attempt here to illustrate and combine these two points of view by looking at certain historical group projects, and comparing them with another project that was born in the present century – Wikipedia.

What sparked off my interest in these particular 'communities of practice' in history and on the Internet was the fact that I have myself for several years been a member of just such a community. In our village there is a flourishing archaeology/local history group whose members share the fruits of their efforts and collaborate in joint publications much as wikipedians do, though admittedly the international dimension is somewhat lacking. Recently we too have set up a 'wiki' site, <www.greatayton.wikidot.com>, to which anyone in the group may make a contribution. From these experiences it has been brought home to me that sharing and participation, while immensely enjoyable in themselves, are also just as efficient and productive a way to operate as is the more usual path of the solitary researcher.

I want to thank Simon and Tom O'Sullivan and Janus Olsen for reading drafts of the book and making numerous useful suggestions. I should also like to thank my wife Hazel for her patience and moral support during the writing of it.

Dan O'Sullivan
Great Ayton, 2009

Introduction

This is a book about Wikipedia, the wildly successful online encyclopaedia, and about wikipedians, the community responsible for it. Wikipedia may be successful in terms of its size and the numbers who consult it, but it is also alien to our cultural traditions in several ways. In the first place it is operated on the whole by ordinary people rather than academics or professional writers, whereas we live in a society in which the authority to pronounce on matters of fact of any complexity is regarded as the province of experts. Secondly, Wikipedia is non-proprietary and free of use, whereas we tend to measure any large enterprise in financial terms. And thirdly, it is run by a group, and an anonymous one at that.

The narrative models available for describing the lives of groups are generally lacking in our culture. We are addicted to heroes, and the myth of rugged individualism strikes a powerful chord in the Western psyche, aided and abetted by a consumer society that operates on the basis of atomized (and often alienated) individuals. In both history and literature the individual has always taken precedence, and groups have had short shrift. Nor is anonymity much favoured in the media. It is remarkable that whenever journalists have to file copy about Wikipedia, their first instinct is to get behind the curtain and find someone willing to discuss their motives for contributing to the project. As Michel Foucault has pointed out, if a text today should be discovered in a state of anonymity, the game becomes one of rediscovering the author. The 'author function', as literary regulator, plays a role characteristic of our era of individualism and private property.[1]

Before starting on Wikipedia, I take a brief look at some other communities of practice that might be understood in some sense as its precursors. Enthusiasts for the large-scale social projects which the technology of the Internet makes possible today have tended to exaggerate the obstacles confronting any kind of similar group activity in the past. About the pre-Internet era, Clay Shirky, a journalist and academic specializing in the Internet, writes: 'Our basic human desires and talents for group effort are stymied by the complexities of group action at every turn. Coordination, organization, even communication in groups is hard and gets harder as the group grows.'[2] And Don Tapscott, another internet luminary, argues that throughout history hierarchies of one sort or another have been the primary

---

1   Michel Foucault (1969), 'What is an author?', *The Foucault Reader*, ed. Paul Rabinow (1991), London: Penguin Books, 109, 119.

2   Clay Shirky (2008), *Here Comes Everybody: The Power of Organizing without Organizations*, London: Allen Lane, 45.

engines of wealth creation and, by implication, of cultural progress.[3] It is, of course, quite true that the Internet makes all kinds of mass and group collaboration far easier than before, but this is not to say that earlier, non-hierarchical groups did not achieve great things, in spite of the obstacles mentioned by Shirky.

I have chosen five historical groups or communities, all of which had ambitions to make an impact on the society of their time, whether in social, cultural or political terms. More than that, they all, like Wikipedia, aimed to produce what one might term non-linear texts or textual systems. A linear text involves a narrative – something intended to be read from start to finish. Plays, novels and biographies obviously come into this category, as do factual monographs. Non-linear texts, however, are treated quite differently. Their readers pick out the parts they are interested in and ignore the rest. Examples are dictionaries, encyclopaedias and all works of reference, but also libraries and library catalogues, academic journals and in fact any collection of books or articles viewed as a whole.[4] As Stanley Baldwin said when celebrating the publication of the *Oxford English Dictionary* in 1928: 'It is a work of endless fascination. It is true that I have not read it – perhaps I never shall – but that does not mean that I do not often go to it'.[5] Non-linear texts use various means of cataloguing and indexing, such as alphabetizing or the Dewey Decimal system, to enable readers to penetrate or browse their depositories of information. The most recent and by far the most efficient such system is, of course, the hyperlinking on which the entire Internet is based, and which is one of the most obvious features of Wikipedia.[6]

These groups were chosen deliberately to be as different from each other as possible, but also to illustrate the fact that elements of the Wikipedia project were anticipated long before the Internet. Each of the five possesses at least one further feature in common with Wikipedia. The Alexandria library aimed to amass in one place the knowledge of the known world; those who initiated the Royal Society were amateurs who spread their message without any commercial motivation; Diderot's encyclopaedia sought to disseminate relevant and useful information; the editors of the *Oxford English Dictionary* employed an army of unpaid volunteers; the missionary zeal of the founders of the Left Book Club inspired their membership.

As has no doubt often been pointed out, our future is forged from our past. My focus, therefore, is not merely on these particular groups, but also, firstly, on whether it might be possible to devise ways of describing groups, or social movements, in general, and secondly, whether such principles might also apply to

---

3   Don Tapscott and Anthony D. Williams (2007), *Wikinomics: How Mass Collaboration Changes Everything*, London: Atlantic Books, 23, 31.

4   Admittedly, the particular element, the book or article, chosen by a reader from a collection may require a linear treatment, but the collection as a whole is non-linear.

5   Quoted in Simon Winchester (2003), *The Meaning of Everything*, Oxford: Oxford University Press, xxvii.

6   For more on hyperlinks, see Chapter 14.

virtual groups which are linked only through the Internet, as is paradigmatically the case with Wikipedia. Starting in Chapter 7, I then turn my attention to the Internet, and in particular to social sharing sites, as exemplified by Wikipedia. One of my themes is to give the Wikipedia group project the same treatment as the others in order to show up the similarities, and also the discontinuities, between a virtual community and pre-Internet groups. In the final three chapters of the book I alter the perspective slightly, and instead of playing the role of a relatively neutral observer and critic, I turn to suggesting ways in which readers themselves might become personally involved in making Wikipedia better. I feel such a treatment is appropriate since Wikipedia, with all its virtues and its shortcomings, is potentially of use to the whole world, and the world is invited to contribute to it, and try to improve it. It seems inappropriate, therefore, to analyse and criticize the project in an academic way while keeping oneself well clear of the struggle.

In general, then, the book attempts a history of Wikipedia and selected antecedents: a tangential history that might allow for the development of a greater understanding of a technology – and a form of knowledge production and dissemination – that is fast becoming ubiquitous. It is my argument that by looking at communities of practice in the past which were involved in processing information, and especially those perhaps which were partisan, we can come to understand the radical, even political, nature of Wikipedia. This is particularly the case in that Wikipedia, I would argue, does not in fact merely announce a new kind of dissemination of existing knowledge, but a change in the very nature of knowledge itself – which we might describe here in the one word 'participatory'.

PART I
Groups in History

Chapter 1
Group Theory

To attempt to compare the nature and achievements of various groups in history, especially groups widely separated in time and place, would appear at first sight an unfruitful – some might say impossible – project. To start with, 'group' is a vague and all-embracing term. Groups might range from collections of individuals who merely have certain characteristics in common (the set of all red-headed teenagers) to individuals who live side by side and know each other intimately (the community of deep sea fishermen in Blanc Sablon, Labrador). Is size a defining consideration? Could several million people constitute a group? Could two or three? Then again, does a group require a certain temporal continuity, or might it remain a group if its members met once only for a certain purpose, and then ceased to communicate? Groups tend to lack permanent boundaries. Like bubbles, they appear under certain circumstances, persist for a time, and then become reabsorbed into the stream. An individual might belong one day and leave the next. The group itself might expand, then break up into fragments and lose its identity.

I shall be using the term in a restricted way, to mean a number of people who come together, or at least communicate with each other, in furtherance of a particular ambition or project. Even this limiting definition is fairly broad, of course. Some such groups may be highly democratic while others are dominated by certain members, for instance by political or religious leaders. Some may be formally organized, perhaps with a constitution, criteria for membership and regular meetings, while others are looser. Another distinction can be made between bridging and bonding groups. The former are outward-looking and aim to recruit widely. Examples might be political parties or ecumenical religious organizations. Bonding groups are exclusive and inward-looking, and examples include clubs or societies which impose highly specific criteria for new applicants. Bonding groups are good for creating cultural solidarity and mutual reciprocity, while bridging groups or networks are better for information diffusion, and also for linking disparate elements in society. Incidentally, the Internet has not altered these distinctions, but merely made the creation and sustaining of all kinds of groups far easier than before.

Social capital, a term coined comparatively recently but today much employed in areas such as business, economics, political science and public health, involves a concept which might be useful in the study of both historic and modern groups.[1]

---

1 The following two paragraphs rely on Robert Putnam's best-seller about the weakening of community in the United States over the last half century: Robert Putnam (2000), *Bowling Alone*, New York: Simon & Schuster, 15–28.

The term has been used in different ways, but the core idea is that social contacts between individuals have a certain value. This value may accrue to the social network as a whole, suggesting, for instance, that the wider or the more integrated a particular network is, the more productive or fertile in ideas it becomes. Alternatively, social capital might pertain to individuals within the network, the assumption being that the more an individual is in contact with others, the better not only his potential productive capacity, but also his mental health and general well being. Conversely, individuals who are relatively isolated socially may suffer adverse effects. Essential in the formation of social movements are the cultural benefits available for those involved – for example, consciousness-raising, the formation of friendships and the experience of working together with others. A crucial element here is the development of collective identity by the group, and this may bring about new ways of thinking and being for its members, which may even lead to them constructing for themselves new and permanent identities.

There is, too, an assumption that increased social capital diffused throughout a community or nation may be of benefit to that community as a whole, so that it can therefore be simultaneously a private and a public good. One must be careful, however, to see 'social capital' as a neutral term rather than invariably positive. For instance, someone might gain access to a powerful position through the employment of social connections although in fact they were less qualified for the post than rival candidates. Again, certain groups such as criminals could possess a high level of social connectivity. In both these cases social capital might have a negative effect on the community in general. Clay Shirky gives the example of Internet groups of pro-anorexic adolescent girls whose websites encourage anorexia with advice and mutual support.[2] Websites supporting terrorism are other obvious examples. Furthermore, with increased social capital may come increased opportunities for tension and conflict. This is especially true of more ideologically driven groups such as the ones in this study.

From what has been said, it will be evident that social capital is more difficult to estimate than the other variables mentioned above, and especially in a historical context, where the evidence may be hard to come by. One might try to gauge the degree of social capital within a group by looking at the intensity of relationships between its members, how often they communicated, and the degree of harmony or conflict that may have ensued. The members of the groups I have chosen may all have shared a common vision or goal, but this certainly did not preclude rivalries and sometimes bitter arguments.

Another useful approach to the study of groups is the concept of transaction costs. These are costs which may be assessed not just in monetary terms, but in expended time or energy. In buying a particular commodity from a shop, one's transaction costs might include not only the price of the goods themselves, but also the energy and effort it requires to find out which of the various brands on offer are to be preferred, where to find them and at what price, the cost of travelling to

---

2   Clay Shirky (2008), *Here Comes Everybody*, London: Allen Lane, 203–8.

the shop and back, the time spent choosing and paying. The concept of transaction costs was first developed by the economist Ronald Coase in the 1930s in order to predict whether certain tasks could be performed more efficiently within an organization or company, or by out-sourcing them to contractors via the market.[3] He pointed out that any organization needed to spend a considerable portion of its overall expenditure of resources on maintaining its own discipline and structure before it could even proceed towards its stated goals.

However, the term can be applied in a much wider sense, to cover any kind of interaction between individuals, groups or institutions. As I said, the costs involved do not necessarily have to include spending money, but might consist solely in time and energy expended or possibly even in social obligations created. For example, someone might consider the comparative transaction costs of setting up a new book group, joining an existing book group or merely continuing to keep their choice of reading matter separate from their social life.

When considering historical groups, the concept might be applied to the costs of creating and maintaining the group itself, in which case one would look at issues such as how they were funded and whether or not they needed to employ a paid secretary or editor. Also relevant here might be the social, economic or even emotional cost for individuals of belonging to the group. Alternatively, the focus could be on the transaction costs involved for the group in broadcasting their ideas to the world, including perhaps costs of printing and publication. The transaction costs of organizing a large group of like-minded individuals to pursue a common project have historically tended to be large, but with the Internet, such costs have shrunk to almost zero.

Coase and others may have used the concept of transaction costs to compare firms and markets, but a third alternative, often neglected by economists, is social production. This entails projects which are collaborative, voluntary and non-proprietary. In its purest form, social production is based on sharing resources and output among individuals who co-operate with each other without relying either on market profits or managerial commands. Wikipedia is obviously one such project, and it is clear that the Internet has made social sharing, especially in cultural and informational fields, far easier and more attractive than before.[4] However, all the other groups discussed here were also involved to some degree in social production, although this was more often than not combined with a profit motive associated with the publication and sale of texts or other group products.

The transaction costs for social production projects are usually much lower than for commercial enterprises, since many of those involved are likely to donate their skills and energy to the group for ideological reasons rather than for monetary reward. Nevertheless, it is important to realize that there can also be disadvantages to social production. People who are highly motivated by ideology

---

3   Yochai Benkler, 'Coase's Penguin, or, Linux and the Nature of the Firm', *Yale Law Journal*, vol. 112, no. 3 (Winter 2002), 369–446.

4   Social production is also known as peer-to-peer production, or p2p. See Chapter 7.

may well lack the skills necessary for co-operation, and may have a stronger than average tendency to dispute. In other words, the ideological glue binding the group together might be unstable, and it could dissolve into rival factions before achieving its goals. A further disadvantage is that the openness of such groups allows malicious or self-serving contributions which require time and energy to eliminate, and hence raise transaction costs.

A further approach to the study of groups in history is via the concept of the public sphere and its component 'publics', as defined by Jürgen Habermas and Michael Warner.[5] Habermas postulated that the bourgeois public sphere, an arena in which free discussion and polemics could take place, largely but not solely through the medium of print, first appeared in England towards the end of the seventeenth century. The precondition for the establishment of this public sphere was the replacement of the patron, typically aristocratic, by the publisher as the author's mentor and the commercial distributor of literary works. At this time, too, the post-Restoration theatre was in full swing, and the coffee house had emerged in London and other cities as a forum for regular debate. The readers, listeners and spectators of these new forms of media constituted a relatively small elite of propertied and educated, predominantly male, persons, but they were conscious of theoretically representing, in their readings and discussions, a much larger, though as yet inarticulate, public. According to Habermas, a preliminary stage in the formation of the bourgeois public sphere was literary and cultural, under the aegis in particular of Addison and Steele's periodicals, the *Tatler* and *Spectator*. However, within a short time clashes between the interests of various groups of powerful merchants and industrialists led in addition to the development of a political public sphere, in which conflicting parties attempted to influence the government by appealing for support to the new authority of public opinion.

Habermas's thesis has recently been developed by Michael Warner with a slightly modified terminology. Warner's main concern is not so much to date the emergence and evolution of the public sphere as to analyse the nature of particular groups who exploited it to present a particular case. Such a group he terms 'a public', provided it fulfils a fairly rigorous and narrow description, and he follows Habermas in citing Addison's *Spectator* as an early paradigm. Warner defines a public as a group that addresses the outer world, the public sphere, in the hope of being read and understood. Although conscious of itself as a group, a public nevertheless seeks to acquire new members, although the recruitment process must have strict limits if the group is to retain its inner cohesion. A public needs to be distinguished from other forms of community including those who look for members through, for example, birthplace or affiliation to institutions such as churches or political parties. He writes:

---

5   Jürgen Habermas (1962), *The Structural Transformation of the Public Sphere*, Cambridge: Polity Press; Michael Warner (2002), *Publics and Counterpublics*, New York: Zone Books. For more on the public sphere, see Chapter 12.

> The achievement of this cultural form is to allow participants in its discourse to understand themselves as directly and actively belonging to a social entity that exists historically in secular time and has consciousness of itself, though it has no existence apart from the activity of its own discursive circulation. . . A great deal must be postulated for the form to work in the world: not only the material conditions of a circulating medium, but appropriate reading or consuming practices.[6]

Warner makes the point that a single text, however widely disseminated, is not enough to create a public. There has to be continuity, circulation, and above all, feedback, which the *Spectator* ensured through printing letters from readers, both real and imagined, and other devices. Apparently, 'on the west side of Button's Coffee House a lion's head was attached through whose jaws the reader threw his letter'.[7]

'Counterpublic' is another useful term discussed by Warner, who devotes most of his book to the latter type of group, taking his examples from nineteenth- and twentieth-century conflicts involving gender, sexuality or race. He classes counterpublics as groups conscious of their subordinate status, and defined by their tension with the public sphere. As such, they constitute a sub-set of publics. It should be mentioned, however, that feminist writers in particular challenge this entire concept of subordinate groups attempting to influence a purportedly neutral public arena. Nancy Fraser has argued that there was never a single 'public sphere', and that Habermas's 'bourgeois public sphere' was actually an ideological construct that 'functioned to legitimate an emergent form of class (and race) rule. It was a Gramscian vehicle for one stratum of society to rule the rest.'[8] She instances various moments in the nineteenth and twentieth centuries when counterpublics, especially women, blacks and other disadvantaged sectors, created their own public spheres.

Warner's discussion of publics and counterpublics ends with a strong definition which contrasts the latter with groups that merely offer their own 'reform programme'. A counterpublic, he argues, is:

> structured by different dispositions or protocols from those that obtain elsewhere in the culture, making different assumptions about what can be said or what goes without saying. ... The discourse that constitutes it is not merely a different or alternative idiom [to that of the wider public] but one that in other contexts would be regarded with hostility or with a sense of indecorousness.[9]

---

6   Warner, 105.
7   Habermas, 42.
8   Nancy Fraser (1997), *Justice Interruptus*, London: Routledge, 76.
9   Warner, 119.

Habermas sees the functional public sphere in the West as disappearing with the evolution of the mass media in the second half of the nineteenth century. The public at this point turn into passive consumers of what is put before them, in both the cultural and political spheres, and the possibilities for real debate and decision-making gradually evaporate.[10]

I want to determine how far any of the groups I have chosen here can be said to be 'publics' in Warner's sense, and also how far they participated in the 'bourgeois public sphere'. Since the groups chosen range in time between the ancient world and the twenty-first century, clearly not all of them fit into the timescale laid down by Habermas. Nevertheless, with the help of these concepts, perhaps useful comparisons can be made as regards the nature of each group and its relationship with the world outside.

Closely associated with that relationship is the issue of trust. Trust is a somewhat mysterious and elusive entity, and it might be appropriate here to say something about its nature.[11] Clearly, it involves a prediction that someone, or some institution, is to be relied on. The degree to which one party trusts another is a measure of belief in the honesty, benevolence and competence of the other party.[12] Trust is easy to understand when it occurs between members of families or kinship groups, or between those who have known each other for a long time, but when an unknown group, or a group that lacks culturally acceptable credentials, addresses itself to the public sphere with the object of gaining support and adherents, the question of trust arises with particular force. Why should strangers show confidence in this group, or believe what they have to say?

One might distinguish here between trusting particular individuals and system trust, although of course the two overlap. In relation to the latter, everyone relies on there being sufficient controls built in to the various systems and institutions with which they have dealings. It is also assumed that these controls operate in an impersonal fashion, so that one does not need to know personally those working within the system concerned.

The effect of trust is to reduce social complexity and simplify life by the taking of a certain risk. We all have to risk relying on others for the processing of information. I need to know who can mend my car or computer, cure my gastritis or keep me reliably informed about current events in the Middle East. Distrust, however, by declining that risk, narrows down the scope of information that can be relied on. Stratagems of distrust – while they may well be justified in particular cases – in the long run become burdensome to maintain, and they absorb the strength of the person distrusting so as to leave less energy to explore and adapt to the environment, and hence fewer opportunities for learning. Both trust and

---

10   Until re-emerging perhaps with the birth of the Internet. See Chapter 7.

11   The following remarks are largely based on Niklas Luhmann (1979), *Trust and Power: Two Works*, Chichester: Wiley.

12   Though a failure in trust may be forgiven more easily if estimated to be the result of incompetence rather than a lack of benevolence or honesty.

distrust tend to be generalized attitudes which may last for a long time, but which are also especially sensitive to disturbance. For instance, it might only take one key event – perhaps the rumour of a small mistake or misrepresentation – which then becomes 'proof' that a loss of confidence is permanently justified. On the other hand, trust begets trust, and the longer it lasts, the more solid it tends to become.

These somewhat aphoristic remarks are intended to apply to today's world, and perhaps in particular to our relations with the Internet, but they are also relevant when we glance back at previous generations and to whom they gave their trust. My examples show that a certain group might acquire trust owing to the elevated social status or academic reputation of its members. Paradoxically, a different group might also be trusted for opposite reasons – because its members are seen as ordinary, and hence more in touch with the needs and feelings of the public than are the élites who are seen to dominate society. Clearly, because trust is a mental state it cannot be measured directly, but only by the statements or behaviour of the (dis-)trusting parties. In the following chapters, one topic will be – in so far as the evidence allows – how far the various groups were trusted, and the reasons for such trust as there was. It may turn out to be possible to distinguish between two kinds of motive for trust: extrinsic, for example the group's connection with people or institutions which were already trusted, and intrinsic, for example that their addresses to the public were persuasive or fulfilled contemporary truth criteria.

There now follow chapters on each of the five historical groups I have chosen. In these chapters I try to combine a brief narrative of the group and its activities with reference to the concepts mentioned in this chapter. The sub-headings within these first chapters ('Aims', 'The Group', 'Transaction Costs', 'Relations with the Public', 'Legacy') are also carried on into the later discussion of Wikipedia itself. A brief summary at the end of each of the five chapters on the historical groups draws attention to what I see as their respective similarities to Wikipedia.

Chapter 2
The Library of Alexandria

We simply do not know whether present technology will preserve texts even as efficiently as libraries of manuscript and printed books have done. The Alexandrian library may have preserved its books, without substantial loss, for up to 600 years. We should not be too confident that we will preserve our own literature for anything like as long.

Robert Barnes[1]

Aims

The great library of Alexandria has always been the subject of much ill-supported supposition and wishful thinking. Its image, as a repository for all the knowledge of the known world, and as a research centre for groups of dedicated scholars, is irresistibly attractive, but unfortunately the sources available to substantiate this image are highly fragmentary, and often contradictory. Crucial issues, including when the library was founded, how many books it contained, who was responsible for running it and who used it, and above all, the date it was finally destroyed, are all still open to speculation, even after endless debate.[2] Hence, any new attempt to describe it, or produce a narrative of its existence, including this one, must be treated with caution, not to say scepticism. That said, I feel that my brief chapter here is worthwhile since the library, or at least its myth, fits in well with the general theme of this book.

The death of Alexander the Great in 323 BC led to a struggle between his generals for control of the vast swathes of territory he had conquered, and the rich province of Egypt fell to the Macedonian Soter, who as Ptolemy I (282–248 BC) started a dynasty that ruled for three centuries, until Egypt was absorbed into the Roman empire by Augustus. As a foreigner who had seized power by force, the new king needed to establish his rule and provide himself with political and cultural legitimacy, especially in the eyes of his Greek subjects who by now constituted a ruling class, dominating the native Egyptians, and providing the king with soldiers and administrators. Ptolemy made Alexandria, the city recently founded by Alexander, his capital, and emphasized his links with Alexander, and with Hellenic culture generally. As part of this process he – or possibly his

---

1   Robert Barnes, 'Cloistered Bookworms in the Chicken-coop of the Muses', in Roy Macleod (ed.) (2005), *The Library of Alexandria*, London: I.B. Taurus, 75.

2   A pessimistic critique of the available sources is in Roger S. Bagnall's article, 'Alexandria: Library of Dreams', *Proceedings of the American Philosophical Society*, vol. 146, no. 4 (December 2002), 348–64.

son, Ptolemy II (Philadelphus) – created two new institutions, the library and the *Mouseion*, or temple dedicated to the Muses. The intention behind the library was complete coverage of everything written in Greek, ranging from epic poetry and drama to humble cookery books, and there was also to be a search for foreign literature which could be translated into Greek. This was said to include Egyptian and Persian texts, as well as the Jewish Pentateuch.

There are no contemporary descriptions of the library, but scholars believe it may have been housed with the precincts of the *Mouseion*, with its papyrus scrolls stacked on shelves in a series of rooms off covered walkways.[3] These scrolls consisted of sheets made from papyrus stalks, pasted together to form rolls usually three or four metres long. Scribes wrote on them in columns, using reed pens with ink made from lampblack and water.[4] References as to how many scrolls were held vary widely. The frequently cited *Letter of Aristeas*, a Jewish source from about 100 BC, relates that:

> When Demetrius of Phaleron was put in charge of the king's library he was lavished with resources with a view to collecting, if possible, all the books in the world; and by making purchases and copies he carried out the king's intention as far as he could. When he was asked, in my presence, how many thousands of books were there, he said: 'more than 200,000, my king; and I will try in a short time to fill up the number to 500,000'.[5]

It is difficult to know when, if ever, this conversation took place, since the author was writing towards the end of Ptolemy II's reign, whereas Demetrius of Phaleron was an adviser to Ptolemy I, but the historiography of the library is full of such discrepancies. Another source, the Byzantine writer John Tzetzes, complicates matters by specifying two libraries, as well as distinguishing between two kinds of scroll. He is suspiciously precise:

> This King Ptolemy [Ptolemy II], of whom I have spoken, had a truly philosophical and divine soul, and was a lover of everything noble, in sight, deed and word. Through Demetrius of Phaleron and other advisors he collected books from everywhere at royal expense and housed them in two libraries. Of these, the external library had 42,800 books; the internal library of the court and palace had 400,000 mixed books and 90,000 single, unmixed books ....[6]

---

3   This was the case at the recently excavated contemporary library at Pergamon: Lionel Casson (2001), *Libraries in the Ancient World*, New Haven, CT and London: Yale University Press, 48–52.

4   Casson, 35: it was not until the Christian era that bound parchment codices started to supplant papyrus scrolls.

5   Quoted in Barnes, 63.

6   Quoted in Barnes, 64. It is thought that 'mixed' books meant scrolls containing more than one work, whereas the others contained part or all of a single work. That there

Tzetzes was writing in the twelfth century AD, and was certainly copying, or elaborating on, the work of many earlier authors. Other sources give different figures. The estimate of over 500,000 scrolls is highly dubious, not least because far fewer would have been needed to achieve the stated aim of containing the literature available at the time. Roger Bagnall has calculated that it would have taken only 377 rolls, assuming 10,000 words per roll, to include the works of all known authors writing in Greek up to the end of the second century BC.[7] He also speculates about the impossibility, long before the invention of the card catalogue, of cataloguing or indexing half a million items. Admittedly, the library might have contained several copies of the same work, and it is also true that longer works took up several scrolls. In spite of all this, the figures given in the two sources quoted above are quite unrealistic. Perhaps all that can be said is that both contemporaries and later writers acknowledged that the library was uniquely large – much larger than earlier institutions, or than contemporary rivals such as the library at Pergamon.

The spread of Greek language and culture throughout the eastern Mediterranean is the factor lying behind the decision by Ptolemy to found his library. To seek out all the books in the world, even merely all the books in Greek, and store them in one place shows a consciousness of that wider world that would have been impossible in earlier times. Before Alexander, the Greeks had inhabited small, isolated city states, but his conquests dissolved those communities into a far larger world, that of Hellenistic civilization. The aspirations of the library of Alexandria were only conceivable given this political evolution.

The Group

The other institution founded at the same time as the library was the *Mouseion*, a cult centre dedicated to the worship and cultivation of the Muses. Strabo, writing at the end of the first century BC, shortly after the end of the Ptolemaic dynasty, gives a brief description:

> The Mouseion is part of the royal quarter and it has a cloister and an arcade and a large house in which is provided the common meal of the men of learning who share the Mouseion. And this community has common funds, and a priest in charge of the Mouseion, who was appointed previously by the kings, but now by Caesar.[8]

---

existed a second, smaller library, which held copies of some of the books in the main library, is mentioned in other sources.

7   Bagnall, 353.

8   Quoted in P.M. Fraser (1972), *Ptolemaic Alexandria*, Oxford: Clarendon Press, 3 vols, vol. I, 315.

This was a community of perhaps 30–50 men (there were no women), chosen for their learning, and appointed by the Ptolemies for life. They seem to have enjoyed an affluent, carefree and peaceful life under royal patronage, enjoying many perks, such as handsome salaries, free board and lodging and tax-free status. The library was available for their use, and they were free to pursue their individual researches, either scientific or literary. Their duties may have included giving public lectures as well as advising the king. The *Mouseion* has been described as an ancient version of a think-tank, but a closer modern analogy might be an Oxbridge college a century ago.

Similar cult centres dedicated to the Muses are known in other Greek cities, but the most obvious precedent was the Athenian *Lyceum* founded by Aristotle. This, too, was a collegiate institution dedicated to research, and there are a clear links between the *Lyceum* and Alexandria. One such was the Demetrios of Phaleron mentioned above, who had been a disciple of Aristotle's before arriving in Alexandria to become adviser to Ptolemy I, and who may have been responsible for the design of both library and *Mouseion*.

As well as the permanent scholars in the *Mouseion*, the Ptolemies made a habit of searching out scholars from all over the Greek world to study in Alexandria and to stay, sometimes for years.[9] The first three Ptolemies were themselves men of culture, and the visiting scholars not only received royal pensions, but also lived in intimacy with the court, sometimes tutoring the royal children. One such was Eratosthenes, the geographer and mathematician who produced an astonishingly accurate figure for the circumference of the earth. He was working in Athens when Ptolemy III invited him, and he was later appointed director of the Library. Other famous visitors included Archimedes, who spent some time at the *Mouseion* observing the seasonal rise and fall of the Nile, and Euclid who is supposed to have told Ptolemy I in response to a request for coaching that 'there is no royal road to geometry'.[10] Some of these scholars were already living in Egypt when they were invited to Court and offered a pension. Callimachus, who wrote for the library the first subject catalogue in the world was a lowly schoolmaster in a suburb of Alexandria when he was picked out.[11] Callimachus' catalogue, the *Pinakes* or Tables, was a bibliographic survey of the contents of the library. It has not survived except for a few fragments, but it was highly influential and became a model for future library surveys for centuries, not entirely superseded in fact until Melvil Dewey developed the Dewey Decimal system in 1876.[12]

Although in its early years the *Mouseion*'s scholars are thought to have specialized in the study of the natural world, as did those of Aristotle's *Lyceum*, subsequent emphasis seems to have been more on literary studies. One of the

---

9   As many as a hundred came at any one time, thinks one authority: Macleod, 5.

10   Macleod, 4.

11   Fraser, vol. I, 308.

12   Mostafa El Abbadi, *The Library of Alexandria*, <http://www.greece.org/Alexandria/Library/library11.htm>.

main preoccupations of Callimachus and his colleagues was the production of definitive editions of the great works of Greek literature, especially Homer, Hesiod, Pindar and the Athenian dramatists. Assembling copies from all over the Greek world, comparing them and trying to establish correct texts was an immense and important task, and needed special linguistic and editorial skills. As James O'Donnell says, to manipulate 24 four-metre rolls in order to edit one of Homer's epics would be to enter a seriously user-hostile environment.[13] It is probably due to the efforts of these Alexandrine scholars that satisfactory editions have survived into the modern world, even though the copies we possess may not be those of the library of Alexandria.

Transactional Costs

The costs of setting up the *Museion* and library were clearly vast, though how vast one can only speculate. Clearly, to maintain permanently a large group of scholars in comparative luxury must have made considerable demands on the royal treasury, as must the original capital expenditure on the buildings within the palace complex where they were to live. As far as the library was concerned, it may be that many of the books were obtained by the aggressive policies described by Galen.[14] He recounts that customs officials had orders to confiscate from passing ships all the books in their possession, which were then copied. The originals were deposited in the library, the original owners receiving back only the copies.[15] Nevertheless, many other books were bought by royal agents in the two main book markets in the Aegean, Athens and Rhodes. By the beginning of the fourth century BC the copying and selling of books had become a flourishing industry, and the Ptolemies sent their agents to scour the Mediterranean for suitable works. Books were expensive since copyists needed to be highly skilled – obviously, the Library would also have had its own scriptorium.

One indication that the Ptolemies were prepared to spend lavishly when it came to the library comes from another story told by Galen. Ptolemy III is said to have tricked the rulers of Athens by borrowing from them their official copies of Euripides, Sophocles and Aeschylus, and depositing as security for their safe return the sum of 15 talents – the equivalent of millions of dollars today. He then had splendid copies made on the finest papyrus and returned these to Athens instead, thus deliberately forfeiting his deposit.

In the ancient world it required the wealth and ambition of a king or an emperor to conceive of anything like a universal collection of books. For the Alexandria library, what was needed was the determination of several successive monarchs.

---

13 Joseph O'Donnell (1998), *Avatars of the Word*, Cambridge, MA: Harvard University Press, 51.

14 Galen (130–200 AD) was a physician and writer on medical subjects.

15 Fraser, vol. I, 325.

This was not merely a case of royal patronage for particular writers or savants, but of sustaining expensive institutions that needed a continuous injection of capital. The rulers of Hellenistic kingdoms, and especially the Ptolemies, could call on wealth far beyond that available to the earlier Greek city states such as Athens, Corinth or Sparta. Egypt was the granary of the Mediterranean world and could supply the taxation that enriched the Ptolemies, and in addition to grain, Egypt was the sole source of papyrus, another important export. The early Ptolemies extended their empire to take in Cyrene (in present-day Libya), Cyprus, and Aegean islands such as Samos and Cos. But when the Ptolemies eventually started to lose interest in scientific and literary pursuits (or perhaps were forced to direct funds towards the defence of their kingdom instead), the library declined in parallel with the decline of the Ptolemaic empire. It was during the late second century BC that Egypt came under repeated attack from the neighbouring Selucid kingdom of Syria, a period which coincided with a series of weaker rulers in Alexandria and a deterioration in the relationship between ruler and city.[16] At this time, many scholars fled the city for Rome or Athens. Both Library and *Mouseion* continued to exist, probably for several centuries, but their finest days were over.

Relations with the Public

The Greeks who settled in Egypt, especially in Alexandria, were part of a wide diaspora that started before the time of Alexander but increased following his conquests. The new capital of Alexandria contained an assortment of races including Greeks, Egyptians, Syrians, Persians, Jews and slaves of varied nationalities. There was, for instance, a large Jewish colony, perhaps comprising a third of the total population, and which probably occupied a separate part of the city. Nevertheless, it was only Greeks who had citizenship with its accompanying privileges, and not even all of these.[17] Alexandria was primarily a city of Greek culture, and a Greek-speaking bureaucracy was imposed on the native Egyptians, who nevertheless retained their own culture and traditions.

Greek culture helped confirm the identity, and establish the superiority, of this dominant minority in its colonial situation. A parallel might be the role of the English language and of British culture in Victorian India. For these Greeks, cut off from their roots, and coming as they did from every part of the Greek-speaking world, the *Mouseion* and the library must have acted as powerful symbols. They provided a link to their common cultural heritage. But for the other races, and especially for Egyptians, these were symbols of exclusion and subjection. It is no coincidence that later in the city's history, when the proportion of Greeks in the population declined, and when the Alexandrian mob

---

16   Fraser, vol. I, 118–31.
17   Fraser, vol. I, 52–8.

became more unruly and difficult to control, the status of the library also seems to have been reduced.[18]

It was not necessary, of course, for the Greeks in Alexandria actually to enter the library and read the books in order to be aware of its cultural significance. Nevertheless, surviving papyrus documents found in many parts of Egypt show that there was a high level of literacy among Greek-speakers under the Ptolemies. Although no such evidence has survived from the Alexandria region due to the humidity of the Nile delta, it is clear that the reading of books went on vigorously there, as elsewhere in Egypt.[19] Numerous fragments from evidently personal collections of literature have turned up, causing scholars to speculate that there was a flourishing book trade involving the copying and sale of manuscripts whose source in many cases may well have been scrolls in the Alexandria library.

Even among the Greeks, however, both in Alexandria and abroad, we can guess that there was some resentment of the dominant position of the library, and the privileged life of the members of the *Mouseion*. Those who paid their taxes to the royal treasury were hardly likely to look kindly on a pampered élite who were in receipt of tax-free royal pensions for life. Then there were the victims of the Ptolemies' cultural imperialism – those, for instance, who had visited the city by ship, only to have their scrolls confiscated and replaced by inferior copies. Timon of Phlius, a contemporary writer of polemical verse, may have expressed a common point of view when he wrote: 'In the populous land of Egypt there is a crowd of bookish scribblers who get fed as they argue away interminably in the chicken coop of the Muses'.[20]

Through their ambitions for the library, the Ptolemies were exerting power over Greek literature and staking a claim to be cultural leaders. Inevitably, this led to rivalry with other intellectual centres, and in particular with the library at Pergamon, created in the second century by the new Attalid dynasty, one of whom tried to persuade the librarian of Alexandria at the time, Aristophanes of Byzantium, to quit his post and migrate to Pergamon. The Ptolemies reacted to this by imprisoning Aristophanes for the rest of his life. They also tried to strangle the new library by banning the export of papyrus, but this only had the effect of promoting the use of animal skins, parchment and vellum, as a substitute. Pergamon became the main source of parchment for Rome, and the new library continued to increase in status.[21]

---

18   The points made in this paragraph are taken from Andrew Erskine, 'Culture and Power in Ptolemaic Egypt: The Museum and Library of Alexandria', *Greece and Rome*, 2nd ser., vol. 42, no. 1 (April 1995), 38–48.

19   Casson, 56.

20   Quoted in Erskine, 38; other writers have translated 'bookish scribblers' as 'bookworms', but it is hard to imagine worms of any sort lasting long in a chicken coop!

21   Casson, 52: the word 'parchment' is ultimately derived from Pergamon.

Legacy

When and how did the Alexandrine library meet its end? As Roger Bagnall says, this is a murder mystery with a number of suspects, each with opportunity and means.[22] Fraser, an authority on Ptolemaic Alexandria, thinks it likely that the main destruction occurred during the fighting between Julius Caesar and Ptolemy XIV, when a diversionary fire was started by Caesar's soldiers in the dock area and accidentally spread to the rest of the city. Fraser writes: 'we are justified in supposing that the contents of the Royal Library, if not wholly destroyed, were at least seriously diminished in the fire of 48 B.C.'[23] However, there is some evidence that the library was still in existence after this date. Anthony is said to have given a gift to Cleopatra of books from the library at Pergamon to replace others lost from the Alexandria library. And some of the scholarship that went on in Alexandria during the Roman period is difficult to imagine without a substantial library.[24] It has also been argued that in fact the library continued in some form until the Moslem invasion of Egypt in the seventh century AD. There is the famous but probably apocryphal story of the Arab conqueror writing to Caliph Omar asking what to do with all the books, and receiving the reply: 'If what is written in them agrees with the Book of God, they are not required; if it disagrees, they are not desired. Destroy them therefore'. The true date may lie somewhere between these two, and one possibility is 273 AD, when the Roman emperor Aurelian recaptured Alexandria after some bitter fighting. But another possibility is that there never was a decisive moment of destruction, and that what happened was the gradual decay of papyrus scrolls in the humid atmosphere of Alexandria. Those works which were copied onto the newfangled parchment codices may have survived elsewhere, while those which were not copied eventually became illegible and disappeared.

One of the library's bequests to the modern world was the valuable work undertaken in various fields including history, geography, astronomy, mathematics and medicine. To take one example, it was because the existence of the library allowed them to take advantage of earlier Babylonian researches that Aristarchos of Samos could propose a heliocentric basis for the solar system 1,800 years before Copernicus, and Hipparchus was able to employ the 360-degree circle. Another example was medical science, and in particular the study of human anatomy, in which many scholars participated, their discoveries being summarized in the 15 books compiled by Galen in the second century AD.

A second bequest to posterity was the philological achievement of Alexandrine scholars in establishing correct and uncorrupted texts for the Greek classics. Many of these texts were later translated into Arabic and preserved in the Moslem world long after all copies had been lost in Christian Europe. And a third, and perhaps

---

22   Bagnall, 356.
23   Fraser, 335.
24   Bagnall, 357.

the most important bequest of all, was the myth of the library itself, the ideal possibility of a comprehensive library that could embrace all knowledge. This image was passed on via the encyclopaedic authors of the early Middle Ages, such as Isidore of Seville and Cassiodorus, to the Renaissance and to the modern world, and it continues to inspire us today. Two recent projects which have taken inspiration from the example of the library of Alexandria are Wikipedia and the recently constructed *Bibliotheca Alexandrina*.[25]

Summary

The group or community which is the subject of this chapter comprised the members of the *Mouseion* over several centuries, together with visiting scholars who may or may not have also belonged to it. Together these formed a privileged élite protected and supported by the wealth and cultural ambitions of a dynasty of Hellenistic kings. This group was responsible for, and profited from, the adjacent library, which they used in order to pursue their varied studies. With these advantages, successive generations of scholars made Alexandria the cultural centre of the Mediterranean world.

The library was the first and greatest of its kind in the world. Its vast holdings, and its cataloguing system developed by successive librarians made it the forerunner and inspiration for all future libraries and gatherings of information in the West. It was comprehensive, and in a sense public, being open to those with fitting scientific or literary qualifications. Like Wikipedia, this was a project with the ambition to collect all the world's knowledge together in one place. It became a symbol of the universality of intellectual enquiry.

---

25   This new high-tech library, built near the site of the ancient Pharos, is supported by the Egyptian government and UNESCO: <http://www.greece.org/Alexandria/Library/library16.htm>.

Chapter 3
The Royal Society

They have broken down the Partition wall, and made a fair Entrance, for *all Conditions of Men* to engage in these studies; which were heretofore affrighted from them, by a groundless Apprehension of their Chargeableness and Difficulty. Thus they have formed that *Society*, which intends a *Philosophy*, for the use of *Cities,* and not for the Retirements of *Schools*, to resemble the *Cities* themselves; which are compounded of all Sorts of Men, of the *Gown*, of the *Sword*, of the *Shop*, of the *Field*, of the *Court* of the *Sea*; all mutually assisting each other.

Thomas Sprat

Aims

On Wednesday 28 November 1660, 12 men met in a private room at Gresham College, London, following a lecture by Christopher Wren, professor of astronomy there. According to the minutes which were kept, they constituted themselves into an association 'for the promoting of Experimental Philosophy', and arranged to hold regular meetings and defray costs through subscriptions.

What exactly was the 'experimental philosophy' which this group sought to promote? They shared a common interest in discovering how the world worked, and a firm belief that the way to do this was by personal observation and experiment. They refused to rely on the ancient Greek and Roman authorities who provided the bedrock of contemporary education, and in particular they were prepared to criticize Aristotle, who was universally revered as the unquestioned authority on all scientific matters, terrestrial and celestial. It is true that earlier scientists such as Gilbert, Kepler, Galileo, Harvey and others had shared their concern for experimentation, and had achieved much, but this project involved a bold proposal for a concerted attack on a specifically collective basis. That the approach should be corporate whenever possible was stressed by the earliest historian of the society, Thomas Sprat:

the Task was divided amongst them, by one of these two ways. First, it was sometimes refer'd to some *particular men*, to make choice of what *Subject* they pleased, and to follow their own Humor in the *Trial* .... Or else secondly, the *Society*, it self made the Distribution, and deputed whom it thought fit for the Prosecution of such, or such Experiments. And this they did, either by allotting the *same Work* to *several* men, separated from one another; or else by *joining* them into *Committees* (if we may use that word in a philosophical Sense ...).[1]

---

1   Thomas Sprat (1667), *The History of the Royal Society of London for the Improving of Natural Knowledge*, 3rd edn, 1722, reproduced by Elibron Classics, 2005, 84–5.

The group looked especially to Francis Bacon, who half a century earlier had stressed the importance of personal experience rather than authority in the investigation of the natural world. In T*he New Atlantis*, published posthumously in 1627, Bacon had invented a civilization in which experimental science was accorded a priority, as the head of 'Solomon's House', a vast research institute, explained to a traveller visiting this new world:

> The end of our foundation is the knowledge of causes, and secret motions of things; and the enlarging of the bounds of human empire, to the effecting of all things possible. ... [We] collect the experiments of all mechanical arts ... take care, out of them, to direct new experiments, of a higher light, more penetrating into nature than the former ... raise the former discoveries by experiments into greater observations, axioms, and aphorisms.

The members of the new society initiated a regular weekly programme of experiments and demonstrations in various fields, to be made available to all by publication, and not kept under wraps as had often been the case with alchemy and astrology. Their approach was to remain flexible, and they undertook:

> not to prescribe to themselves, any certain *Art* of *Experimenting*, within which to circumscribe their Thoughts; but rather to keep themselves free, and change their Course, according to the different Circumstances, that occur to them in their operations, and the several Alterations of the Bodies on which they work. The true *Experimenting* has this one thing inseparable from it, never to be a *fix'd* and *settled Art*, and never to be *limited* by constant Rules.[2]

They declared a determination to show the utmost caution in reaching conclusions from their observations and experiments, and always to proceed by induction, from facts to possible causes, and not the other way round, as did the Aristotelians:

> they have never affirm'd any thing, concerning the Cause, till the Trial was past: whereas, to do it before, is a most venomous thing in the making of *Sciences*; for whoever has fix'd on his Cause before he has experimented, can hardly avoid fitting his *Experiment*, and his Observations, to his own *Cause*, which he had before imagin'd, rather than the *Cause* to the truth of the *Experiment* it self.[3]

The society also started correspondence with a network of researchers and intellectuals both in England and throughout Europe, in this way fulfilling a real psychological need. Many abroad who felt themselves isolated and unappreciated

---

2 Sprat, 89.
3 Sprat, 108.

in their own countries were encouraged in their work by the feeling they now belonged to an international scientific community. Recent research could be reported to London, where it was recorded permanently so that individuals gained the credit they felt was their due. As the society's first secretary, Henry Oldenburg, wrote in a letter to a German correspondent:

> What we are about is no task for one nation or another singly. It is needful that the resources, labours, and zeal of all regions, princes, and philosophers be united, so that this task of comprehending nature may be pressed forward by their care and industry.[4]

In these ways the society managed to combine the roles of international research institute and clearing house for knowledge, as well as becoming a kind of social and professional London club for its members, who were conscious that they were involved in something altogether new – in fact, if not in so many words, a scientific revolution.[5] The sweeping claims made to this effect undoubtedly antagonized not a few. Here is Henry Power, who was elected a fellow in 1663, addressing '*the generous VIRTUOSI, and Lovers of Experimental Philosophy*' in his book written two years earlier:

> You are the enlarged and Elastical Souls of the world, who, removing all former rubbish, and prejudicial resistances, do make way for the Springy Intellect to flye out into its desired Expansion. When I seriously contemplate the freedom of your Spirits, the excellency of your Principles, the vast reach of your Designs, to unriddle all Nature; methinks, you have done more than men already, and may well be placed in a rank Specifically different from the rest of grovelling Humanity.[6]

From the outset, the members took a long-term view of their own activities, understanding that the revolutionary approach to the natural world which they were initiating might take many years to develop and to gain converts. They therefore grasped that continuity was essential, and kept careful records of their activities, including minute and account books and membership lists, a boon to future historians.

---

4 Quoted by Michael Hunter (1998), 'Promoting the New Science: Henry Oldenburg and the Early Royal Society', *History of Science*, xxvi, 171.

5 Steven Shapin (1996), in the introduction to his book *The Scientific Revolution* (Chicago, IL: University of Chicago Press), writes: 'There was no such thing as the Scientific Revolution, and this is a book about it'; he agrees, however, that its proponents certainly thought they were doing something new.

6 Henry Power (1664), *Experimental Philosophy*, quoted in Margery Purver (1967), *The Royal Society: Concept and Creation*, London: Routledge & Kegan Paul, 94.

The Group

The initial meeting in November 1660 was no spur-of-the moment decision, and in fact the origins of the Royal Society can be traced back to earlier groups with similar objectives, meeting in Oxford and London during the Commonwealth period. The original 12 members came from different backgrounds. Christopher Wren, Robert Boyle, William Petty and John Wilkins were already known as natural philosophers or 'virtuosi' in their respective fields.[7] Others, equally important for the survival of the society, were nobles or courtiers with connections to the king. These included William Viscount Brouckner, who was chancellor to Charles II's queen, Catherine, and who became the first president of the society. Early on, it was decided to widen the society by listing 'the names of such persons as were known to those present, whom they judged willing and fit to joyne with them in their designe, who, if they should desire it, might be admitted before any other'.[8]

Among those invited to join over the next three years were others well connected in aristocratic society, as well as savants such as Kenelm Digby, John Evelyn and Elias Ashmole. Over the next few years the membership expanded, until by May 1663 there had been 135 elections, and it is these earliest members who form the group known as the founder members. In fact, the society was actually run during this period by an inner core of about twenty, although the identity of this core changed over the years.

According to the rhetoric of the early Royal Society, membership was open to all. In the quotation at the head of this chapter, Thomas Sprat writes that all conditions of men, including even those 'of the shop' and 'of the field', might engage in these studies.[9] However, this was optimistic. The fellows possessed the circumstances, education and cultural heritage of early modern English gentlemen.[10] It was true that anyone could write to the Royal Society, could report on an experiment they had undertaken, just as anyone could buy the books written by Hooke, Boyle and – a few years later – Newton.[11] However, to have one's experiment accepted and recorded, or to become a fellow of the society, was different. In practice, there were strict limits as to who was acceptable. Firstly, recommendations from people known to the society were required. Steven Shapin instances the problems faced by the Delft draper Antoni van Leeuwenhoek, who reported to the society about

---

7   The word 'scientist' was not coined until the nineteenth century. 'Virtuosi' was the contemporary term for rich amateurs who took an interest in scientific matters.

8   'Journal Book of the Royal Society', quoted by John Gribbin (2005), *The Fellowship: The Story of a Revolution*, London: Allen Lane, 129.

9   Sprat, 76.

10   Steven Shapin (1994), *A Social History of Truth*, Chicago, IL: University of Chicago Press, 123.

11   But very few did buy, or read, such books. Newton's *Principia Mathematica* was probably read by fewer than a hundred contemporaries: Shapin (1996), 123.

the vast numbers of little swimming animals he had seen in pond water through microscopes of his own construction.[12] Leeuwenhoek had been to no university, knew no Latin, French or English, and was a tradesman. In spite of his unique achievements, it took him several years to gain the society's trust. Social realities meant that the membership was very restricted. This was an exclusively male group drawn mainly from the upper echelons of society, and there were very few craftsmen, tradesmen, or even merchants and financiers among them. In turn, this also meant that in spite of rhetoric about the society's utility to the nation, there was some difficulty when it came to passing on suggestions for technical improvements to those actually involved in manufacturing processes. A society of gentlemen was always going to have problems communicating with artisans and mechanics lower down the social scale.

Transaction Costs

From the start, the Royal Society faced major financial problems. Many of the early members, including Wilkins and Oldenburg, had been supporters of the Commonwealth, but they nevertheless hoped and expected that the new king, Charles II, who was known to be interested in scientific questions, would provide them with a permanent income. They therefore spent considerable sums during 1662 and 1663 in setting up an elaborate constitutional structure, which included petitioning the king for a royal charter to give the society a status comparable to other incorporated bodies such as the chartered livery companies of the City of London.[13] But all this effort came to practically nothing. Either Charles was feeling parsimonious, or he was influenced by some of the contemporary satirical attacks directed against the society, and perhaps in particular by Thomas Hobbes, an especially hostile philosopher who was close to the Court. In any case, regular funding was not forthcoming, although there was a royal gift of a piece of land in Chelsea on which to build a headquarters. Initially, this gift proved useless owing to legal difficulties and also the lack of available finance for building. However, twenty years later Charles bought the land back for the sum of £1,200 in order to build a royal hospital, and this helped stave off a financial crisis in the 1680s.[14]

During these early years the society had great difficulty in finding suitable premises. At the start it was suggested that the College of Physicians could rent them accommodation, but this was refused. The regular meetings at certain fellows' rooms at Gresham College continued until the college building was needed as a temporary Royal Exchange after the Fire of London in 1666. Various plans for

---

12   Shapin (1994), 306–7.

13   Michael Hunter (1995), *Science and the Shape of Orthodoxy: Intellectual Change in Late Seventeenth-century Britain*, London: Boydell Press, 122.

14   Gribbin, 232; this hospital became the home of the Chelsea Pensioners.

building their own headquarters came to nothing, and as Oldenburg wrote to Boyle in 1668:

> the building a college for the Royal Society is conceived to be by the council, as being that, which will in all likelihood establish our institution, and fix us (who are now looked upon but as wanderers, and using precariously the lodgings of other men) in a certain place, where we may meet, prepare and make our experiments and observations, lodge our curators and operators, have our laboratory, and operatory all together.[15]

So the society had to rely from the start on its own initiative for funding, and it became a purely voluntary institution, unlike the French Académie des Sciences, founded four years later, which was well supported by Louis XIV. It also differed from 'Solomon's House', in which Bacon had envisaged scientists as paid employees of the state. This private status had the advantage of comparative freedom from government interference, but the drawback was that the early society conducted its affairs on a shoestring. There were many expenses, including legal fees, the cost of scientific equipment, and of renting accommodation. Some of this was met by subscription. Members were expected to pay 10 shillings on first admission, and thereafter 'one shilling weekly, whether present or absent, whilst he shall please to keep his relation to this Company'.[16] However, this still left a large gap, especially since some failed to pay, and by the end of the 1660s there were arrears of more than £1,000. Employees including Oldenburg were paid little, and often in arrears. One solution was to look for donations from the rich and famous, a policy which involved encouraging government ministers and aristocrats to join without any enquiry as to their possible intellectual contribution. This no doubt raised the status of the society in the eyes of the public, but did little for its scientific credentials, especially when there were visits by those who understood little of what was being demonstrated, but came 'only as to a Play to amuse themselves for an hour or so'.[17] When Sir Christopher Wren became president of the society in 1680 he purged more than sixty Fellows, thereafter ensuring that future candidates had to be capable of making a genuine contribution.[18]

The private means of the active members of the group was another source of finance, and here it was fortunate that Robert Boyle, son of the earl of Cork and possessor of large estates, was a leading member. Boyle was prepared to spend part of his fortune on his own chemical researches and publications, and he also paid salaries to various employees, including Henry Oldenburg and Robert Hooke, both of whom were crucial in their different ways to the survival of the society. Oldenburg devoted his great talents and energy to setting up the

---

15   Oldenburg to Boyle, March 1667/68, quoted in Purver, 135.
16   Gribbin, 129.
17   Hunter (1995), 125.
18   Gribbin, 232.

international network of correspondents mentioned above, and Hooke, having been Boyle's leading technician, developed as a notable researcher in his own right.

Relations with the Public

The early Royal Society saw itself as a society of gentlemen, and it was this above all which gave it credible status in the eyes of contemporaries. A gentleman possessed integrity – his word was to be believed, and the higher his social status, the more trustworthy his pronouncements. Early modern English culture tended to make an important distinction between gentlemen and professional scholars. A gentleman was someone of independent means, and hence also of independent mind, since he had no need to curry favour with, or appease, employers. Those who earned their living, on the other hand, whether by scholarship or any other means, were likely to defer to the opinions of employers or patrons. The contemporary image of a scholar, or 'gown-man', was of someone dependent, impoverished and also, very likely, pedantic and disputatious. It was one of the great cultural achievements of the Royal Society to blur this perceived distinction, and to create a new image, that of the scholar-gentleman.

The society therefore fully appreciated the value, not only of royal and aristocratic patronage, but also of having noblemen among its own ranks. Boyle, especially, was an acknowledged expert in natural philosophy and a prolific author. He also added a reputation for modesty, piety and integrity to high birth and great wealth, all of which factors carried weight in contemporary eyes. As Steven Shapin explains, Boyle's image, his 'presentation of self', was 'intensively appropriated and celebrated by the early Royal Society. From the mid-1650s until well after his death in 1691, it was Boyle's example – more than that of any other practitioner – which was mobilized to give public legitimacy to the experimental philosophy'.[19]

Nevertheless, in spite of its social standing, it would be a mistake to think that the society was universally admired and trusted. To convince the public of the legitimacy of the new experimental philosophy, the group had an uphill public relations task to perform. There was considerable scepticism and even ridicule among contemporaries about their aims and methods. Thomas Hobbes criticized the experimental programme as unfruitful, and also undignified for 'philosophers': 'Not every one that brings from beyond seas a new gin, or other jaunty device, is therefore a philosopher. For if you reckon that way, not only apothecaries and gardeners, but many other sorts of workmen, will put in for, and get the prize'.[20] Others, including Henry Stubbe, a persistent critic, held that the Royal Society's

---

19   Shapin (1994), 185. This role of Robert Boyle is one of the main themes of Shapin's book.

20   Quoted in Shapin (1994), 396.

iconoclastic attitude towards Aristotle implied disrespect for traditional learning, the universities and even the established Church. Many felt that the Christian revelation and the authority of the Bible would be next among their targets. However, when it came to religion these natural philosophers had a powerful defence. They argued that God had produced two books, the scriptures and the natural world, and of this second book they were the priests. Every experiment, every discovery made, helped reveal the wonders of the divine purpose. In such ways the charge of atheism was easily repudiated. In fact, one outcome of the new science was to bolster the argument from design, that most powerful pre-Darwinian argument for the existence of God. Perhaps more wounding than intellectual attacks was public ridicule. According to Pepys, even the king, patron of the society, occasionally joined in this sport.[21] Pamphleteers and dramatists sharpened their wits on the material they found in the society's various publications, such as accounts of attempted blood transfusions between humans and animals, or speculations about one day travelling to the moon. The leading character in Shadwell's play, *The Virtuoso*, was Sir Nicholas Gimcrack, who was said to have 'broken his brains about the nature of maggots', and to have 'studied these twenty years to find out the several sorts of spiders, and never cares for understanding mankind'.[22] Towards the end of his account of the Royal Society, Sprat acknowledges that it was 'the *Wits* and *Railleurs* of this *Age*' that most disconcerted him:

> I acknowledge that we ought to have a great Dread of their Power: I confess I believe that *new Philosophy* need not fear the pale or the melancholy, as much as the humorous and the merry: For they perhaps by making it ridiculous because it is *new*, and because they themselves are unwilling to take pains about it, may do it more Injury than all the Arguments of our severe and frowning and dogmatical *Adversaries*.[23]

In spite of critics and satirists, the society gradually succeeded in spreading its influence, both in England and abroad. This was largely due to Oldenburg, who until his death in 1677 single-handedly maintained the extensive network of correspondents at home and abroad.[24]

In 1665 Oldenburg also launched the journal *Philosophical Transactions*, the world's first scientific periodical, to publish the results of research far more widely

---

21   'Gresham College he mightily laughed at for spending time only in weighing of ayre, and doing nothing else since they sat.': Pepys' Diary, 1 Feb. 1663/64.

22   Satirical attacks on the early Royal Society are described in Dorothy Stimson (1949), *Scientists and Amateurs*, London: Sigma Books.

23   Sprat, 417.

24   See A. Rupert and Marie Boas Hall (eds) (1965–86), *The Correspondence of Henry Oldenburg*, 13 vols, Madison, WI and Milwaukee, WI: University of Wisconsin Press.

than would have been possible merely through personal letters.[25] This was a truly international venture, and versions in Latin were regularly published in Amsterdam and Leipzig. In 1663 Hooke described what the new journal would do:

> And that you may understand what parts of naturall knowledge they are most inquisitive for at this present, they designe to print a Paper of advertisements once every week, or fortnight at furthest, wherein will be contained the heads or substance of the inquiries they are most solicitous about, together with the progress they have made and the information they have received from other hands, together with a short account of such other philosophicall matters as accidentally occur, and a brief discourse of what is new and considerable in their letters from all parts of the world, and what the learned and inquisitive are doing or have done in physick, mathematicks, mechanicks, opticks, astronomy, medicine, chymistry, anatomy, both abroad and at home.[26]

Legacy

After four and a half centuries of continuous existence the Royal Society is today the oldest scientific society in the world. It has evolved from a small London club of gentlemen virtuosi to a national institution representing the best of British science to the world. But the principles of the society remain the same as they were in the days of Boyle and Oldenburg – to promote reliance on experiment and observation rather than authority, and to further international scientific co-operation.

The society has always tried to follow the precepts of its founders, who 'openly profess, not to lay the Foundation of an *English, Scotch, Irish, Popish,* or *Protestant* Philosophy; but a Philosophy of *Mankind*'.[27] To take two examples from recent history, in 1918 a motion to remove the names of 'enemy aliens' from the list of Foreign Members of the society was rejected, and during the Cold War there were continuous exchanges of scientists and research workers between Britain and the USSR.[28]

Over the years the Royal Society has had its ups and downs. The age of Newton, who became president of the society in 1671, was succeeded by a period of decline in activity and reputation during the first half of the eighteenth century, but after 1760 there was a revival, with scientists such as Henry Cavendish, Joseph

---

25   The French *Journal des Sçavants* appeared two months earlier, but was not a truly scientific journal as it included much literary, legal and even theological matter.

26   Quoted in Charles Richard Weld, *A History of the Royal Society*, London, 1848, 2 vols, vol. I, 148. The *Philosophical Transactions* were actually to be issued monthly.

27   Sprat, 417.

28   E.N. da C. Andrade (1960), *A Brief History of the Royal Society*, London: The Royal Society, 27.

Priestley, John Hunter and William Herschel making their mark. This was the time, too, when the long-serving and energetic Sir Joseph Banks was president, under the enthusiastic patronage of his friend, George III.[29] Another relatively somnolent period followed, until the reforms of the 1840s changed the society from a club open to anyone of sufficient social standing to the modern scientific institution of today, when entry is based on merit. During the twentieth century the Royal Society increased steadily in activity, and has come to be consulted regularly by the government on a range of issues in times of peace and war.

Summary

Here were a group of savants who organized themselves into an association to investigate nature without reliance on hitherto accepted authority. They aimed to spread the Baconian experimental philosophy to the world at large through practical demonstrations. A neutrality uncharacteristic of the age was cultivated as to questions of religion and politics, and a cautious public was partially reassured as to the group's purposes by the social status of some of its members. As does Wikipedia today, they publicized their efforts internationally by means of the latest technology, employing a network of correspondents and a new scientific journal. Like wikipedians, these were enthusiastic amateurs inspired by zeal for their project, and without pecuniary motives or patronage.

---

29   Banks was president from 1778 until his death in 1820, the same year as George III died.

Chapter 4
The Republic of Letters

May the Encyclopedia become a sanctuary, where the knowledge of man is protected from time and from revolutions ... let us do for centuries to come what we regret that past centuries did not do for ours.

Jean Le Rond d'Alembert[1]

Aims

In 1745 some leading Parisian printers were on the lookout for someone to mastermind a new project. This was to be a four-volume French translation of Ephraim Chambers' highly successful *Cyclopaedia*, first published in 1728. The editor they eventually chose was a 28-year-old garret-dwelling Parisian hack writer named Denis Diderot. However, before he could start work properly, Diderot found himself in trouble with the authorities. He was incarcerated in the state prison of Vincennes, where he remained for three months. A contemporary police report on him has survived:

[from the dossier of Joseph d'Hémery, Inspector of the book trade]

NAME: Diderot, author.
AGE: 36.
BIRTHPLACE: Langres.
DESCRIPTION: Medium size, a fairly decent physiognomy.
ADDRESS: Place de l'Estrapade, in the house of an upholsterer.
STORY: He is the son of a cutler from Langres.
He is a very clever boy but extremely dangerous.
He wrote *Les Pensées philosophiques*, *Les Bijoux*, and other books of that sort.
He also did *L'Allée des idées*, which he has in manuscript at his house and which he has promised not to publish.
He is working on a *Dictionnaire encyclopédique* with Toussaint and Eidous.
9 June 1749. He did a book entitled *Lettres sur les aveugles à l'usage de ceux qui voient*.
24 July. He was arrested and taken to Vincennes on that account.
He is married, yet had Mme de Puysieux as a mistress for some time.

---

1   Jean Le Rond d'Alembert (1751), *Preliminary Discourse to the Encyclopaedia of Diderot*, trans. Richard N. Schwab, Chicago, IL: University of Chicago Press, 1995, 121.

A supplementary sheet adds:

> He is a young man who plays the wit and prides himself on his impiety; very
> dangerous; speaks of the holy mysteries with scorn. He said that when he gets
> to the end of his life, he will confess and receive [in communion] what they call
> God, but not from any obligation; merely out of regard for his family, so that
> they will not be reproached with the fact that he died without religion.[2]

Diderot's first published work was *Les bijoux indiscrètes*, a pornographic best-
seller, but the book which led to his imprisonment, *Lettres sur les aveugles*
('Letters on the blind for those who can see'), had been published anonymously in
England. In it he described the case of Nicholas Saunderson, the blind professor
of mathematics at Cambridge, who had recently died. Diderot used Saunderson
as a peg on which to hang a thesis about the relativity of morals and religion, and
he composed for the professor an entirely fictitious deathbed speech. Here it was
argued that the blind usually lack human feelings as they have never experienced
the sight of suffering, and by the same token, 'if a being should have a sense more
than we have, how woefully imperfect would he find our morality!' The French
authorities, who saw free-thinking in religion as a possible threat to state security,
reacted accordingly.

Once out of prison and back at work, Diderot soon showed the flair and dedicated
vision which was to transform the projected translation of Chambers into something
totally different. By the time Diderot, his colleague, d'Alembert, and his co-workers
had finished, over twenty years later, it had become the famous *Encyclopédie*,
subtitled *A Reasoned Dictionary of the Sciences, Arts and Crafts, by a Society
of Writers*. There were 17 volumes of text incorporating 70,000 articles, plus 11
volumes of plates. The purpose of the enterprise, according to Diderot, was:

> to assemble the knowledge scattered over the face of the earth, to expound its
> general system to the men with whom we live, and to transmit it to the men
> who will come after us; in order that the labours of past centuries will not have
> been in vain for the centuries to come; and that our children, becoming better
> instructed than we, may at the same time become more virtuous and happy and
> that we may not die without having deserved well of humankind.[3]

This was a response to what was then being seen as a knowledge explosion, as
witnessed in the contemporary growth of the sciences, geographical exploration,
and the proliferation of books and periodicals. The idea was to summarize all
available facts and theories, especially in the physical and natural sciences.
Knowledge was to be made public, available to everyone, not kept secret or

---

2   Quoted in Robert Darnton (1984), *The Great Cat Massacre*, reprinted
Harmondsworth: Penguin Books, 1991, 180–81.
3   *Encyclopédie*, vol. v, 635 (article, 'Encyclopédie').

exclusively in the hands of an élite, as it had often been in the past. At about this time, too, a new readership was becoming available in France and elsewhere. Historians have noticed a shift in the reading patterns of educated readers. Instead of the 'intensive', often repeated, and sometimes communal reading of particular works such as the Bible, reading was now becoming 'extensive', with more being read and at greater speed.[4]

Even this ambitious aim, however – to assemble and communicate 'knowledge scattered over the face of the earth' – hardly does justice to the *Encyclopédie*'s real purpose, which was to transform knowledge, rather than just collecting it. Whereas the role of earlier encyclopaedias and books of reference had been to store and preserve traditional knowledge, these authors stressed the need to find and record *new* facts and ideas. There was an awareness that the world was changing before men's eyes, and that merely preserving the heritage of the past would not do.

The most important way to communicate this new knowledge was to record in detail, and for the first time, the industrial techniques and crafts of the day. To do this, explained d'Alembert, it was necessary for the authors to get some hands-on experience:

> Everything impelled us to go directly to the workers. We approached the most capable of them in Paris and in the realm. We took the trouble of going into their shops, of questioning them, of writing at their dictation, of developing their thoughts and of drawing out the terms peculiar to their professions .... But there are some trades so unusual and some operations so subtle that unless one does the work oneself, unless one operates a machine with one's own hands, and sees the work being created under one's own eyes, it is difficult to speak of it with precision. Thus, several times we had to get possession of the machines, to construct them, and to put a hand to the work.[5]

How was all this knowledge to be organized to make it accessible and readable? As Chambers had done in his *Cyclopaedia*, Diderot and d'Alembert followed the fashionable technique of producing a diagram of the tree of knowledge, allotting the arts and sciences to its various branches. Unlike Chambers, and in keeping with their general anti-religious stance, they put 'Theology' on a rather distant twig close to 'Divination' and 'Black Magic'. However, as d'Alembert admitted, readers tended not to set much store by maps of knowledge, and anyway, it would be difficult to make such a map the ground plan for an encyclopaedia. So instead, the authors turned to the alphabetical system on which dictionaries and encyclopaedias have traditionally been based, and still are. This has the advantage of being egalitarian as regards items of information, and also easy

---

4   John Brewer (1997), *The Pleasures of the Imagination: English Culture in the Eighteenth Century*, New York: Farrar, Straus & Giroux, 167–97.

5   D'Alembert, 122–3.

to extend when new articles come along. However, it also has disadvantages, as Gwen Raverat points out in her 1950s autobiography, *Period Piece*. Once, at the age of 17, she consulted Chambers in order to find out how babies were made, but drew a complete blank. 'You have no idea if you have not tried', she writes, 'how difficult it is to find out anything whatever from an encyclopaedia, unless you know all about it already, and I did not even know what words to look up'.[6] Another problem with an alphabetic system, to which the *Encyclopédie* itself was somewhat prone, is that it can easily end up as a disconnected rag-bag of knowledge difficult for the reader to digest. This danger is satirized by Dickens when Mr Pickwick hears of a man who became an expert in Chinese metaphysics via the *Encyclopaedia Britannica*:

> 'Indeed!' said Mr. Pickwick; 'I was not aware that that valuable work contained any information respecting Chinese metaphysics.'
> 'He read, sir,' rejoined Pott, laying his hand on Mr. Pickwick's knee, and looking round with a smile of intellectual superiority – 'he read for metaphysics under the letter M, and for China under the letter C, and combined his information, sir!'[7]

Diderot tried to reduce the problem of putting articles in alphabetical order by introducing a system of *renvois* (cross-references) to direct the reader to other articles relevant to the one he happened to be reading. One advantage of this arrangement was that it could also be used for sly digs against ideas or institutions which the authors disapproved of, one example being the article entitled 'Anthropophagy' (that is, cannibalism) where there was a link, 'See Eucharist, Communion, Altar, etc.' In his article on the *Encyclopédie*, Diderot himself admitted that these cross-references sometimes had this purpose: 'they [the links] will attack, shake and secretly overturn certain ridiculous opinions which we would not dare to insult openly'.[8]

All the contributors were, however, revolutionary in a less overt way, since they believed in collaboration. Chambers' *Cyclopaedia*, which had started off as the model for the early *Encyclopédie*, had been written entirely by one man, the polymath, Ephraim Chambers, and the earliest editions of the *Encyclopaedia Britannica* (1st edition 1768–71) were also researched and composed entirely by one, or at most two, authors.[9] But the *Encyclopédie* involved hundreds of contributors. This difference reveals a new awareness that the sum of knowledge was becoming too vast for any one person to cope with. An encyclopaedia had now become a substitute for individual human memory, rather than a mirror of what an educated person ought to know, and ideally remember. The human

---

6   Gwen Raverat (1952), *Period Piece: A Cambridge Childhood*, London: Faber, 112.
7   Charles Dickens (1837), *The Pickwick Papers*, London: Chapman & Hall, ch. 51, 715.
8   Quoted in Darnton, 177.
9   See Richard Yeo (2001), *Encyclopaedic Visions*, Cambridge: Cambridge University Press, esp. 176–81.

memory, from ancient times until the high Renaissance so crucial and so respected as a storehouse of knowledge, was now seen as fallible, inadequate in face of the contemporary knowledge explosion.

In common with similar works of the day, the *Encyclopédie* concerned itself with science, crafts and philosophy, rather than history or biography. Nevertheless, the authors did have a clearly worked out attitude to history. Theirs was a 'great man' view of the past, but the great men they valued were writers and philosophers, rather than kings and generals. History, they thought, advanced not through nations and their wars, but by progress in the arts and sciences, and this progress came about through the efforts of men of letters. Clearly, the contributors also saw themselves in this category. They were the heirs of Bacon and Descartes, Newton and Locke.[10] In other words, history was made by people like themselves, who were involved in the most exciting project of the age.

The Group

Frank Kafker has profiled 139 contributors to the *Encyclopédie*, and there were others not identified.[11] He has shown that they were not in any sense a homogeneous group, since they differed widely in social background, occupation, age and ideology. There were many medical men, and also lawyers, army officers and government officials. There was even a policeman, François-Jacques Guillotte, once Diderot's landlord, and whom he used as a character reference when in trouble. Unexpectedly, there were also a number of ministers of religion, both Protestant and Catholic, including three young abbés who shared lodgings, one of whom was the notorious de Prades, mentioned below.[12]

Many contributors were authorities in their fields, whether academic, including linguistics, economics, history and architecture, or practical, such as clock-making, bridge-building or wood-engraving. Inevitably, they varied widely in their ability to communicate, as well as their expertise and their commitment. Diderot was aware that many had their weaknesses: 'Among many excellent men, there were some who were weak, some mediocre, and some thoroughly bad'.[13]

10　D'Alembert's special praise for Bacon, Locke and Newton may, however, have been a cover for a more radical 'Spinosist' ideology which he could not acknowledge openly. On this, see Jonathan Israel (2001), *Radical Enlightenment: Philosophy and the Making of Modernity 1650–1750*, Oxford: Oxford University Press, 711–12.

11　Frank A. Kafker (1988), *The Encyclopedists as Individuals: A Biographical Dictionary of the Authors of the Encyclopédie*, Studies on Voltaire and the Eighteenth Century, no. 257, Oxford: Voltaire Foundation.

12　Robert Shackleton (1970), *The 'Encyclopédie' and the Clerks*, Oxford: Clarendon Press.

13　'Parmi quelques hommes excellents, il y en eut de faibles, de mediocre & de tout à fait mauvais': Kafker, xiv.

A few contributors had volunteered to join the project; most were recruited by the editors, printers, or others. The more radical among them, who saw the *Encyclopédie* as a means of undermining people's faith in the values of their own society, were mainly close to Diderot, and shared his values. They constituted an inner group within the larger community of contributors, most of whom did not meet, or even know, each other. This more militant minority aimed to criticize and hence ultimately to reform the *Ancien Régime*. While most of the encyclopedists merely sought to provide their readers with the best available information, this group took every opportunity to attack the powers wielded by Church and state, to suggest alternatives to absolute monarchy, and in some cases to attack Christianity itself. On the whole, members of this inner ring were, at least in their younger days, of fairly marginal socio-economic status. Like Diderot, many were hand-to-mouth jobbing writers living an insecure existence in their urban environment, and under the watchful eye of the police.

Whereas the encyclopedists generally were scattered throughout France and beyond, the inner group of Diderot's collaborators mostly lived in Paris, and could therefore remain in touch with editors, printers and each other. Some of them used to meet regularly at the Thursday and Sunday dinners given by the baron d'Holbach, who himself was an exception to the rule, in that he possessed a large fortune inherited from his uncle, a rich financier. Other meeting places included the salon of Mme d'Epinay, mistress of Grimm, one of Diderot's closest collaborators, and that of d'Alembert's lover, Julie de Lespinasse. One prominent member of the d'Holbach circle was Jacques-André Naigeon, who wrote several articles on religion, including one entitled *Unitaires* in which, while pretending simply to describe the beliefs of Unitarians, Naigeon actually tried to undermine the main doctrines and organization of the Catholic Church.

Transaction Costs

How was this project, which involved hundreds of authors, proofreaders, printers, binders and distributors, kept going and financed? It was a massive capitalist enterprise, which was designed to make a profit, and finally exceeded all estimates. By 1772, after the last volumes of letterpress and plates had appeared, it is reckoned that the total net profit of the entire edition may have amounted to more than 2,000,000 livres.[14] To put this sum in context, it cost 5,000–6,000 livres a year to live comfortably in Paris during the 1760s, and the incomes of French labourers varied from 100 to 300 livres a year. The profits were shared between the four Parisian publishers who initiated the project, or rather their heirs, since the only one of the four who survived from start to

---

14   Kafker, 198.

finish was André-François Le Breton, whose energy and determination were crucial to the project's success, although he infuriated Diderot by tampering with several articles so as to avoid subversive statements.

The costs were met, and the profits derived, not from the sale of individual volumes, but from the subscriptions of thousands of readers who paid upfront before receiving successive instalments. The *Encyclopédie* was the first major work, either in England or France, to rely so heavily on attracting the public to invest during the ongoing work of production.[15] The price of subscription increased rapidly once the success of the scheme was assured. For instance, in 1759, when the work was condemned by the Parlement de Paris after seven volumes had been issued, the publishers were ordered to return 72 livres to each of approximately 4,000 subscribers.[16] However, when the final volume was issued in 1772, the price of a subscription had risen to 980 livres.

By 1789, it is reckoned that more than 25,000 sets of the *Encyclopédie* had been sold throughout Europe, roughly half of them within France.[17] By this time the entire nature of the enterprise had changed. Publication was in the hands of one highly successful printer, Charles-Joseph Panckoucke, who had formed an unofficial alliance with the state. Panckoucke was allowed to circumvent the continuing hostility of conservatives by using *permissions tacites*, a legal fiction supposed to cover books printed abroad, although everyone knew his *Encyclopédie méthodique*, as the work was then called, was still being produced in Paris. It was now made available in quarto and octavo editions, less expensive than the original folio volumes, but still beyond the purchasing power of peasants or artisans. Robert Darnton has examined subscription lists for the quarto, and he concludes that by the time of the revolution, it had become a best-seller within the bourgeoisie of the *Ancien Régime*, appealing to the upper and middle ranks of French society throughout the nation. Surprisingly, however, its appeal was less in towns where the stirrings of industrialization could already be felt than in the older provincial centres and among the traditional élite. Darnton cites the examples of Lille, a burgeoning industrial city of 61,000 where there were only 28 subscribers, as compared to Besançon, an old-fashioned provincial capital of 28,000, which absorbed 338 quartos. He concludes that although 'nothing could have been more cutthroat and capitalist than the *Encyclopédie*', yet during this period, 'its readership was not capitalist. They came from those sectors of society that were to crumble quickest in 1789.'[18]

---

15 Colin Jones (2003), *The Great Nation: France from Louis XV to Napoleon*, London: Penguin Books, 173.

16 Kafker, 197; in the event, this repayment was cancelled.

17 Jones, 171.

18 Robert Darnton (1979), *The Business of Enlightenment: A Publishing History of the Encyclopédie 1775–1800*, Cambridge, MA: Harvard University Press, 525–6.

Relations with the Public

At this time in France, writers as a category were not particularly respected. The reference to Diderot as a 'boy' in his police report, although he was 37, married and a father, was typical of the authorities' attitude to those whose status within the hierarchical class system seemed ambiguous and slippery. As Darnton explains: 'The police could not situate the writer within any conventional category because he had not yet assumed his modern form, freed from protectors, integrated in the literary marketplace, and committed to a career.'[19] The encyclopedists may have seen themselves as *philosophes* and *gens de lettres*, persons of some consequence and influence within society, but to the majority of the nation this was far from clear. It was only somewhat later, and largely due to the work of the encyclopedists themselves, especially Diderot, d'Alembert and Voltaire, that *philosophe* came to be recognized – and occasionally reviled – as an accepted category.

That the project survived persecution at all was perhaps due to a typically eighteenth-century paradox: the fact that many of its critics were also subscribers. It was because the *Encyclopédie* was sold to government administrators, lawyers and churchmen, the very people who officially condemned it, that the project was able to thrive, and to survive attacks by the authorities. Particular articles in the *Encyclopédie* frequently fell foul of the ruling institutions of Church and state, especially the prestigious and powerful Parlement de Paris. On occasion, contributors found themselves arrested and imprisoned, often in the Bastille, where Voltaire had earlier spent nearly a year as a young man. Nicolas Lenglet du Frenoy, who contributed several articles on history, was named in a police report as 'a dangerous man, who would overthrow a kingdom', and passed several weeks in the Bastille on five separate occasions. The abbé Morellet, on the other hand, another writer on religion, has been described by one historian as 'a prudent man who, when he died in 1819 at the age of ninety-one, had spent no more than seven weeks in the Bastille'![20]

An early crisis blew up in 1752, after only two volumes had been produced, when one of the contributors, the young abbé de Prades, had his doctrinal dissertation condemned for impiety by the Sorbonne. The king, Louis XV, was then said to have declared that:

> in these volumes [of the *Encyclopédie*] a point has been made of inserting several maxims tending to destroy the royal authority, to establish a spirit of independence and revolt, and under cover of obscure and ambiguous terminology to build the foundations of error, of moral corruption and of unbelief.[21]

---

19   Darnton (1984), 167.
20   Shackleton, 11.
21   Quoted in R.J.White (1970), *The Anti-philosophers*, London: Macmillan, 106.

Nevertheless, due to the tacit support of Mme de Pompadour, the king's mistress, and also of certain high-ranking officials, the *Encyclopédie* was allowed to continue. One of those sympathetic officials was Malherbes, director of the book trade, who gave Diderot advance warning of an intended search and arrest, advising him to flee Paris. When Diderot objected that he could hardly leave in a hurry with the mass of papers he was working on, Malherbes even offered his own house as a safe hiding place until the heat was off. Diderot was soon able to carry on with the project, but Prades was made the scapegoat and was forced to flee abroad.

A few years later there was an even more serious challenge, which was due to the publication of an openly atheist work entitled *de l'Esprit* ['Concerning the spirit'] by the *philosophe* Claude-Adrien Helvétius. The Parlement de Paris ordered the public burning of this book, and also, for good measure, of the published volumes of the *Encyclopédie*, even though Helvétius was not actually a contributor. Diderot had his royal licence to print revoked, and was again threatened with imprisonment. By the time of this crisis there were at least 4,000 subscribers who had paid good money and did not want to lose their investment, and these included some of the wealthy *noblesses de robe* of the Parlement de Paris, as well as members of the Court and high-ranking ecclesiastics. It was known, too, that not only Mme de Pompadour, but also Choiseul, the king's leading minister, were not unfavourable. The project was allowed to continue.

Legacy

After the French Revolution and the Terror that followed, a myth grew up that Robespierre and the Jacobins were the heirs of the encyclopedists. Edmund Burke was one of the first to develop this thesis. He wrote of a conspiracy, a 'literary cabal', which 'formed something like a regular plan for the destruction of the Christian religion', and which 'would strike at property, liberty and life'.[22] A few years later, Mme de Genlis, whose husband had been guillotined in 1793, described the authors of the *Encyclopédie* as 'a veritable army of conspirators ... a conspiracy bound by solemn oaths and holding secret meetings'.[23] But all this was highly exaggerated. To start with, nothing had been secret, since the *Encyclopédie* was mainly created under royal licence, and if there had been a conspiracy, it was a very open one. Also, these authors had no desire to start a revolution or bring down the government. They themselves were members of the educated middle classes, however impoverished some of them might have been, and their readers came from the same social bracket. It was true that visits to workshops had been made, and craftsmen interrogated, but a patronizing, even contemptuous, attitude to workers and peasants generally was nevertheless widespread among the

---

22   Edmund Burke (1790), *Reflections on the Revolution in France*, London: Everyman, 1953, 107–8.

23   Quoted in White, 115.

philosophes. They were even pessimistic about the need to educate the masses, and it was actually churchmen, especially the Jesuits, who pressed for popular education, so as to encourage piety and religious vocations. The main targets of Diderot, d'Alembert and the rest were the indolence and wealth of the clergy and nobility, and the various corruptions, mismanagements and superstitions of pre-revolutionary France. Their watchwords were certainly not 'Liberty, Equality and Fraternity', and they neither expected nor wanted a political revolution.

Nevertheless, the widespread popularity of the *Encyclopédie*, with its numerous, if often subtle and insidious, criticisms of political and religious ideas and institutions, must gradually have had a corrosive effect. In any case, it is difficult to see how the actual revolution of 1789 could not have been preceded by a revolution in certain radical ideas which by then had permeated large sections of society. Contemporaries certainly thought so, as witnessed by the special honours paid to the *philosophes* by the revolutionary leaders.[24] According to Jonathan Israel, 'there is no scope for ignoring the universal conviction during the revolutionary age, beginning in the early 1780s, that it was "philosophy" which had demolished the *Ancien Régime*, and in particular the ideas, beliefs and loyalties on which it rested, and that it accomplished this feat long before the first shots were fired at the Bastille.'[25] If this is true, then Diderot and his more radical colleagues may be said to have succeeded in their aim of subverting the status quo, even though they might well have disapproved of many of the actions allegedly committed in their name.[26]

Summary

This was an ambitious, even revolutionary project for its time and place, managed by a socially heterogeneous group of authors led by capable editors. Their aim was to collect, record and update all society's knowledge, and to disseminate it appropriately, including, for the first time, practical information concerning trade and industry. For some, there was also a political agenda – to target repressive institutions of Church and state. The project was commercially successful, but had an ambiguous relationship with government and public. It was condemned by the authorities more than once, but survived because it was bought and read by the leaders of society.

---

24   Such as, for instance, the reburial of Voltaire, Rousseau and others in the newly built Panthéon.

25   Israel, 715.

26   Diderot himself died in 1784, d'Alembert in 1783, and d'Holbach in 1789, but many of the encyclopedists survived to take part in the Revolution, some contributing, for instance, to the *cahiers de doléances*, or 'books of grievances', sent up from the provinces to the king in January 1789.

Like Wikipedia, the Encyclopédie was a collaborative effort involving numerous writers and technicians. As do wikipedians today, Diderot and his colleagues needed to engage with the latest technology in dealing with the problems of designing an up-to-date encyclopaedia. These included what kind of information to include, how to set up links between the various articles, and how to achieve the maximum readership.

Chapter 5

The Making of the
Oxford English Dictionary

It is an embittering consideration for me that while trying to do scholarly work in a way that scholars may be expected to appreciate, circumstances place me commercially in the position of the *bête noir* of the Clarendon Press, who involves them in ruinous expenditure.

James Murray[1]

Aims

In November 1857, Dr Richard Chenevix Trench, dean of Westminster, addressed members of the Philological Society on the subject of dictionaries.[2] Although Trench merely proposed the making of a supplement to existing dictionaries, the following year the society entered into a more ambitious plan for a completely new English dictionary which would show the life history of every word in the language, its origin, and any changes in its form or meaning. They took up the most original feature of Trench's original proposal, which was that teams of voluntary helpers should be employed to read books and send in examples of word usage over the centuries. Trench assured his somewhat sceptical audience that this system, although never before tried out in England, was being used successfully by the brothers Grimm in compiling their *Deutsches Wörterbuch.* He explained:

> this almost boundless field could only be made available for dictionary purposes through the combined action of many. … We do but follow the example of the Grimms, when we call upon Englishmen to come forward and write their own Dictionary for themselves, and we trust that our invitation may be responded to still more effectually than theirs has been.[3]

---

1   Quoted in Simon Winchester (2003), *The Meaning of Everything*, Oxford: Oxford University Press, 174.

2   The Philological Society was founded in 1842 for 'the investigation of the structure, the Affinities and the History of Languages'. It was, said James Murray, 'the only body in England then interesting itself in the language': John Willinsky (1994), *Empire of Words*, Princeton, NJ: Princeton University Press, 27.

3   *Transactions of the Philological Society*, London: Trübner, 1857, quoted in Willinsky, 27; according to Trench, the Grimms had 'eighty-three voluntary co-adjutors'.

Trench suggested that the volunteers be asked to submit their quotations on half sheets, and this, he said, would allow 'the registration of 1200 words at trifling expense', since 600 sheets of notepaper could be purchased for 2 shillings.

Over the next twenty years slow progress was made on the new dictionary under successive editors. The first of these, Herbert Coleridge, grandson of the poet, was an extremely erudite but sickly young man who organized the first group of some 150 volunteers, many from America. Readers could choose which books they wanted to read, or the editor was prepared to suggest titles, and even lend out books from the Philological Society's library. Coleridge is remembered for wildly underestimating the future extent of the project. He designed and had built a piece of furniture with 54 pigeon holes to house the slips that were starting to arrive from the volunteers, believing that its full capacity – to hold 100,000 slips – would never be required. It turned out that before the dictionary was finished they needed space for between five and six million slips.

Coleridge died in 1861, and was succeeded as editor by Frederick Furnival, a gifted, colourful and combative character whose erratic nature proved unsuitable for the 'harmless drudgery' of a lexicographer's work.[4] His main reform was to introduce a new category of volunteer sub-editor to work on the slips sent in by the readers, before in turn forwarding them to the editor-in-chief. Each sub-editor was allotted a letter of the alphabet, and expected to fill in gaps in the slips and provide definitions of meaning for the words. However, Furnival failed to maintain enough control over his readers and sub-editors, with the result that by the time he came to resign in 1879 the system was in a fair state of chaos, with vast numbers of slips lost or misplaced, and many volunteers disillusioned, suspecting all their hard work might disappear and never reach the printed page. Elizabeth Murray, granddaughter of James Murray, the next editor, takes up the story:

> Until the material was handed over, Furnival gave James no hint of its condition. The load delivered to Murray at Mill Hill in the spring of 1879 … was a shock to the newly appointed Editor. Many of the sub-editors had clearly found difficulty in packing up hundred weights of slips. Some were sent in sacks in which they had long been stored, and when opened a dead rat was found in one and a live mouse and her family in another: one sub-editor's work was delivered in a baby's bassinet: there was a 'hamper of *Is*' with the bottom broken, which had been left behind in an empty vicarage at Harrow. Many of the bundles had stood for so many years in unsuitable places that the slips were crumbling with damp and the writing had faded; others had been so illegibly scribbled in the first place that Dr Murray exclaimed in exasperation that Chinese would have been more useful, since for that he could have found a translator. In spite of instructions, the

---

4   'Lexicographer: A writer of dictionaries; a harmless drudge, that busies himself in tracing the original, and detailing the signification of words': Johnson's *Dictionary*.

slips were not always of a standard size: Furnival himself nearly always wrote on scraps of paper or backs of envelopes.[5]

James Murray, the dictionary's third editor, was the epitome of a self-taught Victorian polymath. He had left school at 14, becoming assistant teacher in a village school and then a bank clerk, before his omnivorous reading and knowledge of obscure languages brought him to the attention of the Philological Society, and Frederick Furnival in particular. In 1871, aged 43, he was persuaded to sign the agreement to pursue the project which was to dominate his entire life and those of his large family until he died in 1915. Long hours were spent sorting the slips now pouring in at the rate of about 1,000 a day, and when all the slips had been dealt with by sub-editors, the final responsibility lay with Murray to oversee definitions and etymologies. At this stage he had to seek the advice of experts, and sometimes particular words took weeks to sort out. Every week he had to write twenty to thirty letters in his own hand, and presumably twice over, since copies needed to be kept.[6]

The Group

One of his first initiatives was to issue a new appeal for volunteers. This was particularly necessary because existing readers, Murray discovered, were tending to concentrate too much on rare or obsolete words, and neglecting the more common ones. His advice now included: 'Make as many quotations as you can for ordinary words, especially when they are used significantly, and tend by the context to explain or suggest their own meaning'.[7] Long lists of books still needing to be read were also produced. Two thousand copies of this leaflet were printed and sent off to newspapers, and also in bulk to bookshops and libraries so that they might be inserted into any books sold or borrowed. The immediate result of the appeal was an additional eight hundred readers from Great Britain and four or five hundred from the United States.

The number of readers continued to rise, and in 1884 James Murray presented to the Philological Society a detailed list of 762 contributors who had signed on since 1879, along with a list of the books they had read. The readers included (among overlapping groups) 89 clergymen, 103 Americans and 278 women.[8] The participation of so many women in a public project was unusual in this era, to say the least. Elizabeth Murray notes that there were 'many very intelligent

---

5   K.M. Elizabeth Murray (1977), *Caught in the Web of Words*, New Haven, CT and London: Yale University Press, 174.

6   An example of the letters written during one particular week is given in Murray, 201.

7   *An Appeal to the English-speaking and English-reading Public*, April 1879, quoted in Murray, 178.

8   Willinsky, 42.

ladies, lonely widows or spinsters living at home looking after parents or housekeeping for brothers or sisters, who found some fulfilment in contributing to the work'.[9] Americans, too, responded enthusiastically, especially a number of scholars and academics, which was fortunate because the general response from British universities was disappointing. Murray reported in 1880 that 'only one or two Professors of English in this country have thought the matter of sufficient importance to talk to their students about it and advise them to help me'.[10] Four years later there were 1,300 readers, 800 from Britain and almost all the rest from the United States – and numbers continued to grow. By the turn of the century, well over five million slips had been filled in and received by the editor, and of these approximately one third were eventually used in the dictionary. Two of the most unusual among Murray's helpers are described in Simon Winchester's book about the dictionary, *The Meaning of Everything*.[11] The American Fitzedward Hall, a self-taught philologist who had quarrelled with his academic peers and lived in total seclusion in an East Anglian cottage, nevertheless devoted at least four hours a day for 20 years to this unpaid activity. And another American, William Chester Minor, who was confined to Broadmoor Asylum for the Criminally Insane having murdering a total stranger, was also among Murray's most prolific assistants, although for many years the editor was unaware of his circumstances.

One can only speculate about the motives of the readers. Simon Winchester seems mildly surprised that so many were prepared to put in so much effort for nothing. He writes:

> we do not really know why so many people gave so much time for so little apparent reward. And this is the abiding and most marvellous mystery of the enormously democratic process that was the Dictionary – that hundreds upon hundreds of people ... dedicated in many cases ... years upon years of labour to a project of which they all, buoyed by some set of unfathomable and optimistic notions, insisted on becoming a part.[12]

Searching for particular words in obscure works of literature is, after all, quite a pleasant occupation, and not especially demanding. John Willinsky compares it to doing crossword puzzles, or to writing letters to *The Times* protesting some journalist's linguistic solecism.[13] A major advantage of the hobby of citation-culling, of course, is its modularity – the fact that it can be broken up into small

---

9   Murray, 185.

10   Murray, 183.

11   The same author has written a whole book about Minor: *The Surgeon of Crowthorne*, London: Penguin Books (1999).

12   Winchester, 215.

13   Willinsky, 42.

fragments. One may do as much or as little as one wants – select a single example of a word and send it off on a slip, or go through an entire book.[14]

The use of volunteers was far from unproblematic. As far back as 1860, Herbert Coleridge, who had organized the first small army of volunteers, wrote that only 30 of the 147 he had managed to recruit were of any real use.[15] Many had never sent in any slips, and worse, some of them had failed to return the books they had been lent by the Philological Society. Perhaps worse still, sometimes valuable books had been mutilated by readers cutting out the required quotations and pasting them onto slips. Later on, James Murray was just as scathing about some of his volunteers, especially those who had been selected by Furnival or himself to be sub-editors and devise word definitions. In a 1910 lecture he concluded that:

> On the whole the volunteer sub-editing tho' done with the greatest good-will, and immense diligence, has not been a great help. ... I have had to come to the conclusion that practically the only valuable work that can be done by the average amateur, & out of the Scriptorium, is that of reading books and extracting quotations.[16]

Nevertheless, in spite of such pessimistic conclusions, it seems highly likely that without the hundreds of volunteer readers, sub-editors and proofreaders, the *Oxford English Dictionary*, in a pre-digital age, would never have achieved completion.

Transaction Costs

Given the free labour of the volunteers, one might have expected the dictionary project to be free of financial worries, but this was far from the case. Following Murray's appointment in 1871, there followed several difficult years in which the Philological Society tried to find a suitable publisher for the dictionary, and eventually, after months of sometimes acrimonious negotiation, a contract was drawn up between the editor, the Philological Society and the Oxford University Press (OUP). It is ironic that one sticking point was the future allocation of royalties, considering that no such payments were ever made during the lifetimes of any of those involved. The Press was attached to the university, and had an international reputation as a publisher of academic books, and there was no doubt that publishing the dictionary would enhance that reputation in the long term. But it was also a commercial firm, and its directors (known as delegates) did not intend it to lose money.[17] Was the dictionary a learned, unrenumerative work, or was

---

14 For more on modularity, see p. 86.

15 Winchester, 53.

16 Murray, 200.

17 The delegates included well-known academics such as the Orientalist Max Müller and Benjamin Jowett, Regius professor of Greek, who was for a time a thorn in the side of

it intended to fetch a handsome profit? In 1879, when the contract was finally signed, no one guessed how long and complicated its gestation would be. It was then supposed that it would take about ten years to complete the project, that the dictionary might consist of 7,000 pages in total, and that the entire cost to the OUP would be some £9,000. The editor was to receive £500 a year, out of which he was to pay for his own assistants. An additional bonus was that Gladstone's government agreed to give Murray an extra £250 a year from the Civil List, as the work was clearly of national importance.

The following years were ones involving increasing strain and tension, especially between Murray and the OUP, as it became clear that these figures and estimates were wildly out. The delegates muddled along, sometimes trying to speed up the work by harrying the editor, sometimes showing a *laissez-faire* attitude. One expedient to try and improve cash flow was to publish the dictionary, as it gradually emerged, in small, separate paperback sections which the customer could have bound up on completion. However, this system, which seemed to work for Dickens and Trollope, proved commercially disappointing, and there was increasing impatience with Murray's thorough and painstaking approach. Efforts made to hurry him up nearly led to his nervous breakdown on several occasions, and only dogged dedication allowed him to survive insistent demands that he speed up production. In 1885 he moved with his wife and their nine children to Oxford, and in his new garden he built himself a corrugated iron shed where he, his family and various assistants worked long hours, often suffering excessive heat in summer and cold and damp in winter. He was under constant strain to produce anything like the 704 pages a year specified in his contract, and was always short of money, as he later complained to a wealthy friend who helped him out with a loan:

> I am not a capitalist, but a poor man, and have only saved a few hundred pounds in anticipation of the time when I should have to spend some on the further education & starting in life of my boys, by annual savings to which the Dictionary put a stop. ... I have had to say rather bitterly: 'I took up the Dictionary as a student, asking only to be repaid the income I sacrificed in its behalf, and to be furnished with the necessary assistance, and I find myself ... with an incessant struggle to make ends meet, & failing in the struggle ... it is certain that we have all underestimated the cost to *somebody* ... and that it is I on whom the consequences fall, & whom they threaten to crush.[18]

In spite of these troubles, the process of production went on, gradually matters improved between editor and publisher, and eventually parts started to come off the press rather more rapidly. In 1928 the final volume was published. It had taken

---

the editor: Murray 215–45.

18   James Murray to Henry Hucks Gibbs, 12 February 1882. Gibbs, a merchant banker, later became Lord Aldenham: Murray 255.

not ten years, but 54, the number of pages was not 7,000, but 16,000, and the total cost was not £9,000, but about £300,000.

Relations with the Public

Most of those who volunteered to send in slips probably rated their efforts far higher than the solving of crossword puzzles. It was an age of supreme confidence in the achievements of Britain, not only imperial, commercial and industrial achievements, but also cultural. This project of creating a history of the English language, with citations going back to Chaucer, and even *Beowulf*, was only one of many such ambitious projects undertaken during Victoria's reign. These included, for instance, the creation of a national library at the British Museum, the foundation of the National Portrait Gallery, and Leslie Stephen's *Dictionary of National Biography*. As Willinsky says, 'the period was busy with civic-minded gentlemen keen to assemble cultural cathedrals celebrating the British accomplishment', and here was an opportunity to create another such cathedral, a chance to lend a hand in 'establishing the greatness of the English language, as it had been developed and refined over the centuries into a civilizing instrument of great intellectual suppleness and beauty'.[19] That at least one of the editors of the dictionary thought along similar lines is evident from the excitable statement made by Frederick Furnival in the course of one of his clarion calls for volunteers:

> We have set ourselves to form a National Portrait Gallery, not only of the worthies, but of all the members, of the race of English words which is to form the dominant speech of the world. No winged messenger who bears to us the thoughts and aspirations, the weakness and the littleness, of our forefathers; who is to carry ours to our descendants: is to be absent, – Fling our doors wide! all, all, not one, but all, must enter.[20]

Many volunteers and others may also have shared the ideals of Robert Trench, the man responsible for the initial inspiration for the project. Trench, an ordained minister of the Church of England and shortly to become archbishop of Dublin, saw a close link between lexicography and religion. In a highly influential set of lectures to students of theology, many of whom were shortly to set out into the world as missionaries, he exhorted them to 'transport abroad the moral superiority of the English and their language'.[21] According to Trench, it was the 'hateful

---

19 Willinsky, 23, 42.

20 Quoted in Murray, 137.

21 The published version of Trench's lectures, *On the Study of Words* (1851), went into 19 editions by 1886: Jonathan Green (1996), *Chasing the Sun*, London: Jonathan Cape, 295. Trench's ideas about the 'decadence' of indigenous cultures was a widely held Victorian assumption.

poverty' of the languages of the savage that tended to keep him in the 'depths to which he has fallen'. There were languages that had lost any linguistic concept of the divine, and others lacking 'any word in the least corresponding to our "thanks"'.[22] Hence, a knowledge of English must be a precondition for conversion and salvation. Trench wanted his students to study the historical record of their native tongue in order to become more effective proselytizers.

Legacy

The dictionary that resulted from Trench's vision and from the efforts of successive editors incorporated both liberal and conservative elements. To start with, the very existence of an academic and comprehensive dictionary of the English language was progressive from the point of view of the emerging Victorian middle class. Until then, classical languages tended to be the main focus for linguistic education and scholarship, but these were the preserve of those who could afford the lengthy process of training they required. Trench himself believed in the virtues of a classical education, admitting 'the inestimable advantage mental and moral' of the study of Greek and Latin, but he understood that such an education was available to a dwindling proportion of his contemporaries. He therefore offered the next best thing, arguing that 'our own language and literature will furnish the best substitutes … for that formation of discipline which these languages would, better than any other have afforded'.[23]

Another liberal, even democratic, feature of the dictionary was its innovative use of volunteers, even though these played a relatively subordinate part in the creation of the text, and no part at all in the management of the project. And another such feature was Trench's and Murray's insistence that the dictionary was descriptive, and not prescriptive. Both were clear that it was to be an inventory of the language and of the ways it had been used in the past, and not a guide to present usage or an arbiter of style. The idea here was to distinguish it from Continental dictionaries, especially the French model of linguistic dictatorship as demonstrated in the successive editions of the *Dictionnaire de l'Académie française*.[24] It might be argued, however, that such an authoritative product as the *Oxford English Dictionary* can hardly escape being seen as prescriptive, that most of those who consult it certainly see it as a guide to present usage, and that to deny this is slightly disingenuous.

A conservative feature of the dictionary, and one common to practically all dictionaries, then and now, is that the evidence it used for the present and past meanings of words was all taken from printed sources. True, the editors said they

---

22   Willinsky, 21.

23   Willinsky, 26.

24   The French Academy issues successive editions of this work. The first edition was in 1694; the ninth was in progress at the time of writing.

were prepared to use ephemera such as railway timetables, and also the daily press, but the actual use of such items seems to have been rare. However, at least Furnival did sometimes use newspapers as a source of quotation – we know this because Jowett, James Murray's youngest son, wrote a reminiscence of his days sorting slips in which he mentions that the children 'enlivened the task by reading out tit-bits from Dr Furnival's newspaper cuttings, & bundles of slips from Dr Furnival were in demand, in spite of the bad handwriting'.[25] At least one critic, the Rev. Derwent Coleridge, attacked the dictionary makers for not including oral evidence. In 1860 he rebuked the Philological Society for treating English as a 'so-called dead language' like Latin, as if all that were left of it were surviving texts, whereas 'in the living language we have the living instinct of those who speak it, to which we can apply'.[26]

Murray himself, in the various prefaces he wrote to successive parts of the dictionary, made much of the distinction between a natural, living language in which new words might appear and survive, and a literary language which was closed to such development. But in practice, and inevitably, his great dictionary was a literary one. For centuries there had been in popular opinion a difference between 'dictionary English' and the spoken word, as is clearly illustrated in some of the quotations selected in the *Oxford English Dictionary* itself to illustrate the meaning of the word 'dictionary':

1632 *J. HAYWARD* I would not ... be taken (or rather mistaken) for a Dictionary-tutred Linguist.

1831 *CARLYLE* He ... Calls many things by their mere dictionary names.

1858 *R.S. SURTEES* His fine dictionary words and laboured expletives.

It would, in any case, have been virtually impossible for Murray to use the spoken word in his dictionary. Not only were his own education and predilections against it, but the available technology would have made it enormously difficult. Modern dictionaries can dispense with volunteer readers and turn instead to vast electronic databases of word usage known as corpora, which may include oral recordings or transcripts. The OUP itself has been a major contributor to the British National Corpus, which consists of 100 million words compiled from over 4,000 texts, 90 per cent written and 10 per cent spoken.[27]

---

25   Murray, 180.

26   Willinsky, 32. Derwent Coleridge was a noted linguist. He was the son of Samuel Taylor Coleridge and uncle of the dictionary editor Herbert Coleridge.

27   Sidney L. Landau (2001), *Dictionaries: The Art and Craft of Lexicography*, 2nd edn, Cambridge: Cambridge University Press, 288–9. The first complete revision of the *Oxford English Dictionary* since its publication in 1928 was started in 1997, and is now approaching completion.

The eventual publication of the *Oxford English Dictionary* in 1928 was certainly a major cultural achievement, and a tribute to its longest-serving editor, James Murray, who had died thirteen years earlier. The dictionary was a highly literary work, conceived and managed by academics, and making few concessions to commercial interests or popular taste. It is all the more remarkable, therefore, that hundreds of volunteers were recruited to help with the production process. This was unusual, possibly unique, for the period, but without these volunteers the project would probably have failed. Nevertheless, looking ahead towards modern times, and to what we now know about the potential of suitably motivated volunteers, it seems clear that the groups recruited by Furnival and Murray were not employed to their full capacity, nor perhaps could they have been given the level of technology and the cultural assumptions of the period.

Summary

This was a highly ambitious venture – to record not only the current meaning, but also the history of every English word. The project started optimistically, but took far longer to achieve than anyone could have guessed at the start, although it did get there in the end. It fell between two stools, the commercial and the academic, and it was plagued with financial problems from start to finish. As with Wikipedia, an innovative use was made of widely dispersed volunteers, since this dictionary could only be completed through 'the combined action of many' (Dr Trench), and there was also an equally innovative use of the postal network that linked often isolated contributors together. Hence, it was an outstanding early example of collective knowledge production, even though the volunteers themselves played a subsidiary and not altogether satisfactory part in the venture.

Chapter 6

The Left Book Club

Forced to make the choice ourselves
Our rude forefathers loaded shelves
With Tennyson and Walter Scott
And Meredith and Lord knows what!
But we don't have to hum and ha,
Nous avons changé tout cela –
Our books are chosen for us – Thanks
To Strachey, Laski and Gollancz!

Paul Laity[1]

Aims

In early 1936 a successful publisher, Victor Gollancz, teamed up with an academic, Harold Laski, and a political writer, John Strachey, to form the Left Book Club (LBC). The club survived until after the Second World War, but its glory days were from its start to the outbreak of war in September 1939, by which time it had achieved a membership approaching 60,000. During these initial three and a half years it was amazingly successful in its own terms, bringing political awareness backed up by factual knowledge, to a wide audience. In fact, largely as a result of the LBC's activities, the late 1930s was the one and only period in modern British history when large numbers of people, from every walk of life, started calling themselves socialist, even Marxist, and wondering whether the problems they faced were not endemic to the capitalist system itself.

The period 1936–39 was one of growing international tension and menace as the world seemed to be moving inexorably towards war. Germany under Hitler rearmed rapidly, and the invasion of the Rhineland was followed successively by the assimilation of Austria into the Third Reich, Munich, and the invasion of Czechoslovakia. Hitler's ally, Mussolini, had successfully taken over Abyssinia, while in Spain Franco, with the help of his fellow dictators, was proceeding to overwhelm the republican government. On the far side of the world, Japan, having occupied Manchuria, was turning its brutal attention to mainland China. Throughout these events, the League of Nations appeared impotent, and the Western democracies pursued policies of non-intervention and appeasement, mesmerized on the one hand by fear of provoking Hitler, and on the other by their disdain and distrust for Stalinist Russia, whose offers of a collective security pact against the

---

1   From introduction to Paul Laity (ed.) (2001), *Left Book Club Anthology*, London: Victor Gollancz.

fascist powers they repeatedly rejected. Meanwhile, in Britain the consequences of the world depression of the early 1930s, particularly with regard to heavy industry, had led to a low-wage economy and a permanent unemployment rate of over 10 per cent of the workforce. The national government, headed by Baldwin and then Chamberlain, seemed powerless, unable to deal with the consequent problems of poverty, ill-health and inadequate housing in the so-called distressed areas. As guardians of economic orthodoxy, their only solutions involved free markets, wage cuts and the hated means test. Nor did the Liberal and Labour opposition parties appear to have much to contribute, either at home or abroad.

Nevertheless, during these years there arose, spontaneously and without direction from political parties or government, a new awakening of public concern and a critical attitude to hitherto accepted authority. Many who had previously only been concerned with their own personal circumstances now started to take an interest in the state of their country and the world, to discuss political issues and search for solutions. Playing a crucial part in this new movement was the LBC.

The club's initial purpose was to produce a series of books dealing with what was seen as three related issues – fascism, the threat of war, and poverty. The objectives were: effective resistance to the first, the removal of the second, and the elimination of the third through the introduction of socialism. In the first brochure distributed to potential members, Gollancz wrote:

> The aim of the Club is a simple one: it is to help in the struggle *for* World Peace
> and a better social and economic order and *against* Fascism, by *(a)* increasing
> the knowledge of those who already see the importance of this struggle, and *(b)*
> adding to their number the very many who, being fundamentally well disposed,
> hold aloof from the fight by reason of ignorance or apathy.
> That the success of this aim is of terrible urgency at the present time, when
> the world is drifting into war, and when Fascism is triumphing in country after
> country, needs no emphasis.[2]

From the start, the LBC issued to subscribers a book each month together with a copy of *Left News*, which carried reviews of supplementary books which could be purchased at a discount, and also editorials by Gollancz and short articles on political topics. Many of the books of the month were concerned with current events, but there were also books on a wide range of topics – sociological, philosophical, biographical, even a few novels by authors considered suitable, such as André Malraux. The majority of publications were concerned with world events, though there were also books on domestic issues, especially poverty, unemployment and health. Two of the most popular of these were George Orwell's *The Road to Wigan Pier*, and *The Town that was Murdered* by Ellen Wilkinson, MP for Jarrow, who had led the famous march of the unemployed from there to London. There were

---

2 Quoted in Ruth Dudley Edwards (1987), *Victor Gollancz: A Biography*, London: Victor Gollancz, 232.

also books on theory that attempted to provide a leftist framework to help their readers make sense of the complexities of the modern world. Among these, by far the most influential was *The Theory and Practice of Socialism* by John Strachey, which was the November 1936 book of the month. 'I suppose', wrote John Lewis, 'no single book more completely fulfilled the basic aim of the Club: to provide that disciplined study, rooted in fact and illuminated by theory, which was what the Club wanted to give its members'.[3] One crucial element in this theoretical framework was the argument that Nazism and fascism were the predictable outcome of 'monopoly-capitalist' societies in terminal decline.[4] Hitler's demand for *Lebensraum* was thus seen as a logical search for the new markets and sources of raw materials required by those pulling his puppet strings. The LBC set up a training school for leaders to go out to the regions and run study courses on Strachey's book.

The club was strongly involved in promoting support for Republican Spain, and several books about Spain were published, the most influential of which was Arthur Koestler's *Spanish Testament*. Koestler, who at this time was a member of the German Communist Party, had been imprisoned and threatened with execution under Franco. This gave his account an immediacy which was followed up by his speaking tour of LBC groups throughout the country. Support for the Spanish government was seen as one issue where individuals could make a difference. Meetings and rallies were held, funds contributed, orphans from Spain looked after, and those enlisting in the International Brigades given enthusiastic support. Strong feelings were also aroused over news of Japanese atrocities in China, although here there seemed less opportunity for individual action. One of the most popular books issued by the club was Edgar Snow's *Red Star over China*, a moving account of the Red Army's Long March of 1934–35. The nation most discussed in LBC literature, however, was Soviet Russia, about which there were no less than 15 books, some commissioned by Gollancz from Russians, and all uncritical and even adulatory of Stalin and his policies. For instance, the infamous show trials of Zinoviev, Bukharin and other leaders were defended, with no qualms expressed about the executions that followed.

The club's principal purpose may have been to disseminate knowledge through its publications, but its main political aim was to encourage the development of a popular front at home, which might then lead to collective security abroad, implying an alliance between the democratic nations and the Soviet Union against the fascist powers.[5] There were, however, considerable difficulties in the way,

---

3   John Lewis (1970), *The Left Book Club: An Historical Record*, London: Victor Gollancz, 37.

4   'Fascism is an artificial conglomeration of featureless individuals, driven by the external power of monopoly capitalism': Victor Gollancz, addressing an LBC mass rally at the Albert Hall in February 1937, quoted in Edwards, 240.

5   Strictly speaking, one should distinguish between a United Front, which meant an alliance between the Communist Party of Great Britain and the Labour Party, and a Popular

not the least being that not only Baldwin's government but also the leadership of the Labour Party were strongly opposed to any alliance with communists or rapprochement with Russia. True, the Labour leader, Clement Attlee, had shown mild approval of the club when it started, and had even written one, not particularly well received, book for it.[6] However, he and his colleagues soon cooled off, coming to regard the LBC's enormous popularity as a threat. Consequently, the club's policy was to bypass the Labour leadership and instead try to attract individual members of the party as well as those of other parties, or none. At rallies and in their propaganda they made much of the fact that the demand for a popular front cut across party divisions, and it is true that some well-known figures from across the political spectrum were supportive, including the Liberal Richard Acland and the Tory Robert Boothby.[7] Yet it was clear to many at the time, and has become even clearer since, that, in spite of the LBC claiming to represent a broad church, it was in fact something of a front organization for the Communist Party.[8] Neither a popular front alliance between Labour and communists nor a collective security pact involving Russia was ever achieved before the war, and in this sense the LBC may be said to have failed.[9]

The Group

The Left Book Club was run by the formidable trio of Gollancz, Laski and Strachey, who between them were responsible for promoting – and vetting – the choice of books to be published. Gollancz was an inspired publicist who had already commissioned various left-wing books through the profitable publishing firm he had set up in 1927. He was a passionate idealist, a moralist and even a pacifist, a deeply emotional man who put profound conviction into everything he did. However, during the 1930s he found himself moving ever closer to the Communist Party since it alone was firmly in favour of the collective security policy which, so it seemed to him, could be the only bulwark against the growing fascist threat. He was, in other words, driven to associate with those who tended to hold his idealism and his pacifist views in some contempt. The tireless energy and enthusiasm of Gollancz were the real force behind the club. He controlled its

---

Front, which might involve all opponents of government appeasement, from dissident Tory to communist.

6   Attlee's *The Labour Party in Perspective* was the club choice for August 1937.

7   One problem for advocates of collective security was that the leading Conservative supporting that policy was Winston Churchill, who was deeply unpopular on the left owing to his actions during the General Strike and his attitude towards Indian independence.

8   During the 1930s the Communist Party of Great Britain was a growing force in British politics. The first Communist MP, Willie Gallacher, was elected in 1935.

9   One success, however, was the Bridgewater by-election of 1938, which was won by a Popular Front advocate with much support from local LBC groups: Lewis, 95.

finances, commissioned new authors, wrote long editorials in the monthly *Left News*, and made numerous speeches at rallies and meetings. It was he who turned a mere book club into a powerful political movement that for a time rivalled the existing political parties in membership and influence.

John Strachey was a suitable partner for Gollancz. He was easily the most influential Marxist writer of the 1930s, with a genius for explaining complex ideas in lucid and popular form. He had been a young Labour Party MP in the 1920s, and had then joined forces with Oswald Mosley, who broke with Labour over the issue of unemployment to found his New Party. Strachey withdrew when it became clear which way Mosley was headed, and turned instead to Marxism, though he was never actually a member of the Communist Party – probably because the party felt he would be of more use to them as an independent. He was the intellectual force behind the LBC, and his speeches, articles in *Left News* and the seven books he wrote for the club set out a Marxist framework intended to make sense of contemporary events.

The third member of the triumvirate, Harold Laski, was professor of political science at the London School of Economics, and perhaps the most influential left-wing teacher of his day. He too had arrived at a Marxist position, although he remained a member of the Labour Party and was even at one time chairman of its National Executive. Like Strachey, it was his conviction that socialism could only ever come to Britain through revolution. But Laski held himself aloof from the day-to-day running of the club, and played a much smaller part than the other two, who sometimes deliberately failed to keep him up to date with problems requiring decisions.

Another important leader was John Lewis, an ex-Presbyterian minister employed by Gollancz to take charge of the LBC groups which mushroomed up and down the country. Lewis was a communist sympathizer although, like Strachey, he was not a formal member of the party.[10] Working with Lewis and Gollancz were two members of the Communist Party, Betty Reid, whom Lewis later married, and Sheila Lynd. Because they saw the LBC as furthering the communist cause, all three were prepared to work long hours for small pay. Thus Gollancz was surrounded at work by communist sympathizers, not to mention his close relations with Harry Pollitt, General Secretary of the Communist Party, and Ivan Maisky, the Soviet ambassador.

The first adverts for the LBC appeared in February 1936. Those interested sent in their names and received a 12-page booklet setting out the aims of the new club. Gollancz said he hoped to balance the books by recruiting 2,000 by May, but in the event the number was 9,000. The membership rapidly increased until it peaked at 57,000 in August, 1939. Over the same period the club evolved from being a mere book club to a political movement that took over the lives of many of its members. Local study groups sprang up in practically every town throughout the country and in many villages, and there were also groups relating to particular jobs or

---

10   Lewis joined the Communist Party of Great Britain in 1939: Edwards, 237.

professions. For instance, there was an important actors' group which put on left-wing plays, and a musicians' group that provided music at rallies and meetings, as well as groups in factories, groups of bus drivers, postal workers, teachers, lawyers and scientists. Many were promoted by the leadership in London, while others set themselves up spontaneously. Some, in the larger cities, even had their own premises. Altogether, there were some 1,500 such groups by the summer of 1939.[11]

Under Lewis in his Groups department, there were four regional organizers who spent their time travelling round the country visiting groups and making suggestions for new ventures, but often it was the local groups themselves that took the initiative here. A typical small suburban group might well have regular fortnightly meetings, distribute leaflets in the vicinity, organize theatre trips, social events and countryside rambles in summer, and take up a particular cause such as the housing of Spanish orphans whose parents had been displaced or killed in the war. One historian of the LBC paints a deliberately exaggerated picture of how the day-to-day life of an enthusiastic member of an urban group might in theory be entirely taken over by club activities. The member's day might:

> consist of waking to find his Left Book Club monthly selection on his doorstep; attending a Left Book Club Russian language class; going to the local Left Book Club travel agency to arrange for a Left Book Club tour to the Soviet Union; spending the remainder of the morning selling Left Book Club publications in the town marketplace; attending a Left Book Club luncheon, organized by some local businessmen; then going to the Left Book Club Centre to play ping-pong and to relax reading left periodicals; selling Left Book Club pamphlets and leaflets for the remainder of the afternoon; in the evening attending a Left Book Club discussion meeting, followed by a Left Book Club film-showing on Spain and a one-act play performed by the local Left Book Club Theatre Guild group; chalking a few slogans on the way home; reading his *Left News* and then dozing off to sleep, secure in the knowledge that the Left Book Club was Not So Much a Book Club, More a Way of Life.[12]

In addition to local activities there were more ambitious central events such as summer schools, public lectures, delegations abroad and regular mass rallies at the Albert Hall or Queen's Hall in central London. And all such events, local and national, were faithfully recorded in the LBC's monthly magazine, *Left News*.

Nevertheless, in spite of its large membership and ceaseless activity, the club never turned into the mass movement that Gollancz hoped for, the kind of movement which might have forced the British government to alter course. In the November 1939 *Left News*, Gollancz wrote sadly and bitterly:

---

11 Lewis, 7.

12 Stuart Samuels (1966), 'The Left Book Club', *Journal of Contemporary History*, vol. 1, no. 2, 65–86.

If we had had half a million members the Government would have been replaced by a People's Government long before the war came and the Anglo-Soviet alliance would have been consummated. Hitler would have been overthrown ... and the war would never have happened.[13]

Transaction Costs

The Left Book Club could hardly have developed as it did without capital backing. Gollancz used the resources of his publishing firm to subsidize it. Many alleged at the time that he was onto a goldmine and was exploiting the credulous masses for his own profit, but his biographer believes he actually lost money from the club. Certainly, this is what he himself maintained, although he apparently did not keep accounts separate from the rest of his business, and was generally secretive about financial matters. However, one letter has survived which he wrote in May 1938 to the communist scientist J.B.S. Haldane, a friend from university days, which, if true, is revealing about the club's accounts. He wrote that:

> the Left Book Club, with its 50,000 individual members operating through 5,000 agents, not only has overheads disproportionate to those of any publishing business, but is also now, of course, an expensive political organisation – and all the money has to come from somewhere. We spend £12,000 a year on advertising and general publicity (absolutely essential in order to keep up the increase in Club membership): £3,000 a year on the free 'Left News': and about £5,000 a year on Dr Lewis's department (which involves huge circularisation, travelling expenses, etc.) for the local groups. These three items alone amount to £20,000 per annum. The total number of books in a year is between 500,000 and 600,000 (i.e. an average of about 48,000 a month multiplied by twelve months): and if you take into consideration the authors' royalty and the booksellers' discount of 33⅓ per cent, you will find *the three items alone* that I have mentioned themselves amount to something like 1/4d of the 2/6d.
> And we haven't begun to consider the colossal overhead expenses (an army of girls working on the cards alone), or the manufacture of the books themselves! The fact is that at the end of the first two years of the Club's existence there is a very considerable loss. *But this is absolutely confidential ....*[14]

One issue which is somewhat unclear is the relationship between the LBC and bookshops. At the start, Gollancz was keen to get the booksellers on his side, especially since as a profession they had always been wary of displaying and selling left-wing books. The early method was therefore to dispatch books to the shops, where the individual members might claim them after showing proof

---

13   Lewis, 122.
14   Quoted in Edwards, 257.

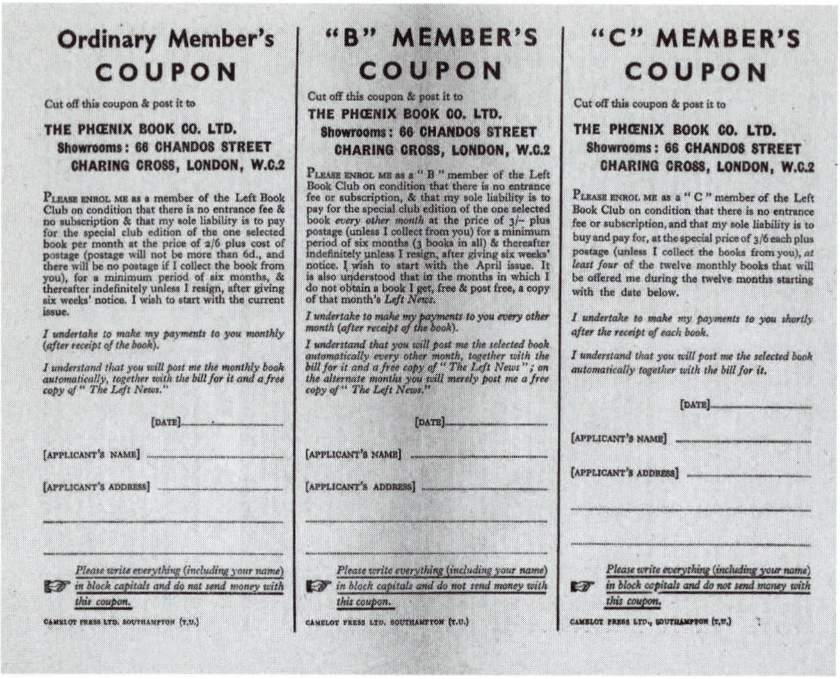

Ordinary Member's COUPON

Cut off this coupon & post it to

THE PHŒNIX BOOK CO. LTD.
Showrooms: 66 CHANDOS STREET
CHARING CROSS, LONDON, W.C.2

Please enrol me as a member of the Left Book Club on condition that there is no entrance fee & no subscription & that my sole liability is to pay for the special club edition of the one selected book per month at the price of 2/6 plus cost of postage (postage will not be more than 6d., and there will be no postage if I collect the book from you), for a minimum period of six months, & thereafter indefinitely unless I resign, after giving six weeks' notice. I wish to start with the current issue.

I undertake to make my payments to you monthly (after receipt of the book).

I understand that you will post me the monthly book automatically, together with the bill for it and a free copy of "The Left News."

[DATE] ______

[APPLICANT'S NAME] ______

[APPLICANT'S ADDRESS] ______

Please write everything (including your name) in block capitals and do not send money with this coupon.

CAMELOT PRESS LTD. SOUTHAMPTON (T.U.)

"B" MEMBER'S COUPON

Cut off this coupon & post it to

THE PHŒNIX BOOK CO. LTD.
Showrooms: 66 CHANDOS STREET
CHARING CROSS, LONDON, W.C.2

Please enrol me as a "B" member of the Left Book Club on condition that there is no entrance fee or subscription, & that my sole liability is to pay for the special club edition of the one selected book *every other month* at the price of 3/– plus postage (unless I collect from you) for a minimum period of six months (3 books in all) & thereafter indefinitely unless I resign, after giving six weeks' notice. I wish to start with the April issue. It is also understood that in the months in which I do not obtain a book I get, free & post free, a copy of that month's *Left News*.

I undertake to make my payments to you every other month (after receipt of the book).

I understand that you will post me the selected book automatically every other month, together with the bill for it and a free copy of "The Left News"; on the alternate months you will merely post me a free copy of "The Left News."

[DATE] ______

[APPLICANT'S NAME] ______

[APPLICANT'S ADDRESS] ______

Please write everything (including your name) in block capitals and do not send money with this coupon.

CAMELOT PRESS LTD. SOUTHAMPTON (T.U.)

"C" MEMBER'S COUPON

Cut off this coupon & post it to

THE PHŒNIX BOOK CO. LTD.
Showrooms: 66 CHANDOS STREET
CHARING CROSS, LONDON, W.C.2

Please enrol me as a "C" member of the Left Book Club on condition that there is no entrance fee or subscription, and that my sole liability is to buy and pay for, at the special price of 3/6 each plus postage (unless I collect the books from you), *at least four* of the twelve monthly books that will be offered me during the twelve months starting with the date below.

I undertake to make my payments to you shortly after the receipt of each book.

I understand that you will post me the selected book automatically together with the bill for it.

[DATE] ______

[APPLICANT'S NAME] ______

[APPLICANT'S ADDRESS] ______

Please write everything (including your name) in block capitals and do not send money with this coupon.

CAMELOT PRESS LTD., SOUTHAMPTON (T.U.)

Figure 6.1 Member's Coupons

of membership and paying. Booksellers then sent up the proceeds, presumably minus their share, to Victor Gollancz Ltd. As the letter quoted above makes clear, they received the customary one third discount. However, later on this system was apparently abandoned in favour of bypassing bookshops to deal directly with members. This at least is implied by the entry forms which the club were sending out from 1938 onwards, after the creation of two new categories of member, 'B' and 'C', who were allowed to choose fewer books annually than the regular membership (see Figure 6.1).

However much the LBC cost Gollancz, it would doubtless have been far more without the efforts of thousands of unpaid volunteers. All the activities initiated by the local groups were freely undertaken by the members themselves, who enlisted new recruits, raised funds and distributed leaflets. One outstanding example of the selfless role of volunteers was in 1938, when it was decided to put out a series of booklets at the absurdly low price of 2d. a copy. The entire membership was mobilized for door-to-door sales, and several millions of the leaflets were sold.

Such were the costs of running the club; one might also briefly consider things from the point of view of an individual author commissioned by Gollancz. What were the transactional costs involved in writing for the LBC? It was certainly a lucrative experience. Authors received standard royalties and were practically guaranteed huge sales compared to books from ordinary publishers. To take one example, George Orwell's *The Road to Wigan Pier*, admittedly one of the more successful LBC choices, sold 42,000, whereas his next book, *Homage to Catalonia*, having been rejected because of its account of communist attacks on the Spanish anarchists, sold 1,500 when published by Secker and Warburg.

However, potential authors were often subject to rejection or censorship when they diverged from the communist line or criticized Russia. *Wigan Pier* itself was published unaltered, but was only allowed to appear accompanied by a highly critical introduction by Gollancz himself. Orwell was pilloried for looking down on the working class from a privileged position. 'I know, in fact,' wrote Gollancz, 'of no other book in which a member of the middle class exposes with such complete frankness the shameful way in which he was brought up to think of large numbers of his fellow men'.[15]

Relations with the Public

Victor Gollancz ran the LBC in the belief that there must be organized resistance to the rise of fascism, including an alliance with Soviet Russia. This ambition threw him inevitably into the arms of the communists, and it could be argued that this was where he got the balance wrong. He managed to convince himself there must be no whiff of criticism of Russia or the Communist Party, and in so doing he gained a reputation for extremism in the eyes of all moderates. His propaganda alienated from the start all Tories and most Liberals, as well as anti-communist members of the Labour Party – in other words, at least three quarters of the British political spectrum. The repeated overtures made by the LBC to the strongly anti-communist leaders of the Labour Party were all rejected. For instance, in 1937 an offer to hand over two special numbers of *Left News* to that party was turned down by Hugh Dalton, chairman of the Labour National Executive Committee, who asked in addition that two or three representatives of his party be added to the LBC triumvirate that selected future books. Negotiations were broken off. Labour was clearly worried about the disruptive and growing influence of the LBC, whose members they regarded as dangerous zealots. Ernest Bevin declared that the real object of the club was 'to undermine and destroy the Trade Unions and the Labour Party as an effective force', and there were threats that Labour Party members might find themselves expelled if they continued to buy LBC books.[16]

Paradoxically, another reason why the membership of the club failed ever to approach the half million mark sought after by Gollancz was because, in spite of the factory groups and many working-class members, it was basically a middle-class organization. This was perhaps inevitable given that it was, after all, a book club, and that most factory workers, miners, agricultural workers and their families

---

15 Quoted in Laity, 9.
16 Lewis, 94.

had neither the education nor the time and money to buy and read the books on offer. Efforts were made to recruit working-class authors, but success was rare. One exception was B.L. Coombes, who wrote a moving account of the life of a Welsh coal miner from personal experience.[17] There were laudable attempts to provide the middle-class membership with authentic glimpses of life at the bottom end, but these appear today, and no doubt did to many at the time, patronizing and even embarrassing. There were, for instance, conducted tours of poverty-stricken districts of London, and there were also 'distressed areas summer schools' where those attending could board with unemployed families (and pack their overalls if they wanted to go down a pit). One such was adjudged a triumph: 'the people, *all* the people, were entirely charming. I think none of us could speak too highly of their genuine kindness and simple dignity. Of course, the gap of class difference lay between us and them'.[18]

In the final analysis, the failure of the LBC to increase its membership and turn into an effective political force was perhaps due, not so much to the failings of Gollancz and others, or to middle-class bias, but to something more fundamental within British culture. The average Briton's pragmatism and suspicion of Continental theory-making went back centuries, as did the ingrained loyalty to the establishment, and deference of British workers. Given all this, the only surprise is that the Left Book Club, with its Marxist orthodoxy, had the success it did – due entirely to the quite exceptional circumstances of the times.

Legacy

Two events caused the decline of the club. One was Gollancz's resolve, after Munich, to rely less on the Communist Party. He admitted in *Left News*: 'I have allowed myself ... to become too much of a propagandist and too little of an educator'.[19] The other event was Britain's declaration of war against Germany, and the subsequent pact between Hitler and Stalin. This resulted in a directive from Moscow to all communist parties that the war should be seen as a mere struggle between imperialist powers, and therefore communists should not support the war effort. This in turn created a deep division in the leadership of the LBC, with Gollancz and Laski urging support for the war, while Strachey, Lewis and others took the Communist Party line.[20] One immediate fruit of Gollancz's new policy of supporting the war while distancing himself from the communists was the publication of Leonard Woolf's *Barbarians at the Gate*, which attacked not

---

17   *These Poor Hands*, LBC book of the month for June 1939.

18   Laity, xxv.

19   Quoted in Edwards, 285.

20   Strachey changed his position after Hitler's invasion of Holland and France. He rejoined Gollancz and Laski, supported the Labour Party, and ultimately became a minister in Attlee's post-war Labour government.

only fascists but also communists, and included a diatribe against the theory and practice of the Soviet government. After a tense meeting between Woolf and the three LBC leaders, as described in Woolf's autobiography, Gollancz finally agreed to publish this book unaltered.[21] Naturally, his decision was bitterly attacked, and the LBC thenceforth became a battleground between pro- and anti-war factions, anti-communists and communists.

The LBC may have failed in all its political objectives, but in a broader, educational sense it might be labelled a success. It acted as a kind of Open University for the 1930s in helping to broaden the outlook of a generation 'by giving (to all who are determined to play their part in this struggle) such knowledge as will immediately increase their efficiency'.[22] More specifically, it helped prepare the way for the Labour landslide which defeated Churchill in 1945. The millions of LBC books in circulation, and their thousands of readers, exerted an immense influence during the war, not least in the armed forces, where the Education Corps and the Army Bureau of Current Affairs were hotbeds of left-wing discussion. Probably, the club's influence was felt more over domestic issues, such as the need for full employment, socialized medicine and proper housing, than in world affairs, where events tended to shift rapidly, with the Soviet Union changing from trusted ally to global adversary in the space of a few years. Several of those who had written for the club became ministers in the 1945 government, including Attlee, Cripps, Bevin, Shinwell and Strachey. Although it went out of existence in 1948, the LBC's influence persisted, not least in the welfare state set up during that government.

Summary

This was a project to distribute polemic and information in the shape of books and a monthly journal to as large a number of people as possible. The information disseminated was highly partisan, designed to promote a particular point of view and a specific position on the political spectrum. Readers were expected to convert to a Marxist version of socialism, and to align themselves with the Soviet Union in a universal struggle against fascism.

Subscribers quickly ceased to be mere passive recipients of information, and took the opportunity to organize and engage in a wide range of supplementary activities. These had the effect of enriching individual lives, creating a sense of solidarity, and attracting more people to the project. However, the pro-communist line taken by the club's leaders caused many in Britain, including the leaders of

---

21   Leonard Woolf (1969), *The Journey Not the Arrival Matters*, London: Hogarth Press, 11–13.

22   As Gollancz wrote in an LBC leaflet in 1938; there were, of course, other contemporary influences and other publications which contributed, not least the Penguin Specials.

the main political parties, to regard it with suspicion. The club declined after a relatively short life span, mainly due to the changing world situation brought on by the outbreak of war, followed by the pact between Hitler and Stalin.

It might be argued that the Left Book Club was a 'counterpublic' under Warner's definition, in so far as its leaders were hostile to the dominant ideology of their society.[23] The founders of the club and many of its members shared with wikipedians a determination to extend their readership and influence, and also to keep up with fast-moving contemporary events. Above all, they shared a missionary zeal in their respective causes.

---

23 For counterpublics, see Chapter 1.

PART II
Wikipedia

Chapter 7

Social Sites

There is a well-known passage in the memoirs of the nineteenth-century Russian writer and activist Peter Kropotkin (1842–1921) in which he describes how he learnt to work with others on equal terms:

> Having been brought up in a serf-owner's family, I entered active life, like all young men of my time, with a great deal of confidence in the necessity of commanding, ordering, scolding, punishing, and the like. But when, at an early stage, I had to manage serious enterprises and to deal with men, and when each mistake would lead at once to heavy consequences, I began to appreciate the difference between acting on the principle of command and discipline and acting on the principle of common understanding. The former works admirably in a military parade, but it is worth nothing where real life is concerned, and the aim can be achieved only through the severe effort of many converging wills.[1]

'The severe effort of many converging wills' is an excellent description of the co-operative ideal, and not only in nineteenth-century Russia. The principle is simple: many hands make light work, or as Eric Raymond puts it in the context of software development: 'Given enough eyeballs, all bugs are shallow'. The best-known recent example of a successful group project is probably the free software movement which was started in the early 1990s by Richard Stallman, who wanted an alternative to the proprietary software then starting to dominate the market. Stallman, as an experienced programmer, thought it only his right to be able to develop or modify any software he used, and he was frustrated by corporations which did their research behind closed doors, refusing to allow their products to be copied, customized or altered in any way. Since then, many thousands have joined him in setting up the free GNU/Linux system which has become a viable alternative to Microsoft Windows, and threatens to surpass it in certain areas. Numerous other free software projects have also been developed. As Raymond explains, this has come about because 'Linux was the first project for which a conscious and successful effort to use the entire *world* as its talent pool was made'.[2] He argues that the closed-source world of the corporation can never win an evolutionary arms race with an open source community that can call on such a wide pool of talent.

---

1   Peter Kropotkin (1899), *Memoirs of a Revolutionist*, New York: Dover Publications, 1988, 7.

2   <http://catb.org/~esr/writings/cathedral-bazaar/cathedral-bazaar/ar01s11.html>.

To return to Kropotkin, however, it is the 'principle of command and discipline' rather than the co-operative principle that has tended to dominate history. Hierarchical forms of organization, including governments, armies and churches, have been involved in most human endeavours since the building of the pyramids and beyond. In recent times, too, wealth creation has been predominantly in the hands of national or multinational corporations run on hierarchical lines. Nevertheless, hierarchies have always been less conspicuous in the cultural arena than they have in the industrial, commercial and military sectors of society, and group collaboration on terms of equality has frequently been a feature of artistic and scientific achievement.

Any kind of mass movement that involves recruiting or galvanizing large numbers of people for a particular cause is hugely facilitated by the Internet, and earlier movements would have been strengthened by its availability. To take one particular example, in 1981 a number of women set up a peace camp at Greenham Common in Berkshire to protest against the imminent arrival of cruise missiles there. The women chose the symbol of a spider's web to represent the network of support groups that soon sprung up to back their anti-nuclear protest in Britain and throughout the world. These groups raised funds, distributed leaflets and operated 'telephone trees' on behalf of the peace camp. A historian of the movement describes their activities as 'a sort of political and social internet before the actual electronic system was invented'.[3] However, this comparison merely highlights how much easier such mobilization of support would have been quarter of a century later. Fibre-optics and broadband are far more effective than leaflets and telephones for the recruitment or continuity of any social enterprise.[4]

New information technology has facilitated not only large-scale movements, but also every possible variety of smaller niche project. All kinds of social interaction which before the Internet would have been out of the question are now feasible, and today there are dozens of ways in which people can participate in reporting news, questioning, debating, and creating cultural products. Politically, for instance, citizens need no longer merely try to inform themselves about current matters so that they can vote intelligently. Now they may also participate in an ongoing conversation. This development, according to Yochai Benkler, signifies the re-emergence of a genuine public sphere, hitherto lacking in Western society due to the dominance of the mass media.[5]

---

3   David Fairhall (2006), *Common Ground: The Story of Greenham*, London: I.B. Taurus, 188.

4   Admittedly, the possession of mobile phones would have helped the Greenham Common women even more. At the time of writing, the most effective way to mobilize a large group rapidly is probably via mobile phones linking to a website such as Twitter. It is said that the first head of state in history to lose power to a 'smart mob' assembled via texting was President Joseph Estrada of the Philippines in January 2001: Howard Rheingold (2002), *Smart Mobs: The Next Social Revolution,* Cambridge, MA: Basic Books, 157.

5   Yochai Benkler (2006), *The Wealth of Networks*, New Haven, CT: Yale University Press, 177.

What Benkler calls the networked information economy is displacing the industrial information economy which has prevailed in Western nations for the last century and a half. The latter tended to concentrate and centralize the production and exchange of cultural products and information. For example, by the mid-nineteenth century newspapers required ever-increasing capital investment. The increasing costs of mechanical presses together with the much larger circulation they permitted meant mass circulation, with a consequent lowering of certain standards and shift of content towards the blander and more popular. Newspapers reached larger and more dispersed audiences. This model of press centralization was taken up in their turn by radio and television. The cinema became an apt metaphor for the relationship which consumers had towards their information environment. Later, the passivity of television culture increasingly took over, while cultural production entailed the production and delivery of high-production value products to ever larger, passive audiences. The mass-media model became the dominant form of public communication in the twentieth century.[6]

Today, the network information economy leads to the possible emergence of a more active culture, making the process of cultural production more participatory and giving individuals a greater role in authoring their own lives. Some of the time that used to be given over to the passive reception of packaged cultural goods, especially television programmes, may now be reoriented towards communication and activity via the Internet.[7] Of course, predictions are foolhardy in a fast-changing environment, and some enthusiasts have exaggerated the likelihood of sweeping cultural changes in the immediate future. In a recent book, *Wikimania*, directed principally at the world of business, Don Tapscott writes about 'the age of participation', and prophesies that 'in the years to come, this new mode of peer production will displace traditional corporation hierarchies as the key engine of wealth creation in the economy'.[8]

One factor which perhaps makes it unlikely that most cultural production will become participatory in the near future is the competitive, individualistic nature of present-day culture. With rare exceptions, writers, artists and intellectual producers of every kind are accustomed to working in comparative isolation, and to being rewarded for their individual labours, supported by the laws concerning copyright and intellectual property. It is difficult to see this attitude changing unless accompanied by fundamental changes in society as a whole, and especially concerning the career structures of professionals. To take one example, Roy Rosenzweig, director of the Center of History and New Media at George Mason University, Virginia, believes that academic historians ought to take a leaf from the success of interactive and open source projects. Why not recruit 'distributed

6   Benkler, 135, 188. For a powerful, pre-Internet attack on television culture, see Neil Postman (1985), *Amusing Ourselves to Death*, London: Methuen.
7   Benkler, 467.
8   Don Tapscott and Anthony D. Williams (2007), *Wikinomics*, London: Atlantic Books, 18.

transcribers' to work on some of the thousands of hand-written documents gathering dust in archives, and which otherwise would very likely never be digitized? Or again, could there not be a collaborative project involving volunteers and professionals working together to write textbooks on, say, American history? But then Rosenzweig wonders whether the academics would ever really be prepared to join in such projects. Might this not involve them having to shed their professional pride? 'How would we allocate credit, which is so integral to professional culture? Could you get a promotion based on having "contributed" to a collaborative project?' Noting that many academics already serve anonymously on editorial and university committees, he asks: 'But are they also willing to take the further step of abandoning individual credit and individual ownership of intellectual property as do Wikipedia authors?'

Social production means collaborating with others, and giving one's labour freely without expecting a financial reward. Clearly, people have always done this, whether on behalf of family and friends, or as part of what is now called the voluntary sector. Throughout human history, unpaid social work has been ubiquitous, though often unacknowledged in economic textbooks. It is, as Benkler puts it, 'the dark matter of our economic production universe', sometimes substituting for, and sometimes complementing, market and state production.[9] The difference today is that in the emerging network economy, social voluntary efforts via the Internet have become simple, straightforward, yet often highly useful and productive. To participate in such a virtual community is life-enhancing for many, and the value of what can be achieved by such non-institutional, voluntary groups is often as great as it is unexpected, though not easy to calculate in monetary terms. Because it is non-commercial, Wikipedia, for example, does not figure in any statistics about gross national product or balance of trade, yet it adds to our collective wealth and to the quality of life of millions.

Wikipedians aim to create a new, universally accessible source of knowledge. But Wikipedia is not merely a product, but also a thriving community, and a secondary aim of that community is effective collaboration. When Tim Berners-Lee devised the World Wide Web, he envisaged it as a means of changing people's lives. He wrote: 'The Web is more a social creation than a technical one. I designed it for a social effect – to help people work together – and not as a technical toy. The ultimate goal of the Web is to support and improve our weblike existence in the world'.[10] His vision concerned interactivity, but 'my definition of interactive includes not just the ability to choose, but also the ability to create. We ought to be able not only to find any kind of document on the Web, but also to create any kind of document, easily'.[11] Berners-Lee wrote this in 1999, and he was at that time pessimistic about the existence of real opportunities for such inter-creativity. Since

---

9   Benkler, 117.
10   Tim Berners-Lee (2000), *Weaving the Web*, London: Texere, 133.
11   Berners-Lee, 182.

then, Web 2.0 and wiki technology, and the success of Wikipedia in particular, are developments which have helped turn his vision into reality.[12]

The economist Ronald Coase was the first to study the relative transaction costs of markets and firms under certain conditions.[13] Coase produced a theory about exactly when one mode becomes more attractive than the other. Such estimates require precise calculation of the respective costs of each system. However, one advantage of social production is that such exact book-keeping becomes irrelevant, since inefficiency and wasted effort are minor considerations in a system in which most people contribute because they enjoy doing so and expect no financial reward. But the biggest advantage of peer-to-peer over hierarchical firms or markets is when it comes to deciding who does what. Here, the principle of spontaneous division of labour applies. Peer-to-peer projects use self-identification, meaning that if someone considers they are capable and willing to undertake a particular task, then they can do it without needing to seek permission or contract from another. In any commercial organization it would be quite impossible to allow employees to work when they liked and at whatever tasks they fancied. In Wikipedia, it is possible to allow contributors this freedom since they are not employees. It is not even necessary to make sure such contributions are competent when they are first made – always provided relevant checking procedures are in place at a later stage. In other words, failure and wasted effort are not a problem, because they cost nothing.

In 2000, the Harvard sociologist Robert Putnam wrote a best-selling book about the decline of community in America over the previous half-century.[14] He drew on a variety of data to show that Americans were increasingly becoming disconnected from each other, and that active membership of all kinds of social groups, from bowling clubs to political parties, was in serious decline. A major reason for this decline was the simple increase in the difficulty of people getting together – in other words, the transaction costs of meeting up. Several trends had contributed to this decline, including smaller households, delayed marriage, two-worker families, the spread of television, and suburbanization, all of which increased the problems of co-ordinating group activities outside work. Putnam postulated that this reduction in community activities constituted a loss of social capital which impoverished the average citizen's quality of life. Clearly, such a loss is not confined to America In our time, which Zygmunt Bauman has christened the era of liquid modernity, permanent communities are at a premium. Bauman writes: 'the harness by which collectivities tie their members to a joint history, custom, language or schooling is getting more threadbare by the year. In the liquid stage of modernity, only zipped

---

12   Wiki technology was devised by Ward Cunningham in 1995. A wiki is a collection of Web pages that anyone, or alternatively a chosen group of people, can edit. It thus allows a shared experience of joint creativity.

13   Yochai Benkler, 'Coase's Penguin or Linux and the Nature of the Firm': <http://www.benkler.org/CoasesPenguin.html>. For more on transaction costs, see Chapter 1.

14   Robert Putnam (2000), *Bowling Alone*, New York: Simon & Schuster.

harnesses are supplied, and their selling point is the facility with which they can be put on in the morning and taken off in the evening'.[15]

Optimistic commentators believe that the virtual communities made possible by the Internet will to some degree fill the gap left by the decline noted by Putnam and Bauman. And even if such 'weak-tie' relationships with people who may be geographically distant are no substitute for the loss of real community feeling, at the very least they need not affect the stronger relationships we have with members of our family or our close friends. Virtual communities have the effect of increasing social capital, and thus adding another dimension to our lives. The Wikipedia project in particular can then be celebrated, not only because it involves such a community, but also because its objectives are so clearly beneficial to society in general.

---

15   Zygmunt Bauman (2000), *Liquid Modernity*, Cambridge: Polity Press, 169.

Chapter 8
Wikipedia: Aims

The Empire will vanish, and all its good with it. Its accumulated knowledge will decay and the order it has imposed will vanish. A Second Empire will rise, but between it and our civilization will be one thousand generations of suffering humanity. We must fight that.

How do you propose to do this?

By saving the knowledge of the race ... my thirty thousand men with their wives and children are devoting themselves to the preparation of an Encyclopaedia Galactica. They will not complete it in their life-times. I will not even live to see it fairly begun. But by the time [the Empire] falls, it will be complete and copies will exist in every major library in the Galaxy.

Isaac Asimov[1]

The great library of Alexandria is said to have aimed at complete coverage of everything written (in Greek, at least). However, this was not the only attempt, or suggested attempt, to corner all the world's knowledge. In 1403, the Chinese emperor Yongle, of the Ming dynasty, commissioned a vast encyclopaedia, said to have included over 11,000 volumes, practically all of which have subsequently disappeared. And in our times, H.G. Wells, writing during the world depression of the 1930s, proposed the creation of a 'Permanent World Encyclopaedia'. Wells believed that the evils of his era were principally caused by incoherent and divisive teaching of the young. If only scientists and savants from all over the world could come together, rising above their various nationalistic prejudices, and create such an encyclopaedia, then it might form the basis of a truly objective education. Wells was particularly taken with the microfilm, the latest communication technology of the day, and hoped his world encyclopaedia could be reproduced cheaply and universally via this method.

More recently, too, there have been various efforts to build an online encyclopaedia. However, none of them has come anywhere near the amazing growth that has turned Wikipedia into the world-wide phenomenon it is today. Jimmy Wales and Larry Sanger, the founders of Wikipedia, have inherited the ambitions of the Alexandrian librarians and the dreams of H.G. Wells, but modern technology has now turned those ambitions and dreams into a real possibility. This, at least, is how Wales sees it. In a recent interview, he said: 'Imagine a world in which every single person on the planet is given free access to the

---

1   From Isaac Asimov (1953), *Foundation*, New York: Del Rey.

sum of all human knowledge. That's what we're doing'.[2] The mission statement of the Wikimedia Foundation, the body which provides the essential infrastructure for Wikipedia and its sister enterprises, announces, more legalistically, that its intention is:

> to empower and engage people around the world to collect and develop educational content under a free licence or in the public domain, and to disseminate it effectively and globally. ... The Foundation will make and keep useful information from its projects available on the Internet free of charge, in perpetuity.[3]

But what exactly is meant by 'the sum of all human knowledge', and is it congruent with 'educational content' and 'useful information'? It might be argued that there are two types of knowledge: propositional or theoretical knowledge, and prescriptive, technical or empirical knowledge. If propositional knowledge is concerned with 'what' and 'why', prescriptive knowledge is rather about 'how'.[4] One assumes that Wikipedia is mainly concerned with the former rather than the latter, since a guideline states emphatically that it is not 'a manual, guidebook or textbook'.[5] There is a major difference here between Wikipedia and Diderot's *Encyclopédie*, which specifically aimed to incorporate hands-on technical information about manufacturing processes.

Propositional knowledge resides either in people's minds or in external storage devices such as books or computers. The aggregate propositional knowledge of a society is the total of all the statements of such knowledge contained in living persons' minds or in storage devices.[6] From the point of view of society as a whole, it is this general aggregate that counts, but equally important from an individual perspective is the efficiency and cost of access to society's knowledge. If, for instance, those who possess special knowledge regard it as a source of wealth or privilege, as was certainly the case in earlier epochs of history, and is to some extent still true today, this will hinder such access for everyone else.

---

2   From a 2004 interview on Slashdot: Phoebe Ayers, Charles Matthews and Ben Yates (2008), *How Wikipedia Works*, San Francisco, CA: No Starch Press, 32.

3   <http://wikimediafoundation.org/wiki/Mission_statement>.

4   This distinction is taken from Joel Mokyr (2005), *The Gifts of Athena*, Princeton, NJ: Princeton University Press, 4, as is much of the following paragraph.

5   <http://en.wikipedia.org/wiki/Wikipedia:NOT>.

6   Karl Popper, however, has made a distinction between these two components. According to Popper, a modern definition of knowledge should not contain any reference to individuals. He divides reality into three worlds: the first is the physical world; the second, the contents of human minds, which to some degree reflect that world; the third, 'the world of objective contents of thought', including 'the contents of journals, books and libraries'. Popper, of course, was writing before the Internet: Karl R. Popper (1972), 'Epistemology Without a Knowing Subject', in *Objective Knowledge*, Oxford: Oxford University Press, 106–7.

Even in a relatively democratic society such as ours there may, for instance, be a gap between the academic community and the rest of society which acts as an inhibiting factor in the free circulation of knowledge. After all, as the saying goes, knowledge is power. Commercial interests may also impose charges on access to information.[7] However, the digital revolution in communications, and in particular the Internet, has on balance vastly increased access to knowledge, and speeded up the flows of information in and out of people's minds, and Wikipedia surely plays an important part here. If knowledge is indeed power, then we are perhaps witnessing the embryonic beginnings of a massive decentring of power.

Nobody could dispute the importance of Wikipedia's proclaimed aim – to disseminate information globally, and give everyone access to it free of charge.[8] Societies that succeed in spreading the maximum amount of meaningful and useful information as widely as possible are likely to be freer, more open societies, and also more successful than those which lag behind. Information underlies all possibilities of social, cultural or political action. It allows for decisions as to which paths of action are feasible and which are not, and what has been attempted in other times and places, and by earlier generations. Access to information widens the options open to individuals and allows them a basis on which to form critical judgements about how to live their lives. Jürgen Habermas has employed the concept of the 'life world' for the untested, often unconscious assumptions about the nature of the world made by individuals during the course of their lives or inherited uncritically from others:

> The life world embraces us as an unmediated certainty, out of whose immediate proximity we live and speak. This all-penetrating, yet latent and unnoticed presence of the background of communicative action can be described as a more intense, yet deficient form of knowledge and ability. ... As background knowledge, it lacks the possibility of being challenged, that is, of being raised to the level of criticisable validity claims. One can do this only by converting it from a resource into a topic of discussion.[9]

Such 'unmediated' views and attitudes, which we may share with others around us, can be challenged and examined rationally when occasion arises, and the vast pool

---

7   Most academic journals are only available to the general public by subscription. However, many academics are coming to embrace the philosophy of the Creative Commons, whereby rights holders allow their material to be freely accessed and used, providing it is not for commercial purposes. John Willinsky has suggested that one way to contribute to Wikipedia is to edit articles by adding references to relevant open access sources: <http://firstmonday.org/issues/issue12_3/willinsky/>.

8   I am here using the term 'information' as a synonym for propositional knowledge.

9   Jürgen Habermas (1998), *Between Facts and Norms: Contributions to a Discourse Theory of Law and Democracy*, 22–3, quoted in Yochai Benkler (2006), *The Wealth of Nations*, New Haven, CT: Yale University Press, 281–2.

of factual knowledge available at the touch of a button in Wikipedia provides many such occasions. Inherited or otherwise passively acquired cultural assumptions are revisable through critical examination, at which point they may be either rejected or confirmed as part of an individual's stock of conscious knowledge.

Is it realistic, now or in the foreseeable future, to talk about passing on such knowledge to 'every single person on the planet'? This question is clearly related to the much-discussed global digital divide. Developed nations today have the resources to invest in relevant IT infrastructure, and their populations, for the most part, can afford the declining costs of computers or other devices with access to the Internet. The case is very different, however, for the vast majority of the world's inhabitants. Apart from persistent poverty, many other factors including low literacy, linguistic diversity and culture-based inhibitions preclude such access. Optimists might assume that this gap between haves and have-nots will gradually narrow, but the opposite may well be the case. The increasing rate of technological development surely tends, other things being equal, to widen the economic disparity between developed and developing nations, as well as between rich and poor within nations. While some learn how to run faster, others remain standing still. Can it be that babies born today in remote villages in the Yemen or the slums of Sao Paulo will one day embrace the Internet and contribute to Wikipedia, or its future equivalent? On present evidence, this seems improbable.

Access to 'the sum of all human knowledge' is Jimmy Wales's ambitious claim. Diderot's *Encyclopédie* was premised on the idea that the world, both natural and cultural, formed a bounded and finite system which was orderly, knowable and recordable. Diderot, too, had the ambition:

> to collect all knowledge scattered over the face of the earth, to present its general outlines and structure to the men with whom we live, and to transmit this to those who will come after us, so that the work of the past centuries may be useful to the following centuries.[10]

Today, however, our culture no longer appears to have anything like the same level of stability as in Diderot's time, or even much more recently, and this instability can be linked to numerous factors, one of which is globalization. It may be the case that we increasingly live in one world, but within that world contradictory processes are taking place, including the growing visibility of different cultures and traditions. We have been made aware of different accounts of global history and various alternative modernities, and it has become apparent that any encyclopaedic project originating in the West may have cultural limitations. It cannot be assumed any longer that the developed nations hold a monopoly licensing them to accumulate and transmit knowledge on behalf of all the rest of the world.

How far might this charge of cultural limitation apply to Wikipedia? Here, it is important to remember that the English version of the encyclopaedia is not

---

10   *L'Encyclopédie*, entry 'Encyclopedia'.

the only one. At the time of writing there were 269 Wikipedias, including, for instance, one in the Lak language, spoken by approximately 150,000 people in the northern Caucasus. This particular Wikipedia has increased its user base from 20 at the end of 2006 to 451 by November, 2008. For some of the minority languages now served by their own Wikipedia, there was little or no factual material in that language previously available on the Internet. Admittedly, most of the newest Wikipedias are tiny, but the hope and expectation is that they will serve the growing proportion of native speakers who have access to the Internet. In some cases, too, some of these languages now counted as endangered will then be better placed for survival.[11] This proliferation of Wikipedias does go some way to emphasize the cultural breadth of the project, as compared to more traditional, nationally based encyclopaedias. However, it is also true that the English Wikipedia is vast in comparison to any of the others, and for this reason many native speakers of other languages tend to use it in preference to their own. When wikipedians held their annual conference in Alexandria in 2008, Arab journalists complained to Jimmy Wales that the Arabic Wikipedia was comparatively undernourished; he merely replied that the answer lay in their hands. It could be argued that, in spite of admirable intentions, and the promotion of minority language versions, the net effect of the entire enterprise is to contribute to the increasing power and scope of the English language throughout the world. In this, of course, Wikipedia is only following a pattern set by the Internet in general.

When one looks, too, at the characteristics of those responsible for the English version, the charge of cultural bias becomes hard to shrug off. Statistics are hard to come by, but it seems likely that a large majority of the leading editors on this Wikipedia have a very specific demographic. By and large, they tend to be male, American, highly computer-literate, and aged in their late teens or twenties. Consequently, what interests them is much better covered in the encyclopaedia than are other subjects more remote from their interests and education. The geography and history of the United States as compared with that of, say, Africa or China is a case in point.[12] Popular culture of all kinds is massively represented. For example, there are long articles on each of the 144 episodes of the American television series *Buffy the Vampire Slayer*, which ran from 1997 to 2003, plus numerous other articles on the actors, the characters and anything else to do with the series. Again, the game franchise Pokemon has about 500 articles on its fictional characters, and there are 600 different articles devoted to *The Simpsons*.

There is an ongoing debate among wikipedians over articles on trivial subjects, especially popular culture. Those calling themselves exclusionists hold that the presence of so many such articles lowers the tone, and makes it likely that the

---

11 Andrew Dalby, 'Wikipedia(s) on the language map of the world', *English Today*, vol. 23, no. 2 (April 2007), 3–8.

12 'The space devoted to the glamour model Jordan's breast implants is as long as the entire entry for the Yi language, spoken by 6.6 million Chinese': Ben MacIntyre, *The Times*, 21 July 2006.

world will take Wikipedia less seriously as a repository of genuine knowledge. They want a more stringent editorial policy regarding trivia, and also the deletion of articles whose status as encyclopaedic material cannot be demonstrated, for instance, by citation to reputable sources. Inclusionists, on the other hand, believe that, since the costs are negligible, any articles which interest even a small minority should be kept. Applying strict editorial criteria would dampen contributors' enthusiasm. Jimmy Wales, himself a self-confessed inclusionist, created a short article about a certain restaurant in South Africa where he once dined, only to have the article deleted as 'not noteworthy'. On this occasion, his point of view eventually prevailed, with the result that there are now numerous articles about restaurants and bars in different countries. Another keen wikipedian, the novelist Nicholson Baker, recently wrote a piece in the *New York Review of Books* about his efforts as an inclusionist:

> But the work that really drew me in was trying to save articles from deletion. This became my chosen mission. Here's how it happened. I read a short article on a post-Beat poet and small-press editor named Richard Denner, who had been a student at Berkeley in the Sixties and then, after some lost years, had published many chapbooks on a hand press in the Pacific Northwest. The article was proposed for deletion by a user named PirateMink, who claimed that Denner wasn't a notable figure, whatever that means. (There are quires, reams, bales of controversy over what constitutes notability in Wikipedia: nobody will ever sort it out.) Another user, Stormbay, agreed with PirateMink: no third-party sources, ergo not notable.
>
> Denner was in serious trouble. I tried to make the article less deletable by incorporating a quote from an interview in the Berkeley *Daily Planet* – Denner told the reporter that in the Sixties he'd tried to be a street poet, 'using magic markers to write on napkins at Cafe Med for espressos, on girls' arms and feet.' (If an article bristles with some quotes from external sources these may, like the bushy hairs on a caterpillar, make it harder to kill.) And I voted 'keep' on the deletion-discussion page, pointing out that many poets publish only chapbooks: 'What harm does it do to anyone or anything to keep this entry?'
>
> An administrator named Nakon – one of about a thousand peer-nominated volunteer administrators – took a minute to survey the two 'delete' votes and my 'keep' vote and then killed the article. Denner was gone.[13]

Another hotly debated topic is whether Wikipedia should operate as an up-to-date news forum for current events. That is certainly the case at present, since reports are placed within minutes of the event taking place, but there seems a potential conflict here between this speed of reaction and an encyclopaedia's duty to be as

---

13   Nicholson Baker, 'The Charms of Wikipedia', *New York Review of Books*, vol. 55, no. 4 (20 March 2008): <http://www.nybooks.com/articles/21131>.

measured and accurate as possible. A recent example of such conflict occurred on the evening of 20 January 2009, after Senator Edward Kennedy collapsed at a lunch celebrating the inauguration of Barack Obama as president. An anonymous vandal inserted into the article on Kennedy a message that he had died in hospital that evening, a statement which was removed and then reinstated several times. The entire episode lasted only 18 minutes, but no doubt could have caused considerable harm and distress to those seeking up-to-the-minute information. Sensitive articles do carry warnings about the possibility of vandalism, and the need for vigilance, such as the following, which were placed above the beginning of the Kennedy article:

> This article must adhere to the policy on biographies of living persons. Controversial material about living persons that is unsourced or poorly sourced must be removed immediately, especially if potentially libellous. If such material is repeatedly inserted or if there are other concerns relative to this policy, report it on the living persons biographies noticeboard.

> This page is about an active politician who is running for office, is in office and campaigning for re-election, or is involved in some current political conflict or controversy. Because of this, this article is at increased risk of biased editing, talk-page trolling, and simple vandalism.

Jimmy Wales reacted strongly to the adverse publicity generated by the Kennedy incident by demanding that unregistered users should be immediately barred from editing all controversial or current topics. This proposal aroused considerable opposition, and has not been implemented at the time of writing.[14]

Wales's stated aim is *free* access to knowledge, and the mission statement of the Wikimedia Foundation pledges that information from its projects will be available 'free of charge, in perpetuity'. This formal guarantee that the consumer is never going to be charged for finding information on Wikipedia helps create the trust necessary for users to commit themselves to the project.[15] It also, of course, provides a vital service to the world. As Charles Leadbeater points out: 'Most people in the world cannot afford to compare Wikipedia with the *Britannica*. They will not be able to afford an encyclopaedia in any form for many years to come'.[16]

---

14   For more about this proposed reform, see p. 110.

15   Note that this pledge does not specifically rule out the use of the site for commercial purposes, say for advertising, but this prospect, which has often been mooted, seems unlikely in the foreseeable future. It, too, would certainly affront many wikipedians. In *How Wikipedia Works*, p. 40, it is stated that freedom in Wikipedia includes being 'free of commercial influences', but this statement does not seem borne out by the references given there. On this question, see also p. 120.

16   Charles Leadbeater (2008), *We-think*, London: Profile Books, 18.

The free provision of information to the public in the shape of encyclopaedic articles is made possible, firstly, by the labour of volunteers, and secondly, by the availability of the sources of that information to the volunteers in the first place. It is not true, of course, that all the information required to build an encyclopaedia is freely obtainable. The laws of copyright mean that much is unavailable, or at least needs to be paid for. Furthermore, the task of determining which items of information, or which images, are free of copyright and which are not is demanding, and is part of the unavoidable costs of the project. To take one example, the 1911 edition of the *Encyclopaedia Britannica* is out of copyright, available online, and material from it has been widely used by wikipedians, but a source like this clearly needs to be updated by more recent research.

Another dimension of the 'freedom' which attracts so many volunteer editors is that they are aware their work can never in the future be appropriated by any single individual or commercial organization. This promise is spelt out in the GNU Free Documentation Licence cited at the bottom of every article in Wikipedia, which ensures that anyone who copies or modifies the document concerned for their own purposes must do so under the same licence.[17] Content remains permanently part of the commons, and cannot be turned into private property. This licence, a form of what is known as 'copyleft', was devised by Richard Stallman and is similar to that used by the free software movement. It creates the trust necessary for long-term commitment by volunteers, and its absence would mean that contributing to Wikipedia lost some of its attraction.

---

17   <http://en.wikipedia.org/wiki/Wikipedia:Text_of_the_GNU_Free_Documentation_License>.

Chapter 9

Wikipedia: The Community

To the average user, Wikipedia is a useful work of reference, a vast, free, online encyclopaedia. Behind the scenes, however, it is also a community of enthusiasts devoted to discussion and argument. Admittedly, 'community' has become a rather hackneyed term in recent times. As Eric Hobsbawm remarks in another context: 'Never was the word "community" used more indiscriminately and emptily than in the decades when communities in the sociological sense became hard to find in real life'.[1] Wikipedia is merely a community in the Internet sense: a loose, world-wide grouping of otherwise unrelated members. It might be classed as a bridging group, that is, a group one of whose aims is to recruit as many members as possible.

The boundaries and precise membership of this network are not easy to establish. It would be absurd to try and define it as consisting of all users of the encyclopaedia when one is informed that the website sometimes receives up to 65,000 hits per second.[2] Fewer than 2 per cent of Wikipedia users ever contribute, and in one sense, therefore, it is this 2 per cent that makes up the Wikipedia community. However, among these there are enormous differences as to the extent of their contribution, since the overwhelming majority edit only one or at the most very few items. In other words, there is a steep decline from a few highly active contributors to a very large group of barely active ones. This is a system which can be described as a power law distribution – a distribution very different from the usual bell-shaped curve in which the average is at the top of the bell curve and represents the largest number. It is true that the active contributors could hardly run Wikipedia without the help of the larger group. Nevertheless, it is this core of active members, a few thousand dedicated wikipedians, who constitute the real community, carry out essential housekeeping and generally keep the project running. Recently, there has been debate over whether or not there is an even smaller inner core or perhaps five hundred or so who create most of the new text in articles. Jimmy Wales has argued that it is this dedicated band, of whom 'I know all of them and they all know each other', that do most of the work. Recent research, however, has shown that this may not entirely be the case. There are large numbers of so-called 'good Samaritans', that is, people who have made valuable contributions but who contribute relatively rarely, and then often

---

1   Eric Hobsbawm (1994), *The Age of Extremes*, London: Michael Joseph, 428.

2   <http://wikimediafoundation.org/wiki/Press_releases//UNU_survey_agreement>, 24 January 2008. The following comments and figures apply only to the English Wikipedia.

without even registering as users.[3] Another complication that arises when trying to estimate the size of the Wikipedia community is that the inner group itself, however constituted, includes many closely bonded smaller communities which interest themselves in particular subjects but may never communicate with other users outside their particular speciality. The small bank of editors who watch over and create articles on Irish history, for example, form one such community, and those interested in *Star Wars* make up another.

Of course, even Wikipedia, discourse-centred and democratic as it is, requires some form of leadership or overseeing. This is provided by a small number of editors who have system administrator privileges such as the right to protect articles that have been subject to repeated vandalism.[4] These administrators, or 'sysops', have been elected by a peer review process, and are people who have proved their engagement with Wikipedia over time. Hence, the system is based on a hierarchy of mutual respect, as well as a general recognition by most users that it is to everyone's advantage to have some decision-makers with certain privileges. Wikipedia's founder, Jimmy Wales, has warned against the danger inherent in any hierarchical system, of the administrator's role becoming a matter of prestige: 'I just wanted to say that becoming a sysop is not a big deal. I don't like that there's the apparent feeling here that being granted sysop status is a really special thing'.[5]

What can be said about why people choose to become wikipedians? Before considering the motivation of the inner community, one might first look at why anyone might start wanting to contribute in the first place. Clay Shirky has tried to analyse how he came to make his first edit, an improvement in the style of an existing article (on the Koch snowflake). He concluded he had three motives, the first being 'the chance to exercise some unused mental capacities – I studied fractals in a college physics course in the 1980s and was pleased to remember enough about the Koch snowflake to be able to say something useful about it, however modest'. The second motive was vanity – 'making a mark on the world' – and the third, 'the desire to do a good thing', which he describes as 'both the most surprising and the most obvious'.[6]

Shirky also mentions modularity, a key factor for a project which seeks to harness the voluntary efforts of large numbers of people. This is the capacity to break down a particular task into small elements so that individuals can choose to

3   Aaron Schwartz (2006), 'Raw Thoughts: Who Writes Wikipedia?': <http://www.aaronsw.com/weblog/whowriteswikipedia>; Denise Anthony, Sean W. Smith and Tim Williamson (2005), 'Explaining Quality in Internet Collective Goods: Zealots and Good Samaritans in the Case of *Wikipedia*': <http://web.mit.edu/iandeseminar/Papers/Fall2005/anthony.pdf>.

4   As of November, 2008 there were 1,554 administrators on the English Wikipedia.

5   <http://en.wikipedia.org/wiki/Wikipedia.Administrators>; Wales said this in February 2003, and has since often repeated it.

6   Clay Shirky (2008), *Here Comes Everybody*, London: Allen Lane, 131–2.

contribute even on a small scale. For instance, if the project involved planning and writing a whole book, it is difficult to conceive how large numbers could usefully get involved. This would most likely have to be undertaken by a single individual, or at most a very small team of highly motivated individuals. But Wikipedia has extreme modularity. One might set out to write an entire article from scratch, but it is also possible merely to alter the odd spelling or punctuation error, or modify one or two sentences in an existing article.

However, none of the reasons mentioned by Shirky really explain why so many confirmed wikipedians are prepared to devote up to several hours a day to the project for no financial gain or public recognition. It is true there are many other social networking sites on which people spend hours every day – MySpace, Facebook, Bebo, YouTube. But writing an article for an encyclopaedia is much harder work than making contact with friends or downloading videos. Wikipedia requires not merely co-operation between individuals, but discipline and a commitment to norms, for instance to a particular style of writing which may be far from intuitive or natural to many potential editors. In his book about the making of the *Oxford English Dictionary*, Simon Winchester expressed surprise that 'so many people gave so much time for so little apparent reward'. Today, however, the Internet furnishes us with many examples of similar behaviour on a large scale.[7]

The answer must surely involve the attractions of belonging to a community, and of being recognized and valued by that community, especially one which offers a non-hierarchical and collaborative form of organization. Membership gives participants a sense of belonging, of common purpose, and offers mutual support in achieving the aims of the group. Charles Leadbeater, another enthusiast for peer-production systems such as Wikipedia, puts such feelings in a historical context:

> It is vital to our psychological well-being that we are held in esteem, valued and recognised for what we do. Our identities – what we are good at and what matters to us – depend on the recognition of other people. In the past, certainly in the rich world, many people acquired a sense of identity from their position in a bounded local community. In the 20th century, occupation and position in an organizational hierarchy often provided the key. Now, people increasingly get a sense of identity from the relationships they form and the interests they share with others. ... The web matters not least because by allowing people to participate and share, it also gives them a route to recognition. ... People are drawn to share, not only to air their ideas, but in the hope their contributions will be recognised by a community of their peers.[8]

---

7 One obvious example, not too different from the work on the *Oxford English Dictionary* performed by volunteers, is proofreading for Project Gutenberg: see <http://www.pgdp.net/c/>.

8 Charles Leadbeater (2008), *We-think*, London: Profile Books, 229–30.

Practically all the contributors to Wikipedia are anonymous, or at least anonymous to the public at large, in that when first registering on the site they are asked to choose a 'user name' by which they are then known to their colleagues.[9] Contributors are free to give out information about themselves on the user page allocated to each editor, and in a very few cases the user name chosen is the contributor's real name. It was one of these rare cases that Andrew Keen, the author of a recent polemic about the evils of the Internet, was able to use when he accused Wikipedia of failing to defer to expertise. Keen chose as his example Dr William Connelly, whose special area of expertise included global warming, and whom he said had been unfairly treated by other editors, who had disregarded his qualifications.[10] It could be argued, however, that in broadcasting his real name and his various qualifications on his user page, Connelley was going against the spirit of Wikipedia, and that if his example were widely followed, the project would rapidly grind to a halt. This, at any rate, is the opinion of most wikipedians, who see anonymity as important because it allows all contributions to be judged on their intrinsic merit rather than by their source, and means, crucially for the community, that contributors are judged by their track record of service to Wikipedia rather than by any formal or 'real world' qualifications. It is undoubtedly also a reason for the vast numbers who volunteer their services. If every contributor were asked to state their name and qualifications, the result would probably be that most contributors completely abandoned their efforts in deference to a handful of highly qualified editors who would soon find they had neither the time nor the inclination to run a massive encyclopaedia.

Another major benefit of anonymity is that it tends to produce a more constraint-free communication than is usually the case in ordinary life. The reasoning here is that real space is permeated with the various rules and conventions that govern social intercourse. As an individual, one takes part in a variety of communicative relationships, ranging from those between family members and friends to those with professional bodies or persons in authority. In each case, we are aware of, and likely to comply with, the cultural and social norms that govern any particular group. In other words, the consciousness of whom we are addressing may affect the style and content of the message itself. Communication between anonymous individuals, on the other hand, is to a large extent exempt from this inhibitive process. Hence efforts by wikipedians to reach consensus can rely on the authority of the better argument rather than being influenced by some trait of the recipient such as gender, social background or educational qualification. This is not to say that what might be termed power relationships between wikipedians do not play some part in behind-the-scenes discussions. The factor affecting relationships here, however, will tend to be the degree of experience and commitment of a particular

---

9   Under a recently introduced rule, those choosing not to register may not start new articles, but may edit existing ones. This, however, may change shortly: see p. 110.

10   Andrew Keen (2007), *The Cult of the Amateur*, London: Nicholas Brealey, 43–4.

editor. Those who have only recently joined the system may be expected to defer to those whose wikipedian pedigree stretches back further.

Paradoxically, in view of the anonymity of the members and their physical separation the Wikipedia community exhibits a high degree of social bonding.[11] But, as in all close-knit communities, disagreements and even factions within the group are common. These are particularly inevitable in what is really a giant arena for argument. Nevertheless, the relationships between those highly involved in the project tend to develop and strengthen over time, and it is remarkable how these ties can thicken even though contributors remain anonymous. Reputation matters, and for many becomes an important part of editing on Wikipedia. Undoubtedly, some editors are highly competitive, looking for instance at the well-publicized list of those with the highest edit counts. Others may seek administrator status, or a role on the Mediation or Arbitration committees which have been set up to handle intractable disputes. There is enough of a sense of ownership of articles that editors may keep close track via their watchlists of articles they started or contributed to, and one way in which high-quality editing can be publicly rewarded is when articles achieve 'Good Article', and especially 'Featured Article' status.[12] Editors interact and get to know each other through discussions on article and user talk pages. On these pages there is a continuous flow of communication between editors, ranging from bitter reproaches and accusations to admiration and the award of 'barnstars', which are commendations sent by one editor to another for work considered especially meritorious.

The Special Barnstar

I award you this Special Barnstar for correcting all of the minor mistakes to articles that no one else thinks about...for being a great asset to the LGBT project...for staying neutral and offering fair advice in article disputes...for helping me out when I've had questions about NPOV edits and other WP issues.

User A

The Random Acts of Kindness Barnstar

I've come across your comments on various talk and user talk pages, whether explaining policy to inexperienced users, dealing with disruptive behaviour, or discussing article content. Every time you've been friendly, often offering extra help to struggling users instead of just chiding them for mistakes, and I've never seen you lose your cool when exposed to incivility. Keep up the good work!

User B

---

11 Wikipedians do occasionally come together at locally arranged meetings, and there is an annual conference entitled 'Wikimania' which is held at varying locations. Recent such conferences have been in Taiwan, Frankfurt and the new Library of Alexandria.

12 For watchlists and Featured Articles, see Chapter 10.

On the Wikipedia site, two different languages are used. There is the style of the articles themselves, the public encyclopaedia, and there is the style of the various discussion pages. The articles are in a formal style quite suitable for its purposes, though it has been criticized as somewhat bland and anaemic. For instance, Mark Bauerlein, an American professor of literature, writes: 'I can tell when my students have consulted Wikipedia when writing their papers. Sentences lose their singularity, transitions go flat, diction pales. The discourse sounds like information coming from a neutral platform, not interpretation coming from an angle of vision'.[13] Bauerlein may be right to point out the relatively restricted style and vocabulary of many contributors to Wikipedia compared to those of more literary authors, but nevertheless his criticisms seem a little unfair. After all, wikipedians merely try to convey information as clearly and unambiguously as possible, and do not aim to produce literature.

Antonella Elia has made a comparison between what she terms 'WikiLanguage', the formal style of the encyclopaedia, and 'WikiSpeak', 'the spoken-written language used by wikipedians in their backstage and informal community'. She gives examples:

> WikiSpeak is an unofficial and high-content language which can be considered as a new variety of the Netspeak, one of the most creative domains of contemporary English. ... A large number of new words have emerged. WikiSpeak is an informal and colloquial language rich, for example, in acronyms (NPOV – Neutral Point Of View, COTW – Collaboration Of The Week, IFD – Image For Deletion). ... Many word processes take place in WikiSpeak including several ludic innovations. A popular method of creating *wikilogisms* is to combine two separate words to make new compound words (WikiPage, WikiBooks, WikiLink, WikiStress, etc.). In addition WikiSpeak makes large use of blends (namespace, infobox, quickpoll, etc.) and semantic shifts (orphan, mirror, stub, etc.).[14]

The following brief example of WikiSpeak is taken from the talk page of the article 'Meh'. Apparently, 'meh' is an interjection, an expression of apathy, indifference or boredom, which is heard frequently on *The Simpsons*. This article was nominated for deletion on 3 December 2008, but the result of the ensuing discussion was to retain it:

> **User A**: I note that this article ['Meh'] was subject to VfDs in 2004 and 2005 (1 and 2). I've written a stub that I humbly suggest passes WP:V and have overwritten the redirect. Happy for anyone querying the verifiability of the new article to list it at AfD. I thought that DRV was inappropriate, as the article was

---

13   Mark Bauerlein, 'REPN TRI to the FULLEST!!!', *Education Next* (Summer 2008), 81.

14   Antonella Elia (2006), 'An analysis of digital writing': <http://acl.ldc.upenn.edu/W/W06/W06-2804.pdf>.

a redirect, not deleted and furthermore, I didn't want to recreate any of the old deleted versions – all the verified information in the article is from the last few days.

User B: Looks good, nice job.

This rather esoteric language, with its innumerable abbreviations and shortcuts, constitutes no doubt an obstacle facing newcomers seeking to join the community. However, once mastered, it probably also contributes towards the bonding process within the community, as does any special dialect or vocabulary common to a particular group.

Three crucial factors behind the exponential growth of Wikipedia and the number of its contributors are: the comparative lack of hierarchy, the anonymity, and the absence of commercialization. It is likely that if any of these were substantially modified, the result would be a rapid exodus of contributors. Nevertheless, the main reason why people choose to become wikipedians, and hence a major factor in the success of the project, is surely the close bonding within a vibrant community, with the attendant peer recognition that follows.

Chapter 10
Wikipedia: Structure

A common misapprehension about Wikipedia is that it consists of a chaotic free-for-all to which anyone can add whatever they fancy. This is far from the case. Behind its public face lies a vast and complex organization containing, for instance, dozens of pages of rules, conventions and advice to potential editors, and further pages involving discussion of each of these. Most of those consulting the encyclopaedia will only be interested in the article pages, but these are like the visible part of an iceberg. At the time of writing there were two and a half million article pages on the English Wikipedia, but also another ten million pages related to the articles in one way or another.[1] These ancillary pages include discussion (or 'talk') pages, user and user talk pages, policy, procedure and help pages, image description pages, and category and list pages. Pages are categorized into different types known as 'namespaces', of which there are 20. Each namespace has a separate prefix which comes before the actual page name, and is separated from it by a colon.[2] The Wikipedia namespace (abbreviation: WP) is for pages that are specifically about running the site and the encyclopaedia. For example, Wikipedia: Statistics refers to a place for describing the project's statistics. Practically every page on the site is accompanied by a talk page, so that Wikipedia_Talk:Statistics brings one to a page discussing these statistics. It is easy to see how the total number of ancillary pages mounts up towards the figure of ten million when one considers that a lengthy article might have a dozen further pages attached to it, including a history page, a discussion page, and various image and image-talk pages. Furthermore, when editors first register on the site they are automatically allocated five new pages for various purposes, including a record of all their future edits. Of course, the creation of new pages does not mean that these pages are necessarily ever used, and no doubt the majority are not.

Recently, activity has increased in those spaces where editors co-ordinate and debate possible changes, these being also the spaces used by the community for general communication and bonding. Many of these ancillary spaces hardly

---

1   A digital 'page' may be far longer than a page in a book; the 'page' on George W. Bush, for instance, might take up about 18 pages if printed out, as also might the 'page' on the 'Great Fire of London': see Chapter 15.

2   However, the 'main', or article, namespace pages have no prefix. Thus, for example, 'Phoebe' might refer to an encyclopaedia article, 'Image:Phoebe' to a page referring to a particular image within that article, 'Image_talk:Phoebe' to a page of discussion about that image, 'User:Phoebe' to the personal page of an editor who uses this name as a pseudonym, and 'User_talk:Phoebe' to that editor's discussion page.

existed when Wikipedia started, and have developed within the last few years. The fastest-growing sections include image pages and Wikipedia (guideline) pages, as well as all kinds of talk pages. Talk pages are produced using the same wiki technology as article pages, but as is the case in other parts of the site, rules have been developed by the community as to their use. For instance, contributors are expected to sign every post with their user name and the date, and to indent related postings. Talk pages are never erased, but earlier contributions are archived so as to become dormant records of past discussions. These pages are key areas for resolving conflicts between editors, and for suggesting and planning possible changes to articles. As might be expected, articles with the fullest talk pages tend to be those with the largest number of edits.

I would like here to look at a few excerpts from talk pages to give some idea of their flavour and the kind of topics they deal with.[3] My examples are all chosen from one particular article, 'George W. Bush', which admittedly is one of the longest, most controversial, and hence most edited articles in the entire encyclopaedia. The talk page on this article had, at the time of writing, over sixty archived sections, amounting altogether to about one and a half million words. Most of this vast corpus consists of extended, not to say interminable, arguments involving two, three or at most four editors. The arguments are mostly political or semi-political, occasionally also puerile, and it is usually quite clear where each participant stands along the American political spectrum. Nevertheless, a wide range of external sources are cited as evidence, including the press, both American and international, and numerous websites and blogs. The shorter excerpts chosen here exclude lengthier discussions for obvious reasons, and are merely to illustrate issues typical of talk pages in general.[4]

One issue often aired was whether new material should be placed in this particular article, or elsewhere:

> **User A**: The economic collapse we are currently undergoing is going to be one of the core features of the Bush Administration in the history books, just as Hoover is irretrievably associated with 1929 (whether fair or not). It's time to put something about it into the article. I don't know what though.

---

3   There have been several recent studies of talk pages. For instance, Besiki Stvilia, Michael B. Twidale, Linda C. Smith and Les Gasser (2006) examined them to analyse what types of 'Information Quality' problems were discussed: 'Information Quality Discussions in Wikipedia': <http://www.isrl.uiuc.edu/~stvilia/papers/qualWiki.pdf>; Fernanda B. Viégas, Martin Wattenberg, Jesse Kriss and Frank van Ham (2007) looked at a sample of 25 talk pages and classified their contents along 11 dimensions: 'Talk before you Type: Coordination in Wikipedia': <http://www.research.ibm.com/visual/papers/wikipedia_coordination_final.pdf>.

4   User names have been removed from all extracts in this and following chapters, to preserve anonymity.

User B: I added a sentence summary of the problem and what the administration has proposed. That should really be all that we say though, because we have to be careful as events are still developing and will likely change (see WP: RECENTISM). In addition, this article is about George W. Bush and there is an article specifically dealing with this event.

Mistakes in spelling or style were frequently brought up:

User A: Has no one proofread this? "Affect" should be "effect" when talking about Laura Bush. "liason" is misspelt as "laison" when referring to his oil exploration ventures. There are more I'm sure, and I'll update this as I find them.
User B: I've fixed those, and thanks for the heads up.

User A: ". . . the wars have lead to the deaths of hundreds of thousands of Iraqui civilians and tens of thousands of Afghanistanis" (or is it Afghans?).
User B: Its "Afghanistanis". You were right the first time, the second you make them sound like carpets (!).
User A: I'm pretty sure its Afghans (as in 'List of Afghans'). Afghanistan.org also states "People of Afghanistan are called Afghans, not Afghani" but we're getting off topic.
User B: In the real-world I heard people call them "Afghanistanis", like "Pakistani" but yes we should stop this now.

A frequent topic of discussion was accuracy, for instance, when the legitimacy of statements made in the article was questioned:

User A: Hello. I am not a wikipedia expert, and I am certainly no supporter of George Bush. But the following remark seems exaggerated to me. "Historical American allies such as France and Britain have held remarkably unfavorable opinions of Bush, with many believing him to be more dangerous than Kim Jong-il." I think the article from which this information is taken distorts slightly the results of the poll on which it is based, for the following reasons: this exact poll comparing him to Kim Jong-il was only made in Great Britain (thus contradicts the "many allies" part). Also the polls did not ask which was more dangerous, but which was a greater danger to peace. 'Being a danger to peace' is not the same as 'being dangerous'. I replaced the phrase with the following, which I think reflects more the polls cited as reference in the article 'Historical American allies such as France and Britain have held remarkably unfavorable opinions of Bush, with a 2006 poll even showing that britons were considering him more a danger to peace than Kim Jong-il.'

Probably the most intractable issue faced by editors in a topic such as this was how to sustain a neutral point of view (NPOV) and avoid personal bias (POV).[5]

> **User A**: This has been removed from the article: 'Egyptian President Mubarak commented Bush's policies had led to an "unprecedented hatred" of Arabs for the US.' User B considers this 'aggressively POV against Bush'. Mubarak's comment itself is, of course, his POV, but as an attributed quote I think it was not inappropriate. Comments?
>
> **User C**: I think this quote is appropriate. Being Mubarak is a sovereign, it is a specific and concrete indication of the diplomatic consequences of George W. Bush's actions. There might even be a section under 'diplomatic relations', which takes a quote like this from leaders of important countries. This is a very typical diplomatic statement. Point being, the comment is perfectly appropriate.
>
> **User D**: While I'm usually opposed to such quotes, in this context I'd vote for keeping this one. The president of Egypt is more respectable than Al Franken or Michael Moore.
>
> **User E**: I agree with User A – and Mubarak.

> **User A:** Nobody has referred to George W. Bush's tendency to speak in slogans that people like but that have no substance?
>
> **User B**: Such a phrasing would be POV, and without sources it would be just your opinion. Besides, slogans without substance is a recurring theme in nearly all of politics, not just GWB's administration.
>
> **User C**: Such a phrasing would be POV if it wasn't true. It is, and sources should be easy to come up with. And just because all NFL quarterbacks throw touchdowns, it doesn't mean that Peyton Manning isn't exceptional. The same goes for GWB's slogans (or propaganda if you want to call a spade a spade).
>
> **User D**: I'd tend to agree with User B – you see those cliché sayings with almost every speech that's been made by a politician, or almost everything you see in the media. I don't think that using 'slogans' is something particular to or exceptional to Bush (unlike Bushisms).

Wikipedia has numerous lists and categories in order to help users search for particular articles. These occasionally lead to controversy:

CATEGORY: ALCOHOLICS

> **User A**: Such a category exists (I created it) but I'd expect trouble if I add George [Bush] to it, so I thought I'd discuss it rather than be bold and then deal with the tide of protest. Would there be a problem with me adding GWB? I think his problems with alcohol are well documented.

---

5   For a discussion of NPOV, see Chapter 12.

User B: Well, he himself admitted to 'drinking too much'. I'd say put it in.

User C: I'm opposed to that. There is a difference between someone who 'drinks too much' and an alcoholic, which is a medical diagnosis, unless we have a better source than British tabloids.

User D: Total agreement on my part! I would also caution User A that creating a category like 'Alcoholics' plays with the edge of libel, and not just for GWB. . .

[This particular discussion continued for some time]

User A: It seems to me that Category:Alcoholics is going to be more trouble than it's worth in regards to verifiability. I'm listing it on Wikipedia:Categories for deletion.

User E: I think we should declare this issue dead and forget the category altogether.

One solution to the prolonged arguments that tended to rage round certain sections of the Bush article was to split the article into sections:

User A: A huge amount of the NPOV controversy about this article centers around claims about Bush's alleged drug alcohol use. It's a distraction from more important issues and it's caused a lot of unnecessary edit wars. Since deleting that section is not something I or most editors would support, I think it might be a good idea to split the content about drug and alcohol allegations into a separate article - 'George W. Bush drug and alcohol controversy', perhaps. That'll move all the inevitable edit wars to the new article and give the editors of this article more time to focus on other, more important topics.

The Bush article was vandalized so often that it was decided to 'semi-protect' it, meaning that only certain categories of user would be allowed to edit it. This was done several times, but always created controversy as it was felt to be against the spirit of Wikipedia. The following extract shows an occasion when a number of editors contributed to the discussion. User A was an administrator, with power to semi-protect articles:

User A: Looking at the reduction in vandalism recently, it feels quite promising. I'm testing removal of semi-protection because it's looking so good – this should be tried regularly anyhow.

User B: I support this; its time to remove it and see what happens.

User C: Hear, hear.

User D: I also support this, it has been semi-protected for too long.

User E: Adding to the pile-on; lets see what happens. You never know when someone anon or new might actually improve the article.

User A: [later the same day] I restored semi-protection again because vandalism shot up.

User C: Just for the record: the world did not end for having this page unprotected for a few hours.

User D: I think this is ridiculous, obviously an article like this will get a lot of vandalism. I know this has already been discussed, but leaving an article unprotected for not even 12 hours and then re-protecting it is not how the WP: SEMI [semi-protection] is meant to work. If this is intended to be semi'd for the long term, can we at least remove the notice at the top?

User E: How WP:SEMI is supposed to work is in response to serious vandalism irrelevant of how long it hasn't been applied. After GWB was un-semi'd it got vandalized pretty heavily right afterwards, thus semi-protection was then justified again.

User D: But isn't semi-protection (and full protection, except for the main page) supposed to be a temporary solution? Obviously, this will receive a lot of vandalism, semi-protection here will never be temporary. This is akin to protecting the Featured Article [the different Featured Articles appearing daily on Wikipedia's Home page], something we very rarely do.

User F: That wouldn't work, I don't think. New editors need to know why they can't edit the page.

User G: We MUST test the water, agreed. But if vandalism rushes in, then we protect again and test the water later. It is policy to protect against heavy vandalism. I don't like protecting either . . . Anyway, this is the best we can do.

User A: I propose that semi-protection be lifted regularly – at least once a week – so that we can spend a few hours watching what happens. Unless we do this we won't ever be able to decide whether its a good idea to lift semiprotection for good.

User E: Agreed, it should be a gentleman's rule to un-semi at least once a week.

User H: I'd say maybe a bit more often, perhaps SP for 24 hours, relax it to see what happens, and if vandalism spikes, SP again. A few hours a week doesn't seem to contribute to the 'anyone can edit' mentality. Just my opinion though.

If all else failed, a request for mediation could be made. Here, a long dispute arose over whether to mention in the article that Bush had once been arrested for drunkenness, and also whether it was relevant that much later in his career he excused himself on the grounds that he was young at the time:

User A: I think its time to get a neutral party to look at the issue of pointing out dubya's age in that section. Does anybody here know how to do that? I would appreciate it if someone can do it. User B apparently is going to keep removing it no matter how many different editors insert it.

User C: An informal mediation can be started using the Mediation Cabal under the section "Making a Request for Mediation". It may be a good idea, since no matter how many people remove it, others will keep on adding it back . . .

User D: Greeetings, being a member of the Mediation Cabal, I was asked to give a neutral POV to this discussion. I see no problem with placing the age of the pre-presidential Bush (30 at the time of the incident) on the page. Nor do I see a problem with Bush's quotation characterizing this act as a youthful indiscretion, which is a slight spin of 30 as young. (By the way, was he specifically referring to this incident in that quotation?) As stated above, 30 is considered very young by those in their 60's and very old by those in their teens. If these two statements are facts, then they should stand on their own, stay in the article as encyclopedic, without editorial comment (which would be original research). By the way, it could be helpful to find an independent source in the press taking the President's comment (about 30 being youthful) to task. If not, it seems fine to me to leave the age in there along with the President's quotation on the incident. I suggest that the bickering stop, leave the age in the article (assuming it is fact) and move on.

A clear and more positive example of Wikipedia's procedure for implementing quality control is the process whereby certain articles are given Featured Article (FA) status. At the time of writing, there were 2,340 FAs out of a total of 2,664,536 articles on the English Wikipedia.[6] This process, which was initiated soon after the birth of Wikipedia, has over the years become more complex and more bureaucratic. In the early days there existed merely an invitation for editors to nominate any article they came across, and those chosen are now referred to ironically by the current community as 'brilliant prose' articles, in reference to the somewhat casual rubric that accompanied the list:

> We think the following Wikipedia pages are pretty good. This is a selected list – since there are thousands of pages on Wikipedia, we couldn't possibly keep track of *all* the brilliant prose here! But if you come across a particularly impressive page, why not add it to the list as your way of saying "Thanks, good job"?[7]

Since those days there have emerged various specific criteria for FAs, including topic comprehensiveness and detailed source citation. Before an article is even nominated as a Featured Article Candidate (FAC), it has usually undergone significant editing, including a separate peer review as well as having been the focus of a wikiproject.[8] The FAC director and his delegates determine whether there is a consensus for promoting or rejecting an FAC. Once nominated, the article undergoes further assessment and editing, and again a consensus must be reached

---

6   <http://en.wikipedia.org/wiki/Wikipedia:FA>, retrieved on 17 December 2008.

7   <http://en.wikipedia.org/w/index.php?title=Wikipedia:Featured_articles&direction =prev&oldid=47610>.

8   A wikiproject is a collection of pages devoted to the management of a specific topic within Wikipedia, and, simultaneously, a group of editors who use those pages to collaborate on that topic. It is a resource to help co-ordinate and organize the writing and editing of articles. For instance, the article 'Albert Speer' comes within the following wikiprojects: biography, architecture, Germany, military history.

on whether to grant FA status.[9] For many editors, the FA process undoubtedly acts as a major incentive, since the results of all their hard work are plainly visible, and they acquire a sense of ownership over the article concerned. This is the case for 'Sarah', a 17-year-old committed wikipedian, who was interviewed for an article in *The Times*:

> Sarah likes to focus on one article at a time, nurturing it over a period of weeks while it goes through the rigorous peer review process necessary for it to be Featured Article (FA) standard. Featured Articles are meant to demonstrate the best of Wikipedia and only a tiny proportion of articles – 0.077 per cent of the total number – have such status. Sarah has three: on Jake Gyllenhaal, the actor, Justin Nichols, and the 2003 film *Latter Days*.
>
> 'No resource in the world is as comprehensive as my article on my idol, Jake Gyllenhaal. The pleasure you gain from that is amazing', Sarah says. 'There's a lot of kudos in getting FA. I love it that millions of people are reading the edits that I've made. Although my friends think I'm mad.'[10]

To keep track of this lengthy process, wikipedians have devised a way to communicate the current status of an article, which involves the use of templates. A template is a piece of wiki code that creates a visual marker such as a text box, which in the case of the FA system is placed in the article's Talk page. These are two examples:

> **Albert Speer** is a featured article; it (or a previous version of it) has been identified as one of the best articles produced by the Wikipedia community. Even so, if you can update or improve it, please do so.

> This article is a current featured article candidate. A featured article should exemplify Wikipedia's very best work, and is therefore expected to meet the criteria. Please feel free to leave comments.
>
> Some time after the FAC director or his delegate promotes the article or archives the nomination, a bot will update the nomination page and article talk page. **Do not manually update the {{ArticleHistory}} template** when the FAC closes.

During the FA process, the templates allow participants to see at a glance the status of an article, but they have an additional feature in that by adding templates to his own 'watchlist', any editor is instantly notified of all pages newly tagged with that template.[11]

---

9   This process is described in detail in Stvilia et al.

10   *The Times*, 2 March 2007.

11   All registered editors may have their own watchlists consisting of those articles they are particularly interested in.

User A: Hi User B, we're sorry to bug you but in fact I was showing a friend how quickly even minor changes to Wikipedia get edited. I was doing it to prove how effective the peer-editing system is though, forgive? Your quick change (less than 5 minutes, bravo) was an awesome example. We were wondering, how did you know notice my change so quickly? Were you just browsing around? Best.

User B: Hi User A. The English Language article is on my Watchlist, a feature that comes along with a Wikipedia account. Basically, you can "watch" pages that you're interested in; by clicking a particular link you can see any changes made recently to the pages you've so bookmarked. There's no minimum, and I don't think there's a maximum (I'm pushing 300). And thanks for noticing the reverts.

I reproduce below a few examples of comments on the article 'Albert Speer', taken from the FAC talk page:

User A: Work is underway on this article. I'm concentrating on getting the facts in there, then will add the citations. My goal is to get this to GA [Good Article status] by the end of the year, to FA by the spring, and get this on the front page for the anniversary of Speer's death on 1 September 2009. There were some howling factual errors. Speer's 'rifle club' statement did not have to do with Nuremberg, but an earlier Berlin rally. I've cleared it up.

User A: [some weeks later] I'm nominating this article for featured article because after extensive work, a peer review, and feedback from another editor I've worked with on another FA, I believe it meets the FA criteria. I find it rather ironic that what would be the first FA about a member of the Nazi Party should be done by me, a former synagogue president, but that is how things are sometimes. As I am currently on the road and will be online on a less than continual basis, please allow for some lag with your comments.

User B: Yup, gotta love the irony of User A bringing this to FAC but in a weird way I like the idea of the first FA biography of a Nazi leader being about a somewhat ambiguous figure like Speer than about a more macabre one like Göring, Hess or Himmler (not that this comment has anything to do with the FAC of course). In any case, this is a very interesting read: I don't claim any expertise on the subject so I can't judge comprehensiveness (or for that matter accuracy) but I am going through the article to do a bit of copyediting (update: I'll continue tomorrow).

User C: I thought it was an interesting article. However, I think it can be stronger with some additional details and/or tweaking: I think the article would benefit by having subheadings under Nazi architect and Minister of armaments. I would love to see a paragraph that discusses Speer's background, philosophy and inspiration for those Nazi buildings that are so unique, and quite imposing.

User D: I believe there's something wrong with the Harvard referencing: the links in the citations do not seem to lead anywhere, when in fact they are supposed to link to the works under 'Bibliography', yes? Also, per WP:DASH, dashes for page ranges in the citations need to be changed to en dashes.

User A: I just copied what was already in the article. Can someone point me in the right direction in fixing the refs? I'll fix the dashes after I fix the refs, just in case I have to redo the refs.

User B: 'In his final years, Speer would describe his perspective in 1939 to Gita Sereny, later to become one of his biographers'. Maybe I'm just tired, but the combination of 'final years', 'would describe', '1939', 'become' and 'later' has me completely confused by the timeline. I started to rewrite the sentence but stopped for fear of completely changing its meaning (feel free to ignore if I am just being stupid).

User E: I feel that the lead should be expanded to satisfy the demands of WP: LEAD. Currently, it leaves out details about Speer's early life and only briefly (in two short sentences) discusses his role as Nazi architect. These are vital bits of information which should be expanded upon to give the reader a sufficient overview of the entire article.

One of the most fascinating aspects of Wikipedia is the way this Byzantine structure has evolved since the comparatively simple wiki was first put on line by Wales and Sanger less than a decade ago. It is a good example of the organic, decentralized growth of a self-governing institution. Internet communities, of which Wikipedia is one of the best-known, are continuing a long tradition of self-government that dates back to well before the coming of the Web.[12] Throughout history there have been local communities which devised their own rules and procedures for sharing communal resources without reliance on a central government. In Britain, for instance, before the enclosure movement of the sixteenth to eighteenth centuries, individual villages had their own unique systems of land tenure, evolved over many years. There were complex rules concerning the use of open fields and common lands, and for monitoring the enforcement of such rules. Those accused of infringement came before manorial courts where they faced juries of their peers. More recent examples of self-government are instanced by Elinor Ostrom, who has examined a range of contemporary communities which govern and manage 'common-pool resources' (CPRs).[13] Her examples of successful CPR management include commons-based irrigation in Spain and the Philippines, high mountain meadows in Switzerland, and inshore fisheries in Turkey and Sri Lanka. In a recent article, Fernanda Viégas and her colleagues at IBM have compared the systems used by such communities to Wikipedia's extensive body of rules and guidelines:

---

12   This tradition might include, for instance, friendly societies, sick clubs and trade unions.

13   Elinor Ostrom (1990), *Governing the Commons*, Cambridge: Cambridge University Press.

The policies were written by the [Wikipedia] community to address a set of problems that is common to all efforts to organize collective action: creation of institutions, monitoring mechanisms, arbitration, and conflict resolution. These are exactly the challenges faced by the self-governing communities studied by Elinor Ostrom that succeeded in managing natural resources. There is an impressive degree of overlap between what happens on Wikipedia and the design principles that Ostrom extracted from offline communities. That Wikipedians have independently arrived at some of the same governance answers as in offline communities suggests some of these principles are universal.[14]

Given the history of Wikipedia's development of rules and procedures, one might conjecture that the main danger facing the project in the future may not be anarchy and chaos, but rather the opposite – petrification into stultifying bureaucracy. One of 'Raul's laws' states: 'As time goes on, the rules and informal processes on Wikipedia tend to become less and less plastic and harder and harder to change'.[15] The main safeguard against this threat is the fact that all these complexities and conventions have been developed not by hierarchy or diktat, but by the common consent of the community. What the community has created, it could presumably also modify. As Viégas says, the emergence of these processes is just as magical as the emergence of high-quality articles.

---

14   Fernanda B. Viégas, Martin Wattenberg and Matthew M. McKeon (2007), 'The Hidden Order of Wikipedia', *Lecture Notes in Computer Science*, Berlin: Springer, vol. 4,564.
    15   <http://en.wikipedia.org/wiki/Wikipedia/Raul>; Raul is an administrator on Wikipedia.

Chapter 11

Wikipedia: Transaction Costs

Wikipedia is a prime example of social sharing, since it is exclusively run by volunteers who have come together to produce user generated content. What mainly distinguishes Wikipedia from all the other group projects discussed in this book are its far lower transaction costs due to the technology involved.[1] This dramatic lowering of costs applies both from the point of view of the entire enterprise, and from that of the volunteers who run it. Wikipedia comes into the category of projects which could not even have been considered before the Internet, and specifically before wiki software was conceived. To understand Wikipedia's minimal costs, one might start with Benkler's dissection of communication systems in general. He writes:

> For several years I have been using a very simple, three-layered representation of the basic functions involved in mediated human communications. ... These are the physical, logical and content layers. The physical layer refers to the material things used to connect human beings to each other. These include the computers, phones, handhelds, wires, wireless links, and the like. ... The logical layer represents the algorithms, standards, ways of translating human meaning into something machines can transmit, store, or compute, and something that machines process into communications meaningful to human beings. ... The content layer is the set of humanly meaningful statements that human beings utter to and with one another.[2]

For Wikipedia, or more precisely for the Wikimedia Foundation which operates it, the costs derive almost entirely from the first of these layers, the physical layer.[3] The type of expenses incurred by the foundation are indicated in a recent message from Jimmy Wales after an appeal for funds:

---

1   On the concept of transaction costs, see Chapter 1.

2   Yochai Benkler (2006), *The Wealth of Networks*, London and New Haven, CT: Yale University Press, 392.

3   In addition to Wikipedia, the Wikimedia Foundation manages, among other projects: Wiktionary, a multi-language dictionary and thesaurus; Wikiquote, an encyclopaedia of quotations; Wikisource, a repository of source texts in any language, and Wikibooks, a collection of e-book texts for students. The foundation maintains the technical infrastructure, software and servers for all these sites, and is also responsible for fundraising and outreach activities, spreading awareness of Wikipedia and the others throughout the world.

Dear Reader

Since July 1, more than 125,000 of you have donated $4 million. In addition, we've received major gifts and foundation support totaling $2 million. This combined revenue will cover our operating expenses for the current fiscal year, ending June 30, 2009.
Your donation makes you a key supporter of the free culture movement, and pays for:

1. Day-to-day operations: servers, hosting, bandwidth, our staff of just 23 people.
2. Continued development & improvements of open source software that powers all Wikimedia projects.
3. Outreach events like Wikipedia Academies: in-person workshops where you can learn more about how to use and edit Wikipedia.
4. Volunteer support: helping our international volunteer community to grow and to continue to do amazing work.

Wikipedia owns or leases hundreds of server units grouped in various centres round the world, including Florida, Amsterdam and South Korea. The code layer, which involves the open source software Mediawiki, is largely maintained and developed by volunteers with appropriate programming skills. And, of course, the content layer, which is what meets the eye of the consumer, is again run entirely by volunteers.

As a public charity, the foundation relies on public contributions and grants, and is exempt from US federal and state income tax. Contributions to it qualify as tax-deductible charitable contributions. During the financial year 2007–2008, revenue was about $7 million dollars, which included a grant from the Alfred P. Sloan Foundation, a charitable institution that agreed to donate a million dollars a year over three years.[4] In 2007, both income and expenses nearly doubled, and the foundation ended the year with net assets of $1,700,000.

Because technical costs are relatively low, it is possible to make Wikipedia free to all users, and this of course is a major cause for its popularity. It is also one reason why those who contribute to it are prepared to work for nothing. No doubt a lot of money could be made from the project. One commentator has tried to estimate the billions of dollars that could be generated if space on Wikipedia pages was made available for advertising. 'Endemic advertising opportunities' would be particularly lucrative, meaning, for instance, that entries on countries or cities might attract travel-related adverts, or entries on information technology attract adverts for computers. In this way, enormous sums might be raised which could be spent on worthwhile causes such as preventing malaria in Africa. However, if

---

4   <http://upload.wikimedia.org/wikipedia/foundation/4/4c/Wikimedia_20072008_fs.pdf>.

any moves were made in this direction, to turn Wikipedia into a money-making concern, there is no doubt that the whole ethos of the project would change, and volunteers would quit in droves. The example of Microsoft's online encyclopaedia *Encarta* bears this out. It was suggested to Encarta users that they might edit articles along Wikipedia lines, but since it was generally perceived that those who co-operated would merely be adding to Microsoft's profits, the idea never caught on. This example seems to show that the commercial path, as taken for instance by Diderot and the encyclopedists, is not available to Wikipedia.

In December 2007, Google introduced Google Knol, a rival encyclopaedia to Wikipedia, but one in which users who write an article can agree to include advertisements on it, and share the profits with Google. This site, backed as it might be in the future by favourable treatment from Google's page rank system, appears to pose a real threat to Wikipedia. However, at the time of writing Knol has not attracted as much traffic as its authors hoped.[5]

To sum up, Wikipedia's finances have the advantage of a circuitous logic. Costs are minimal, which allows the encyclopaedia to be offered free to the public. This in turn means that volunteers are attracted to this non-profitmaking, idealistic concern, and the efforts of the volunteers ensure that costs can be kept low.

What has been said so far about costs relates to the Wikimedia Foundation when considered as an economic unit possibly competing in the market with other units. However, another way to investigate transaction costs is to look at them from the point of view of the volunteers themselves, and from that of individual members of the group. Given the technological infrastructure provided by the Wikimedia Foundation, what are the costs of running Wikipedia – for wikipedians? In other words, what are the advantages and disadvantages, the strains and stresses, of belonging to this group?

To start with, no qualifications are needed and it is very easy to join. Individuals merely need a computer and Internet access to turn themselves into wikipedians. There are no deadlines set; editors can work when, and as much as, they wish. The extreme modularity of Wikipedia means that there are tasks available for all, and no one need undertake anything beyond their available time or capacity. One of the great advantages of social production, mentioned above, is that managers are not required to decide who does what – the volunteers do this for themselves. The limited motivation of most participants in large-scale social projects such as Wikipedia is evident, but again this hardly matters given the existence of a self-selecting core group of enthusiasts who are prepared not only to work long hours, but also to co-ordinate the efforts of others. The attractions of participation in the project, either for casual editors who are, as it were, merely passing through or for this core group have already been discussed.

There are various transaction costs resulting from the nature of the project which face participants. Learning to master the complicated vocabulary that

---

5   <http://arstechnica.com/news.ars/post/20090119-google-knol-six-months-later-wikipedia-need-not-worry.html>.

wikipedians tend to use could be daunting for a new recruit, as could the sheer volume of onsite conventions, policies and advice which have accumulated over the years. Another 'cost' is the chances of finding oneself in an edit war – the often protracted, often bitter arguments that sometimes take over a particular article's talk page. No doubt such experiences have been enough to put off many potential contributors. And because of Wikipedia's openness, another major transaction cost, in terms of time, energy and the possibility of disillusionment, is having to deal with all kinds of vandalism and contributions made in bad faith.

Straightforward vandalism, usually committed by younger viewers, is fairly easy for wikipedian editors to spot and deal with. An administrator explains in greater detail:

> Basically the transaction costs for healing Wikipedia are less than those to harm it, over a reasonable period of time. I am an admin and if I see vandalism in an article, it takes about ten total clicks to check that editor has vandalized other articles and made no positive contributions, block the IP address or user-name, and rollback all of the vandalism by that user. It takes more clicks if they edited a lot of articles quickly, but they had to spend more time coming up with stupid crap to put in the articles, hitting edit, submit, etc. After being blocked they have to be really persistent to keep coming back to vandalize. Some are, but luckily many more people are there to notice them and revert the vandalism. It's a beautiful thing.

'Suppose you could go to a big city', writes another editor, 'and whenever you see graffiti click a button and repair a surface. One after another they're gone in ten seconds. It's extremely satisfying'.

In 2005, Alexander Halavais, a lecturer at the State University of New York at Buffalo, conducted an experiment by slipping 13 deliberate errors into various Wikipedia articles. To his surprise, all of them had been deleted within less than three hours. Admittedly, Halavais now understands that once one or two of the errors had been noticed it was fairly simple for the system to grasp who was doing the damage, and then home in on his other alterations. If he had made his changes over a period, and using different computers, they would have been harder to detect.[6] Nevertheless, this experiment seems to confirm the claim that vandalism and obvious mistakes are soon put right, and therefore only pose minor problems for Wikipedia.

More challenging than simple vandalism are deliberate misstatements or distortions. In November 2004 a new entry was posted on the Polish Wikipedia, a brief biography of a leading member of the Polish Communist Party in the mid-twentieth century. In English, the entry translates as follows:

---

6   <http://alex.halavais.net/the-isuzu-experiment/>.

Henryk Batuta, whose real name was Izaak Apfelbaum, was born in 1898 in Odessa, and died in 1947 near Ustrzyki Górne. He was a Polish communist and an activist in the international workers' movement. After involvement in the Russian civil war, he returned to Poland and became a member of the Communist Party of Poland. With the authority of the party, and under instructions from leaders including Waclaw Komar, he organized the killing of various undercover political police informers. This affair was not discovered until the fifties. From 1934 to 1935 Batuta was a prisoner in Bereza Kartuska. Subsequently he emigrated and participated in the Spanish Civil War. During the Second World War he remained in the USSR, where from 1943 he was a member of the Union of Polish Patriots, holding the rank of major in their Internal Security Corps. He died in 1947 near Ustrzyki Górne during a clash with UPA.

His name is commemorated by a street in Warsaw (Służew nad Dolinką). After 1989 numerous voices were heard demanding that the street name be changed, but this change has not yet come about.[7]

There is convincing detail here, but unfortunately Henryk Batuta never existed. The entry was a hoax, and one that remained undetected for fifteen months. It seems that the anonymous perpetrators had wanted to make a protest about the fact that there were still places in Poland named after former communist officials who did not deserve the honour.

The Batuta entry was a comparatively harmless contamination of the encyclopaedia, although the length of time it took to discover it was presumably worrying for the community of wikipedians. More damaging to reputation was another incident in 2006, when Brian Chase, an entirely unremarkable 38-year-old from Nashville, Tennessee decided to play a joke on John Seigenthaler, the ex-editor of his local newspaper. It was, said Chase later, 'a joke that went horribly, horribly wrong'. He made up an entirely fictitious biography for Seigenthaler, writing that he had once lived in the Soviet Union before returning to the USA and founding a public relations company. It was then stated that he might have been implicated in the assassinations of both John and Robert Kennedy. As with the Polish hoax, this item also went undetected, in this case until friends of Seigenthaler told him about it four months later. Volunteer sleuths then traced the libel to its origin, whereupon Chase came clean and made an apology to his victim. Jimmy Wales acted quickly, and the sabotage was removed, but Seigenthaler was unappeased. He submitted a bitter article about Wikipedia in *USA Today*. 'When I was a child,' he wrote, 'my mother lectured me on the evils of gossip. She held a feather pillow and said, "If I tear this open, the feathers will fly to the four winds, and I could never get them back in the pillow. That's how it is when you spread mean things about people." For me, that pillow is a metaphor for Wikipedia'.[8] Some wikipedians thought he

---

7   <http://en.wikipedia.org/wiki/Henryk_Batuta_hoax>.

8   <http://www.usatoday.com/news/opinion/editorials/2005-11-29-wikipedia-edit_ x.htm>.

had over-reacted, and that the correct response would have been just to edit out the misinformation, adding an explanation on the article's talk page. But perhaps this was too much to ask of a 78-year-old retired journalist who had probably never heard of Wikipedia before the outrage occurred. His reputation had been tarnished, and he was entitled to be upset.

Seigenthaler's concern was that on Wikipedia, 'irresponsible – and anonymous – vandals [can] write anything they want about anybody'. Jimmy Wales responded to this charge with an extended simile:

> Imagine that we are designing a restaurant. This restaurant will serve steak. Because we are going to be serving steak, we will have steak knives for the customers. Because the customers will have steak knives, they might stab each other. Therefore, we conclude, we need to put each table into separate metal cages, to prevent the possibility of people stabbing each other. What would such an approach do to our civil society? What does it do to human kindness, benevolence, and a positive sense of community?
>
> When we reject this design for restaurants, and then when, inevitably, someone does get stabbed in a restaurant (it does happen), do we write long editorials to the papers complaining that 'The steakhouse is inviting it by not only allowing irresponsible vandals to stab anyone they please, but by also providing the weapons'? No, instead we acknowledge that the verb 'to allow' does not apply in such a situation. A restaurant is not *allowing* something just because they haven't taken measures to *forcibly prevent it* a priori. It is surely against the rules of the restaurant, and of course against the laws of society. Just. Like. Libel. If someone starts doing bad things in a restaurant, they are forcibly kicked out and, if it's particularly bad, the law can be called. Just. Like. Wikipedia.
>
> I do not accept the spin that Wikipedia 'allows anyone to write anything' just because we do not metaphysically prevent it by putting authors in cages.[9]

One suggested change to Wikipedia – not yet implemented at the end of 2008 – is a software feature called 'flagged revisions' which would allow experienced editors to grade the quality status of articles. Those selected as competent and free of vandalism would not be available for editing by anonymous users, and this, it is hoped, would greatly reduce casual vandalism because vandals would not have the pleasure of being able to view the results of their efforts straight away. This solution runs up against the difficulty of deciding how to choose 'experienced editors', as well as the danger of subverting the ethos of Wikipedia by creating a new status system among editors generally. In any case, flagged revisions would do nothing to stop future Batuta creators or Seigenthaler traducers.

To sum up, the conventional costs of Wikipedia, and hence of the Wikimedia Foundation, are minimal as compared with proprietary sites or enterprises of similar

---

9   <http://many.corante.com/archives/2005/12/17/wikipedia_academia_and_seigenthaler.php>.

size and nature (if such exist), and this is perhaps the main reason for the project's continued existence and growth. However, this is to some degree balanced by less conventional, psychological costs, in particular the need to combat vandalism, which are the result of Wikipedia's openness to all-comers, and which place a real burden on the shoulders of committed supporters.

Chapter 12
Wikipedia and the Public

This chapter considers Wikipedia's relationship to the 'real' world. The question arises how far can the Internet, and more particularly the Wikipedia community, be seen as contributing to a newly emerging public sphere, as defined by Jürgen Habermas and Michael Warner.[1] Habermas postulated that the bourgeois public sphere, an arena in which free discussion and polemics could take place, largely but not solely through the medium of print, first appeared in England towards the end of the seventeenth century. The distinction between Habermasian 'public opinion' and more passive 'mass opinion' might be summarized briefly as follows: public opinion is effective when the public may broadcast opinions as well as receiving them; has a chance to answer back to any opinion expressed publicly; finds outlets for effective and legal action, even in opposition to authority, and remains independent, and protected from penetration by governmental or proprietary interests. Mass opinion prevails when far fewer express than receive opinions, and when political or cultural elites control the process of opinion-formation. According to Habermas:

> By the 'public sphere' we mean first of all a realm of our social life in which something approaching public opinion can be formed. Access is guaranteed to all citizens. A portion of the public sphere comes into being in every conversation in which private individuals assemble to form a public body.[2]

Habermas sees the functional public sphere as disappearing with the evolution of the mass media in the second half of the nineteenth century. The public at this point turn into passive consumers of what is put before them, in both the cultural and political spheres, and the possibilities for real debate and decision-making gradually evaporate. The Western 'public sphere' has been largely structured by the mass media during the twentieth century, and this has resulted in a relatively controlled and weak arena for cultural and political debate. Public communication has tended to be one-way, contained within a hub-and-spoke system in which

---

1 Jürgen Habermas (1962), *The Structural Transformation of the Public Sphere*, Cambridge: Polity Press; Michael Warner (2002), *Publics and Counterpublics*, New York: Zone Books. See also Chapter 1.

2 Habermas, in a 1974 article quoted by Alan E. Rycraft, 'Young Adults and Virtual Public Spheres', [2007]: <http://sunshinecommunications.ca/articles/virtual_public_spheres.pdf>.

cultural content is produced centrally and broadcast to consumers on the periphery. Hence, a genuine public sphere is a rare beast indeed.

Since Habermas first outlined his views on the public sphere, many have been critical of his original narrow framing of a sphere controlled by propertied, male participants, and his assumption that there would be just a single public sphere with the power to influence a government merely through the power of rational discussion. The world of Addison and Steele clearly has little in common with today's globalized world with its corporate mass media.[3] Habermas himself has refined and modified his original thesis in order to apply it to complex modern societies in which the vast majority of citizens can no longer know each other face to face. Many would argue that in today's digital world there are not just one, but many public spheres, operating from the personal and local to the global level, with vastly differing potential levels of influence on public policy.[4] Others caution that previous new technologies, such as radio and television, were widely heralded in the same way as the Internet as ushering in a new era of public debate, only to fail to live up to expectations. Is it evident that the Internet, with its numerous opportunities for political discussion and action, and its relatively low costs, will play a crucial part in the development of informed and democratic debate? This is a major issue for our time, which others have addressed and no doubt will continue to do so; below, I intend to confine my remarks to wikis, and to Wikipedia in particular.

How far does the recent appearance of Internet sites containing user-created content, such as Wikipedia, assist towards the re-creation of a public sphere? There are clearly two ways in which Wikipedia might be construed as achieving this, one being the provision of free and independent information to the public on which to base their opinions. Take, for instance, a previously apolitical young American, who might want to find out something about her new president. The Wikipedia article on Obama is up-to-date and covers every possible aspect of his career and policies, his family life and background, together with images and also dozens of links to other relevant articles and sources of information. In addition, on the article's talk page, various editors argue over numerous controversial points relating to the article, including a discussion of several thousand words about how to describe his ethnic identity.[5] Every year, the number increases of those who consult what have been called 'citizens' media', including Wikipedia, in preference to more traditional sources of information such as newspapers or television. Younger adults especially, who may feel disenfranchised from political parties and from the mass media, often visit a range of online sites to research

---

3   For Addison and Steele, see also p. 10.

4   See, for example, J. Keane, 'Structural Transformations of the Public Sphere', in K.L. Hacker and van Dijk (eds.) (2000), *Digital Democracy: Issues of Theory and Practice*, Thousand Oaks, CA: Sage Publications.

5   In particular, should he be described as 'bi-racial', 'African American', or both?

political positions and engage in dialogue on issues. One blogger compared his use of the media in 2005 with his practice four years earlier:

> I couldn't help but notice how different my media consumption has been surrounding the terrorist attacks in London from September 11th. When my girlfriend came and hammered on my door on the morning of September 11 [2001] I turned on CNN and just watched. When I heard about the bombings in London [2005] I looked it up on Flickr, Nowpublic, Wikipedia, Wikinews to mention a few. It seems the editors/writers/journalists at the dinosaur blogs did the same. In fact, not only did these old school media folks go online for their news gathering, but they took citizen's media and ran front page stories with it.

Another, and perhaps even more significant, way in which Wikipedia may help create a public sphere is through participation, for example in all the arguments that rage on the various talk pages and user pages. Here, perhaps the most important factor is the absence of any controlling authority. The public sphere is at its strongest when individuals share an equal capacity to enter opinions and ideas into public deliberation, and at its weakest when debate is left in the hands of opinion-forming elites. Discussions on Wikipedia are thoroughly democratic, open to anyone, and any contributions made are visible to the entire world as soon as the 'save' button is clicked. Such debates and arguments, constantly repeated, lead to intellectual self-reliance as well as scepticism. Those accustomed to expressing their own point of view in a public arena are less likely to be politically compliant citizens, and more likely to question received opinion in general.

However, before assuming that Wikipedia's contribution to the public sphere is obvious, a few precautionary points are in order. The first of these, which applies not merely to Wikipedia but to the entire Internet, is: how far it can function, or continue to function in the future, as a democratic medium uninfluenced by commercial pressures or government oversight? Net neutrality and independence is constantly threatened in all kinds of ways, including pressures for increasing surveillance and censorship and the possibility of shrinking access to the currently wide diversity of opinion. As far as Wikipedia is concerned, recent attempts by commercial and state institutions to delete criticism or insert self-promotional material are cases in point.[6] The more successful the Wikipedia project, the more special interests will attempt to influence it; the only solution is presumably perpetual vigilance by the community.

Secondly, according to Michael Warner another criterion needed for a group genuinely to participate in the public sphere is an ongoing life. The message that the group brings to the public must not be evanescent, but rather must offer circularity, continuity and feedback. A text, to have a public, must continue to circulate through time, which is why all publics are intertextual. To Warner, writing

---

6   Hence the need for a recent new guideline on conflict of interest: <http://en.wikipedia.org/wiki/Wikipedia:COI>.

in 2002, it seemed unlikely that the Internet could offer such continuity. 'Web discourse', he wrote, 'has very little of the citational field that would allow us to speak of it as discourse unfolding through time. Once a Web site is up, it can be hard to tell how recently it was posted or revised or how long it will continue to be posted'. He concluded: 'it remains unclear to what extent the changing technology will be assimilable to the temporal framework of public discourse'.[7]

Such strictures may be accurate regarding perhaps the majority of blogs, and websites generally. The Internet is highly fluid and changeable, and hence quite unlike the more stable and hierarchical models of traditional print media. However, the criticism of impermanence hardly applies to Wikipedia, with its software that preserves every version of every article, and every argument put forward in accompanying discussions. Wikipedia does offer continuity and feedback. Its record of past events is comprehensive and unrelenting, and its near decade of existence means it is ancient in Internet terms, and gives grounds for anticipating a certain permanence.

A third issue concerns the precise connection between the provision of information and political activism. What might be called a thin or passive idea of citizenship identifies it primarily with the duty to make an informed choice between different party programmes in order to vote in local and national elections. Thicker conceptions see it as full participation in every area of public and communal life. Such an active concept might include, for instance, both the self-organized creativity of cultural or political associations and the right to take part in mass movements or demonstrations against corporate malpractice or governmental failure. As a source of free information, Wikipedia clearly contributes to the requirements of both the passive voter and the engaged activist. As a forum where scepticism and dissent are prominent, however, it might be argued that the project encourages the more active side of citizenship. Not everyone would support this kind of apprenticeship, and some might say it was taking the idea of democracy a step too far. Suzanna Sherry, an American law professor, has written a long article entitled 'Democracy and the Death of Knowledge' in which she criticizes Wikipedia as demonstrating 'the dark side' of the democratization of knowledge. Sherry distinguishes between value judgements, which voters are entitled to make (via their elected representatives), and factual decisions, which should be left to experts. As an example of how this system ought to work, she instances a decision by the United States to go to war – a rather unfortunate example considering she was writing in 2006, three years after the invasion of Iraq:

> we are likely to get better results from a panel of trained experts than from a survey of ordinary citizens. So what is the role of democracy in our constitutional regime? It is to make value choices: the choices that depend not on expertise but on policy preferences. The popularly elected branches decide, for example, whether to go to war. But if we want to wage war *successfully*, we ask military

---

7   Warner, 97–8.

experts and if we want to wage war within constitutional bounds we ask legal experts. In both cases, we might not like what the experts tell us – and their decisions might end up preventing us from acting as we would prefer – but putting those questions to a popular vote is a recipe for disaster.[8]

In other words, Sherry thinks that too much knowledge can be dangerous, as it might lead to 'ordinary citizens' challenging the opinions of the experts. Apart from the fact that 'experts' may have their own axes to grind, the obvious problem here is surely that the ability to make informed value judgements always depends on the relevant factual knowledge being readily available.

If Wikipedia is indeed to play a part in an emerging public sphere, it must be trusted. But why should we, the public, trust it? A page from it appears miraculously on our screen at the touch of a button, but what exactly is its provenance, who created it, and who will vouch for it? How different is the case of that new monograph on the French Revolution which may have recently appeared on a shelf in one's local bookshop. To start with, the book is displayed in a respectable location, surrounded by other reputable works of history with familiar titles. It might have on its spine the logo of a well-known publisher, in which case one can assume it has survived the usual thorough process of peer review, copy editing and so on. On the dust jacket there will no doubt be endorsements from people whose names are recognized, and a glance at the acknowledgements, preface and introduction reassures as to the author's pedigree. The name may be unknown, but one is soon satisfied as to his or her qualifications, the institutions they are associated with, the libraries and archives they have used. It is clear that this text has gone through, and passed, a cultural selection process, and that it therefore has some claim to one's confidence. Its author has, as it were, been granted the right to publish by those whose task it is to know about such things. Academia, in particular, gives its members a source of accreditation. In an era of mass media, the universal distinction between the consuming public and the producer applies just as much to cultural products as to other artefacts.[9]

When it comes to the Internet, however, one often finds that it is not possible to fall back on the trust criteria to which one is accustomed in the case of print. In the absence of the usual context surrounding a printed book, the criteria on which trust is based must be looked for within the text itself rather than extrinsically. Most websites do not, for instance, exhibit the pedigrees of their authors or creators, or give evidence of peer review. In Wikipedia's case, the situation is even more extreme since its numerous authors are anonymous, and the public, by and

---

8   Suzanna Sherry (2006), 'Democracy and the Death of Knowledge': <http://ssrn. com/abstract=947530>.

9   'Modernity guarantees knowledge not by reference to virtue but to *expertise*. ... The expertise of individuals is itself considered to be vouched for by the institutions from which they speak and which are the ultimate sources of that expertise': Steven Shapin (1994), *A Social History of Truth*, Chicago, IL: University of Chicago Press, 412.

large, is wary of anonymity. Furthermore, because every reader is also potentially an author, the usual binary producer/consumer division becomes blurred. The creators of Wikipedia are not, or not clearly, part of that cultural élite to which, it is argued, the authors of printed books usually belong. Hence those signs, extrinsic to the actual text, from which trust is conventionally obtained are absent. In these circumstances, how can we ever be expected to decide who and what to trust?

One way to establish what degree of trust readers should put in Wikipedia articles has been put forward by a team supported by Stanford University, California.[10] It involves a complicated scheme whereby all the articles would be divided into small fragments, and the fragments colour-coded according to their degree of trustfulness. This in turn would depend on which editor last modified the fragment in question, and on the degree of trust that could be placed on that particular author. The question then arises, however, how to judge an editor's trustworthiness, and here the scheme seems to rest on shaky and circular foundations. Editors are to be assessed on all the edits they have ever made in that particular subject area. If they have previously edited generally trustworthy articles, then they are themselves to be trusted. Whether an article is 'generally trustworthy' depends on how many times links have been made to it from other Wikipedia articles. This was a brave attempt to measure trust by using quantifiable information already archived on the Wikipedia site, but there is no sign that it is likely to be implemented. It merely seems to show once again that trust is an elusive quality, never easy to measure.

Apologists for Wikipedia point to the peer review that is presumed to take place whenever new articles, or contributions to existing articles, have been submitted. They compare this process to the peer review that academic articles and books undergo before publication, and it is even claimed that Wikipedia's process is superior because many more eyes scan the contributions, and over a longer period. However, the crucial distinction here is, of course, that those asked to carry out an academic peer review have been picked for their expertise in the subject, whereas Wikipedia editors have not. Again, Wikipedia is often compared to open source software development, which has proven highly successful and is trusted by the public. Both enterprises, it is claimed, profit from Eric Raymond's famous principle concerning eyeballs and bugs which I mentioned at the beginning of this second part of the book.[11] However, the difference between the two is surely that open source programmers are required to test their innovations against reality – in other words, must constantly check whether or not their programs work.

---

10   Deborah L. McGuiness et al. (2006), 'Investigations into Trust for Collaborative Information Repositories: A Wikipedia Case Study': <http://ebiquity.umbc.edu/_file_ directory_/papers/274.pdf>.

11   See p. 71.

Most people probably have an ambivalent attitude to Wikipedia, thankful for its existence, using it frequently, but with reservations about its total reliability.[12] University teachers are by and large wary of it, or at least discourage their students from citing it in their assignments. Danah Boyd of the University of Southern California, a self-confessed Wikipedia enthusiast, writes: 'As a contributor to and user of Wikipedia, there is no doubt that I have a deep appreciation for it. All the same, I roll my eyes whenever students submit papers with Wikipedia as a citation'.[13] Should Wikipedia be trusted? The answer may depend partly on what one is seeking from it, and partly on one's own preconceptions about the nature of knowledge. This debate continues in the next chapter.

---

12   A recent TNS poll found that only 24 per cent of Britons but 52 per cent of Germans said they 'highly trusted' Wikipedia: <http://www.guardian.co.uk/technology/2009/jan/01/internet-web-worldwide-international>.

13   <http://many.corante.com/archives/2005/01/04/academia_and_wikipedia.php>.

Chapter 13
Wikipedia and the Nature of Knowledge

If you think about it, where does all knowledge lie? It's in our heads, really. Sure, it's out there in books somewhere, but that knowledge is dead. What we know is in our heads. Someone is talking about it somewhere. In the case of Wikipedia, it just happens to be on the page. So its common knowledge distilled.

Marshall Poe

Jimmy Wales, founder of Wikipedia, was born in Huntsville, Alabama in 1966. After studying finance at the universities of Alabama and Indiana, he worked as a futures and options market trader in Chicago. At this time the dot.com boom was just getting under way, and Wales came up with Bomis, a search engine or portal through which the customer could access various erotic websites. In later years he downplayed references to the porn traffic on Bomis, describing its content as 'glamour photography', but in any case it was clearly a money-spinner, and income from the site was to help the initial funding of Wikipedia.

But before Wikipedia there was Nupedia. This was another of Wales's schemes – to set up a free, yet academically respectable, Internet encyclopaedia. To assist, he hired Larry Sanger, a computer specialist with a doctorate in philosophy from Ohio State University, who became Nupedia's editor-in-chief, subsidized by Bomis. However, the problem with Nupedia was that the process of finding experts to write articles, which were then checked out by other experts, was extremely laborious and slow, and by the end of 2001, after a year online, they had got together a mere handful of articles – although pretty good ones, according to Sanger.

At this point someone – and it is disputed whether the initiative came from Wales or Sanger – had the bright idea of opening up the writing of the encyclopaedia to anyone at all, by using a wiki, a program that allows anyone to contribute text, or to edit previous contributions, and which keeps a permanent record of all changes made. The initial idea was that although the articles could be written by the public, they would be vetted and edited by the academics who were already involved with Nupedia. But it turned out that these experts were reluctant to lend their names and reputations to a project open to all and sundry, so Wales then went a step further and split off Nupedia altogether from the new venture, which had been christened Wikipedia. The text was now to be not only written but also edited by anyone who cared to log onto the site. By now Sanger, whose funding by Bomis had run out, and who in any case had always been the more academically minded of the pair, had decided to pull out. He went back to university teaching, while claiming to retain a benevolent interest in Wikipedia.

Since then, Sanger has set up Citizendum, yet another Internet encyclopaedia, which involves – and pays – experts, but which will not, he hopes, be stifled by Nupedia's problems of bureaucracy and inertia. Meanwhile, Wikipedia has grown exponentially, and become the world's leading source of reference. The difference in approach between Wikipedia and Citizendum is crucial, and rests on a fundamental disagreement on how knowledge is best produced. The Wikipedia doctrine holds that knowledge-creation is a social process that is fluid and never finally complete. A typical article in Wikipedia might start when an individual user collects information from sources he or she considers trustworthy and pieces these together into a first draft. Subsequently, all active users may criticize, edit or develop the article over an indefinite period. The effectiveness or otherwise of this procedure does not derive so much from the original content as from the extended peer-review process which, it is hoped, converts untested raw material into socially acceptable knowledge.

Sanger, on the other hand, believes that reliable knowledge needs to be produced and overseen by experts, and claims that the root problem with Wikipedia is an engrained culture of 'anti-elitism', or lack of respect for expertise.[1] Academics and specialists do not want to waste time bandying words (on the discussion pages of articles) with obstinate or prejudiced people who might well know little or nothing of the topic concerned. Consequently, until Wikipedia acquires 'a policy of respecting and deferring politely to experts', the experts will stay away. And without them, the quality of articles will continue to suffer, and the general public, especially those who needed a thoroughly reliable source of information, such as researchers, teachers and librarians, will be put off using it. Sanger's solution is to invite panels of academics to oversee the production of articles. 'I hope', he writes, 'that a university, academic consortium, or think-tank can be found to pursue a project to release vetted versions of Wikipedia articles'.

There are various difficulties here. In the first place, Sanger's solution seems counter to the highly democratic spirit of Wikipedia, and would certainly tend to alienate swathes of existing and potential volunteer editors. Secondly, there would be major problems in recruiting such experts, and in defining their spheres of expertise. Nevertheless, Sanger's point about the need for expertise will not go away. As Joel Mokyr, the historian of science, says, 'truth is to a large extent what society believes on the basis of what authorities and experts tell the rest is the truth'.[2] In most areas of knowledge there is a vast difference between the expert and the general public. At present there may well be many among Wikipedia's editors who are experts in their fields, but not nearly enough, surely, to cover even a small proportion of the existing two and a half million articles.

A century ago, James Murray, editor of the *Oxford English Dictionary*, gave a lecture about the kind of knowledge he and his colleagues were engaged in providing. He said: 'Every fact faithfully recorded, and every inference correctly drawn from the facts, become a permanent accession to human knowledge … part

---

1   Larry Sanger (2004), 'Why *Wikipedia* must jettison its anti-elitism': <http://www. kuro5hin.org/story/2004/12/30/142458/25>.

2   Joel Mokyr (2002), *The Gifts of Athena*, Princeton, NJ: Princeton University Press, 7.

of eternal truth, which will never cease to be true'.[3] This Victorian optimism is very different from the attitude to knowledge displayed throughout Wikipedia. The arguments that rage on the history and discussion pages of numerous articles are an important element, and one of the factors making Wikipedia very different from a conventional encyclopaedia. Such disputes reveal to the reader something about the nature of truth and how it is acquired. Knowledge, according to Wikipedia, can be contentious, problematic, controversial – in a word, political. Frequently, disputes about knowledge can never be satisfactorily settled, no agreement or compromise can be found, and final representations come at the expense of others. In other encyclopaedias, and indeed in many other scholarly media, these features are not evident. Early encyclopaedias, including Chambers' *Cyclopaedia*, were composed entirely by one person who took all the editorial decisions and therefore brooked no dispute. Larger projects such as the *Encyclopaedia Britannica* employ numerous experts, but still favour a hierarchical system of working in which the actual process of producing the knowledge is 'blackboxed' and invisible. The results are presented in an unproblematic and one-dimensional manner, with every entry written in the same authoritative voice. The reader can take it or leave it. The problem is that people who consult encyclopaedias are usually fairly ignorant about the subject being investigated, and therefore have to accept what they are given. One Wikipedian puts it like this:

> Suppose that the editors of a well-known and trusted encyclopedia had had a huge vicious war on which point of view would be reflected in the entry on a certain topic, and that one of those editors had won out. How would you as a reader of that encyclopedia know that? With Wikipedia you could. You could see exactly what the alternate views were, you could see which was accepted and why, and most importantly, you would know there was some controversy there.

One of Wikipedia's leading principles, and the one that certainly generates most heat among contributors, is the need to be impartial, to maintain always a neutral point of view (NPOV). At the time of writing, over 400 articles were classified by their authors as possibly lacking neutrality.[4] NPOV mandates that writers refrain from advancing their own opinions or value judgements; one should merely assert facts, perhaps including facts concerning the opinions and value judgements of others. The principle also demands, not that decisions about truth need be made, but rather, decisions about the existence of reputable sources. Articles should fairly represent all significant viewpoints, and should do so in proportion to their representation in reliable sources on the subject. But even with this guidance, neutrality is far from easy to achieve. One editor may write something which

---

3   Quoted in K.M. Elizabeth Murray (1977), *Caught in the Web of Words*, London and New Haven, CT: Yale University Press, 197.

4   Retrieved from <http://en.wikipedia.org/wiki/Category:NPOV_disputes> on 17 November 2008.

another editor classes as POV and wants to delete. Sometimes those with strongly held opinions take up entrenched positions and refuse to budge, and this can lead to an 'edit war', with successive alterations repeatedly cancelling each other out. Meanwhile, on the article's discussion page the contributors try to justify their 'edits' and argue their case. It may end in compromise, or possibly with adjudication from a passing administrator. In the worst scenario, it can lead to someone being temporarily banned altogether from contributing.

Obviously, most argument and most edit wars occur on controversial topics.[5] In the article 'Abortion', a new editor might appear and replace the statement 'to terminate a pregnancy' with 'to destroy a living human foetus', and this predictably kicks off a ferocious battle between pro-choicers and pro-lifers. In the four years since it was first written, this particular article has been subject to over 6,000 edits, with practically every phrase in it subject to intense analysis and debate. To take a different example, one can easily grasp why there was a long and bitter argument about how to describe national borders in the article 'Israel' when one realizes – from their respective user pages – that one recent editor is a Palestinian from Nazareth, and two others are Jewish students at Tel Aviv University. Edit wars can also blow up over seemingly trivial issues. For instance, on the talk page of the article on the artist Francis Bacon, thousands of words, some of them extremely bitter, have been devoted to a discussion as to his nationality – whether he should be classed as Irish, English or British.

There are two important points to make here. Firstly, it is of course highly unlikely that editors with radically differing views on a controversial topic will ever reach an understanding with each other as to the truth of the matter. But, secondly, such a consensus is not required. What they can perhaps agree about is something much less demanding – merely, what should go into the encyclopaedia. The NPOV guidelines state: 'NPOV weights viewpoints in proportion to their prominence. However, when reputable sources contradict one another and *are* relatively equal in prominence, the core of the NPOV policy is to let competing approaches exist on the same page'. The conflicting points of views might, for instance, end up being stated in separate paragraphs without any definite judgement emerging. The danger with this solution is that it can produce a flaccid and unhelpful conclusion. Roy Rosenzweig quotes the ending of an article on the controversial guerrilla fighter William Clarke Quantrill, who fought ruthlessly for the South in the American Civil War: 'Some historians view him as an opportunistic, bloodthirsty outlaw, while others continue to regard him as a daring horse soldier and a local folk hero'.[6] In its early days, according to the authors of *How Wikipedia Works*, 'you could find too much writing on Wikipedia in the form "some say X, while others say Y". This form aims at neutrality but fails. … The phrase should be verifiable,

5   For recent articles in which there have been heroic attempts to preserve neutrality, see '2008 Mumbai attacks', and 'Israel-Gaza conflict', and their respective talk pages.

6   Roy Rosenzweig, 'Can History be Open Source?', *Journal of American History* (June 2006), 130.

reading "A, B, and C say X, while D and E say Y'". It is only fair to mention that the Quantrill conclusion has been improved since Rosenzweig quoted it in 2005.

Alternatively, one side's arguments could be moved to a separate article entirely. This is the case with the article 'Evolution', which a scientific account of the theory is explained, but with a link which takes the reader to 'Creationism'. Here, the view that the earth was created within the last 10,000 years, a belief said to be shared by 47 per cent of Americans, is developed, with links to external sources that support this position.

While the idea that it is possible to adopt an objective or neutral position is an old one, the idea of having multiple voices competing within the encyclopaedia is original. Representing alternative points of view in highly contested areas without critical analysis of the quality and content of argument relieves the need for validation, and may give partial satisfaction to the disputing parties, motivating them perhaps to continue to use or contribute to Wikipedia. However, this approach alters the traditional positivist approach to knowledge which assumes that there is always one truth, and one only.[7] Hitting the history buttons in Wikipedia articles similarly demonstrates that on most topics there exists the possibility of competing points of view. Admittedly, these buttons are more likely to be hit by the various contributors to the article concerned than by readers merely seeking information about the topic. Nevertheless, the archives are available for all the world to read, and those taking the opportunity soon learn that knowledge is not only political, but also provisional, and what is obviously true today will very likely be in dispute tomorrow. In a world that is changing before our eyes at an ever-accelerating rate, this is an important lesson. Zygmunt Bauman's description of how to construct some degree of unity within the pluralism of modern society seems to accord well with the Wikipedia project:

> The most promising kind of unity is one which is *achieved*, and achieved daily anew, by confrontation, debate, negotiation and compromise between values, preferences and chosen ways of life and self-identifications of many and different, but always self-determining members of the *polis*. This is, essentially, the *republican* model of unity ..., a unity put together through negotiation and reconciliation, not the denial, stifling or smothering out of differences.[8]

But there are crucial problems at the heart of this admirably tolerant and democratic approach to knowledge. To start with, is it inevitable that a period of peer review, during which anyone is allowed to make whatever changes they see fit, will inevitably improve a particular article? Must standards rise as time passes? That they must is an article of faith with most wikipedians, but not according

---

7 Besiki Stvilia, Michael B. Twidale, Les Gasser and Linda C. Smith (2005), 'Information Quality Discussions in Wikipedia': <http://www.isrl.uiuc.edu/~stvilia/papers/qualWiki.pdf>.

8 Zygmunt Bauman (2000), *Liquid Modernity*, Cambridge: Polity Press, 178.

to Robert McHenry, ex-editor of the *Encyclopaedia Britannica*, who penned a hostile piece about Wikipedia entitled 'The Faith-based Encyclopedia'.[9] McHenry attacks the belief that articles will steadily improve because better contributions will inevitably prevail in the long run. He describes this optimistic theory as 'some unspecified quasi-Darwinian process' which is 'faith-based'. He thinks, in fact, that the reverse often happens, and that articles can easily start off well and then get 'edited into mediocrity'. However, it should be said that McHenry is short on specific evidence for this claim. He does cite one Wikipedia article – on the eighteenth-century American statesman Alexander Hamilton – which, he says, is 'what might be expected of a high school student and at that it would be a C paper at best. Yet this article has been "edited" over 150 times'. This particular article has in fact been greatly improved of late, no doubt partly because of what McHenry wrote. It has metamorphosed into an essay of considerable length and quality. This, incidentally, is one of the problems about making public criticisms of Wikipedia in detail. Such criticisms quickly become obsolete, since the target will not stand still long enough for the arrows to make their mark.

Even if McHenry is wrong, and articles normally do improve over time, any given article may be faulty when consulted by the viewer, either due to recent vandalism, or because it is at an early stage of development, and hence unreliable. Furthermore, if the topic is obscure enough, it could well be the case that not enough editors have undertaken to revise it, and it remains in its initial unsatisfactory state.

It is clear that the success of the Wikipedia process depends very much on the number and calibre of the users who commit themselves to participate in the editing process. If the Wikipedia community is sufficiently large, active and diverse, then it may claim to represent society at large, in which case the knowledge produced might be taken to be appropriate and acceptable to that society. But can issues involving knowledge really be solved by democracy, that is by counting the heads of those who subscribe to a certain opinion? This perhaps depends on the type of knowledge involved. In his best-seller *The Wisdom of Crowds*, James Surowiecki describes an experiment in which a class of 56 students were asked to estimate the number of beans contained in a jar.[10] It turned out that the average of all the estimates was quite close to the true answer, and also was nearer than all but one of the individual estimates. Another experiment with similar results involved a class trying to guess the temperature of the room they were in. The conclusion in these cases was that if the group consulted is sufficiently large, its combined efforts will probably come up with something better than particular individuals could. In these two experiments, the students concerned were merely being asked to use faculties of judgement which presumably we all possess to a greater or less degree, but in another, even more recent best-seller, Cass Sunstein has subsequently gone so far

---

9   <http://www.tcsdaily.com/printArticle.aspx?ID=111504A>.
10   James Surowiecki (2004), *The Wisdom of Crowds*, London: Little, Brown, 5, 254.

as to erect this result into a general thesis about how to deal with factual questions. He writes:

> Suppose that we want to answer a disputed question of fact. The question might involve past events: When was Calvin Coolidge elected president? How tall is the Eiffel Tower? How many home runs did Babe Ruth hit? ... A great deal of evidence suggests that under certain conditions, a promising way to answer such questions is this: *Ask a large number of people and take the average answer*. As emphasized by James Surowiecki in his engaging and illuminating *The Wisdom of Crowds*, large groups can, in a sense, be wiser than experts.[11]

Many would argue that there are no conditions whatever under which this would be a good method for discovering when Coolidge was elected president, and that one reputable source is worth more than a thousand well-intentioned guesses. The way to discover which year Coolidge was elected president is not to ask a number of people, all of whose opinions are to be considered of equal value, but rather to seek a source of information one thinks one can trust. To be fair to Sunstein, he does devote many pages to exploring instances when the principle is not applicable, for instance, if all those asked are unduly influenced by others, or otherwise collectively biased in some way.

Sunstein's rationale for his knowledge-via-democracy principle is drawn from Friedrich Hayek, an economist who claimed that prices are crucial indexes of value since they aggregate information derived from numerous consumers and suppliers.[12] Taken as a whole, the knowledge held by this multitude is far greater, it is argued, than that held by even the best-informed experts. The price of apples on any particular day is an accurate aggregation of the opinions of millions of apple buyers and apple sellers. Therefore, 'the price is right' – much righter, for instance, than if some government agency had dictated that price.[13] However – and this is the crucial point here – Sunstein includes the kind of cultural information purveyed by Wikipedia as governed by the same laws of supply and demand as are commodities in the market. He writes: 'As we have seen, a price is a result of the judgments and tastes of a large number of consumers. An article on Wikipedia or any other wiki has the same characteristics'.[14] The implication here is that, other things being equal, the collaboration of large numbers of editors on Wikipedia will eventually produce accurate and truthful articles.[15] Such a view of knowledge is,

---

11   Cass R. Sunstein (2006), *Infotopia: How Many Minds Produce Knowledge*, New York: Oxford University Press, 21.

12   Jimmy Wales, founder of Wikipedia, is said to admire Hayek: Sunstein, 156.

13   This example is taken from Surowiecki, 246.

14   Sunstein, 157.

15   This view is spelt out by George Bragues (2007): 'Wikipedia is [best] seen as a test of an economic theory, namely that of competitive markets. It is democratic in that all are equally entitled to input information, but this contribution is then subject to a market

of course, not new. John Dewey, for instance, held that enquiry, whether scientific, technical, sociological, philosophical or cultural, is self-corrective over time *if* openly submitted for testing by a community of enquirers in order to clarify, justify, refine and/or refute proposed truths.[16] Such a pragmatist theory of truth need not preclude the traditional view of truth as correspondence with reality, since when the 'community of enquirers' converges on a particular claim it can properly be said to signal the truth, or at least to approach it as far as we are as a society capable of so doing.

Wikipedia is an amazing achievement, and presents an entirely original way of collecting and distributing information, a method which seems highly suitable to our era. However, Sanger's criticism, that a reputable encyclopaedia run by volunteers can hardly be produced without expert supervision, is valid. The paradox is that although such an encyclopaedia may indeed require visible expertise, it is difficult to foresee a system in which expert supervisors happily coexist with the volunteers, and in any case such coexistence would violate the fundamental principle of equality on which the entire project is based. To solve this paradox, and for Wikipedia to fulfil Dewey's specification and enjoy the public's trust, it might be suggested that the following conditions need to be met:

1. Contributors must come from a wide range of backgrounds, so that as a group they have a real claim to represent society in general.
2. They must have interests across a wide enough spectrum of knowledge to satisfy the public.
3. A critical mass of the contributors must be well-informed (that is, 'expert') about the subjects they write about.

---

test in determining the output, what ends up being presented to the Internet's encyclopedia's audience. For like any market, Wikipedia exhibits buying and selling. When someone contributes to the encyclopedia, they are selling information and when a person accepts what they read there, such that they do not act to change it, they have bought information': 'Wiki-philosophizing in a marketplace of ideas', <http://papers.ssrn.com/sol3/papers.cfm?abstract_id=978177>.

16   'Dewey, John', *Encyclopedia of Philosophy* (1969), vol. 2, London: Macmillan, 383.

PART III
Using Wikipedia

Chapter 14
Browsing Wikipedia

Readers attend to the text. They create images and verbal transformations to represent its meaning. Most impressively, they generate meaning as they read by constructing relations between their knowledge, their memories of experience, and the written sentences, paragraphs and passages.

Merlin C. Wittrock[1]

In the following three chapters I change my orientation towards my subject matter somewhat, in that I take a more pragmatic look at Wikipedia – adopting the point of view of a potential reader or editor. As I mentioned in my introduction, I feel that because Wikipedia belongs to everybody, it is not enough merely to survey it with a dispassionate eye. There is some pressure to get involved. This chapter concerns browsing and digital reading, Chapter 15 is about how to assess Wikipedia articles, and Chapter 16 makes some suggestions about contributing oneself.

In 1968 Roland Barthes wrote a seminal essay entitled 'The Death of the Author'. Here he argued that it is always the reader rather than the author who is responsible for imparting final meaning to any text. Authors, according to Barthes, are mere conduits for passing on some of the various phrases and images, different meanings and fragments of meanings, which they in turn have picked up from other sources, other authors. He wrote:

> A text is not a line of words releasing a single 'theological' meaning (the message of the 'Author-God'), but a multi-dimensional space in which a variety of writings, none of them original, blend and clash. The text is a tissue of quotations drawn from the innumerable centres of culture.[2]

In fact, Barthes saw the author as necessarily having to abdicate control of his text as soon as it was published and had fallen into the hands of the reader. It was, he said, the function of every reader to make their own sense, their own version of any text, out of the diversity of potential meanings available: 'There is one place where this multiplicity is focused and that place is the reader, not, as was hitherto said, the Author' – hence the latter's 'death'. Barthes was writing long before the arrival of the Internet, but one cannot but help see the latter as an extreme and accurate illustration of his thesis. What better description of Wikipedia could there

---

1 Merlin C. Wittrock was professor of education at UCLA.
2 Roland Barthes (1977), 'The Death of the Author', in *Image, Music, Text*, New York: Hill.

be but a 'space in which a variety of writings, none of them original, blend and clash'?

The consumers of cultural products have more power than they perhaps realize, or have conventionally been credited with, and the reader is not, and never has been, a mere passive consumer. On close examination, the actual process of reading turns out to be a highly personal, flexible, and even creative, process. In the course of reading a particular text, one might, for instance, assimilate certain facts, question or doubt what the author is saying, day-dream, go off at a tangent, skip, either deliberately or casually, or re-read a certain passage more than once. Always and inevitably, one finds oneself drawing comparisons and contrasts between the present page and other texts, or between it and remembered conversations and past experiences. As de Certeau says, 'readers are travellers; they move across lands belonging to someone else, like nomads poaching their way across fields they did not write, despoiling the wealth of Egypt to enjoy it themselves'.[3] And of course, such readers always carry with them their own personal histories, their own stories, as it were, that impact not only on what they read, but also how they read.

Since reading is a creative activity, and because every reader is not only different, but different each time they read, no author can control what meanings the reader is likely to derive from the text. A contemporary novelist puts it like this:

> No text can be mastered in a way that abolishes its gaps and indeterminacies, so we can never read closely enough, or often enough, to arrive at any objective statement; the more we rub up against the text, the more we shape it. We seldom study a text in depth without finding that it miraculously reflects our preoccupations; inside every book, we are seeking and finding ourselves.[4]

The argument here is that readers have always worked harder than conventional wisdom gives them credit for. And when surfing the Web with its myriad hyperlinks, another factor comes into play, which is that no two readers are likely ever to follow exactly the same path. Any page of Google, for instance, has been specially created to answer one particular request by one particular reader, and will vanish when that reader has finished with it. In Wikipedia, too, readers cut their own paths through what can appear a jungle of disparate 'information', paths which close again after they have made their passage. Barthes saw the author as having to abdicate control of his text as soon as it was published and had fallen into the hands of the reader. How much more, then, does the author lose control if he cannot even guarantee the path that the reader will choose to follow? The Internet bears out Barthes's prophesy that 'the birth of the reader must be at the

---

3   Michel de Certeau (1984), *The Practice of Everyday Life*, Berkeley, CA: University of California Press, 174.

4   Hilary Mantel, 'In the canon's mouth', *The Guardian*, 5 January 2008: <http://www.guardian.co.uk/books/2008/jan/05/classics.society>.

cost of the death of the Author'. The distinction between writer and reader, usually so clear, and enforced by the medium itself, is blurred in Wikipedia, where one may alternate at will between the two roles.

A prominent aspect of Wikipedia is the number of hyperlinks scattered throughout every article. In total, in the English Wikipedia there are some 60 million of these links, averaging about 25 per article. These links produce a curious effect very different from conventional printed sources, in that they tend to ensure that anyone who browses for long enough gets to create their own text which no one else has read. Take, for example, a Wikipedia experiment involving Tudor history which was performed recently by the author. First, I read about the 'Pilgrimage of Grace', moving from there to 'Catherine of Aragon', and then to that mysterious sixteenth-century illness the 'Sweating Sickness', which is said to have caused her death. I went on to 'John Caius', a doctor who interested himself in that disease, and then to 'Gonville and Caius College, Cambridge', of which he was a co-founder. I finished my browsing session with a short article on the present master of that college, 'Sir Christopher Hum', a former British ambassador to China. In fact, I chose him because I suddenly remembered he was someone I once had the pleasure of meeting.

My journey from the Pilgrimage of Grace to Sir Christopher was nothing very special, and took only five clicks, yet the astonishing fact is that almost certainly, no one else in the history of Wikipedia has ever made the same journey or ever will – unless, of course, some of my readers decide to retrace my footprints. I base this statement on a calculation of the odds against anyone choosing precisely the same hyperlinks as I did. There are over 50 hyperlinks available in the 'Pilgrimage of Grace' article, of which I chose one. 'Catherine of Aragon' has about 60 links, 'Sweating Sickness' about 50, 'John Caius' 26, and 'Gonville and Caius College' about 30. I therefore calculate that the chances of someone else happening to choose my particular path are:

$$1/50 \times 1/60 \times 1/50 \times 1/26 \times 1/30 = 1/117,000,000$$

In other words, the likelihood of that happening randomly is over 100 million to 1 against! The arithmetic is only valid if one assumes that the chances of any particular link being chosen by the reader are equal – possibly a somewhat dubious assumption – but nevertheless, the general principle holds.

But what kind of reader have we in mind? What it means to be literate has constantly shifted throughout history as economic, social and cultural necessities imposed new demands on people. For example, during the eighteenth century there occurred throughout Europe the change from intensive to extensive reading that probably started in England somewhat earlier. Before then, books were scarce, and those who possessed them tended to read them 'intensively', meaning slowly, repeatedly, and often aloud and in groups. By 1800, all kinds of material, from books to periodicals and newspapers, was being read 'extensively' – in other words, more rapidly, and probably more superficially.

In addition, the proportion of the population needing to possess literacy skills has also varied historically. For centuries literacy was the prerogative of an élite, but the Industrial Revolution led to demands for a workforce that could cope with words and figures. The need today is for a digital literacy that would incorporate the entire population. Digital literacy involves the tactile skills and knowledge needed to manipulate digital devices, together with the print literacy of the industrial age. When handling the Internet with its massive amount of information – and this goes also for browsing Wikipedia – what one also needs is the ability to read extremely rapidly, and to skim, and even skip when appropriate. I know that many will see this not so much as a skill, but as typical behaviour by a semi-literate generation with a woefully short attention span. Nevertheless, without knowing when to skim and skip, one can so easily be discouraged and overwhelmed by the sheer mass of material available on the Internet. One also needs, of course, to decide when to stop skimming and start reading carefully. In the next chapter, I discuss how to read a Wikipedia article intensively and critically. The digital reader, in other words, has to be versatile. The point I am trying to make, following on from Barthes, is that on the Internet it is the reader who is in charge. Every reader will have their own priorities, and must decide where to go and how much of what is on the screen to read. The author takes a back seat. In the case of Wikipedia, this is particularly obvious since there are numerous authors, all anonymous, and none of them with the power to stop the others changing or deleting what they have written.

Digital reading is, or should be, a highly creative process. Creativity, in the sense that every reader 'writes' their own text – makes their own connections – is built in to Wikipedia and into the Internet in general. From a biological point of view, it could be argued that such creativity depends on the nature of the links one has succeeded in establishing between the neurons in one's brain. To be human is to make connections. Tim Berners-Lee, inventor of the World Wide Web, might be cited in support of this contention. He writes:

> In an extreme view, the world can be seen as only connections, nothing else. We think of a dictionary as the repository of meaning, but it defines words only in terms of other words. I liked the idea that a piece of information is really defined only by what it's related to, and how it's related. There really is little else to meaning. The structure is everything. There are billions of neurons in our brains, but what are neurons? Just cells. The brain has no knowledge until connections are made between neurons. All that we know, all that we are, comes from the way our neurons are connected.[5]

Wikipedia (like the brain itself) is a rhizomatic structure, a system of nodes and links without a fixed centre or underlying hierarchical pattern. It is the hyperlinks evident on every page that provide the main structure of the site, and allow for the possibility that any of the two and a half million articles may be directly connected

---

5   Tim Berners-Lee (2000), *Weaving the Web*, London: Texere, 14.

up with any other. This makes it quite different from older systems of classification, whether alphabetical, as in the case of works of reference generally, or by topic, as with the Dewey Decimal system used by most libraries. In this latter system, a book has to be classified and put into a particular place even if its subject matter cuts across the existing boundaries. The rhizomatic nature of Wikipedia implies that an article can be, as it were, in several places at the same time. This is ideal for browsing, since the reader is presented with so many possible paths to follow.

Hyperlinks provide the Wikipedia site's main structure, but alternative systems, useful for navigation or browsing, are also available. Authors are encouraged to assign categories to their articles, and at the bottom of most articles can be found a list of the various categories to which that particular article belongs. These categories are themselves included within wider categories, the whole system making up a pyramidal structure – or rather, numerous pyramids, since articles may belong to several categories. For instance, 'Sleeping sickness' belongs to seven different categories, one of which is 'Parasitic diseases', which is in the category 'Infectious diseases', and so to 'Clinical pathology', then 'Medical specialities', 'Medicine', and finally 'Society'.

Categories are useful for navigation or browsing, but at present less useful for those researchers who attempt to mine Wikipedia for information that can easily be interpreted by machine. One such group goes so far as to describe the present category structure as 'haphazard, redundant, incomplete, and inconsistent'.[6] As an example, they cite the category 'Pork', which currently contains, among others, the articles 'Domestic pig', 'Bacon bits', 'Religious restrictions on the consumption of pork', and 'Full breakfast'. Nevertheless, categories provide another way to make connections – to produce new knowledge, as it were. Every category page includes at the bottom a list of the categories to which that category belongs, so that the reader may navigate either up or down a particular pyramid, searching for the category and articles of greatest interest.[7]

Alongside links and categories there are yet other aids to browsing, among which are portals and lists. A portal is a gateway to a particular topic, usually featuring selected articles, relevant links and information about work currently in progress on that topic. On Wikipedia's Main (Home) page there are a number of links to portals on broad topics such as Art, Biography and Mathematics, and each of these leads to other portals on narrower topics. Some Wikipedia articles take the form of lists in which each item links to its own article. Lists, therefore, are

---

6   Olena Medelyan, Catherine Legg, David Milne and Ian H. Witten (2008), 'Mining Meaning from Wikipedia': <http://arxiv.org/ftp/arxiv/papers/0809/0809.4530.pdf>.

7   Categories have also been used to calculate the variety of content on Wikipedia. By tallying articles in the broadest categories, Robert Rohde estimated its composition (in October 2007) as follows: 28% science, 10.5% culture, 16% geography, 6.3% history, 0.8% religion, 5.5% philosophy, 1.8% mathematics, 14.3% nature, 6% fiction and 9.6% biography: Phoebe Ayers, Charles Matthews and Ben Yates (2008), *How Wikipedia Works*, San Francisco, CA: No Starch Press, 92–3.

miniature indexes for particular topics.[8] They mainly differ from categories in that they have to be created or edited by hand like any other article, whereas categories are populated automatically whenever an editor adds a specialized tag to an article. Readers may find especially useful the lists of significant events during a particular date, year, decade or century. For instance, a search for '24 August' will produce a list of events throughout history that took place on that date, from the eruption of Vesuvius in 79 BC to the closing ceremony of the Tokyo Olympics in 2008. There will also be lists of those with birthdays on that date, and of those who died then – another painless way to browse.

The next chapter has a different focus. Instead of navigating purposefully (or flitting aimlessly) around Wikipedia's treasure house of knowledge, let us assume one has alighted somewhere one wishes to remain for a time. But how much reliance should one place on this particular article, and how far does it approximate to the standards of the best of Wikipedia?

---

8   Both lists and portals may be accessed via the 'Contents' button in the left-hand sidebar of the Main page.

Chapter 15
Assessing Wikipedia

At the time of writing the English Wikipedia contained about two million *bona fide* articles, ranging widely in quality from the very short, incomplete articles classified as 'stubs' to the 2372 Featured Articles.[1] The first matter, therefore, for anyone consulting the encyclopaedia is to assess the particular articles they are interested in as to their quality, in order to establish how much faith to put in them. It is clearly possible, if one reads carefully and critically, to make a personal judgement on the merits of a particular Wikipedia article, even on a topic about which one is comparatively ignorant. What follows here is a suggested assessment scheme for grading, and awarding points to various features of an article. This scheme is geared towards articles on historical topics, though there is no reason why it could not be modified for other subjects. The scheme is largely based on the list of attributes said to be required to raise articles to Featured Article status.[2] Obviously, anyone can make their own assessments in a less schematic fashion, but what follows at least has the merit of reminding the reader of the general requirements for a competent and useful article, and might also help when it comes to comparing one article with another.

To make an assessment, first read the article right through to the end, including notes and references. Then take the following headings in turn and grade the article on a scale of 0–5 for each heading. This gives a possible maximum of 50. However, if one or more of the headings seems inappropriate for a particular article, or you find it impossible to judge, then leave it or them out completely. For example, if you felt that *images* would have been quite impossible or irrelevant for a particular article to include, then leave out this assessment and adjust the maximum accordingly. So if this article had scored 20 out of 45, multiplying this fraction by 50 adjusts its score to 22 out of 50. This brings it into line with other articles you might assess. Try to use the full range of points, and do not hesitate to award a 5 when appropriate, or a 0 in dire cases.

1. Length and Structure

Is the article the right kind of length, considering the importance or otherwise of the topic? This is difficult to judge, of course, if one comes fresh to the subject.

---

1 The figure of two million excludes 'redirects' and disambiguation pages. Approximately 70 per cent of Wikipedia articles are stubs. For more on Featured Articles, see Chapter 10.

2 <http://en.wikipedia.org/wiki/Wikipedia:Featured_articles>.

But you may well feel it should have had lengthier treatment, or conversely that it is too long and contains unnecessary or trivial details. On the whole, for example, Wikipedia tends to carry much more detailed treatment of American history than any other.

Is the lead section clear and interesting? Is it a hook to make you want to read the rest, yet also to summarize the topic for those not seeking more detail. What about the other sections of the article? Are they in what seems a logical order, or do they jump around? For many historical items, including biographies, a chronological order might be appropriate, but there may be compelling reasons for varying this. For example, a person may have been involved in several activities which need to be kept separate, even if this involves violating the chronology. Note also whether there is reasonable continuity between one section and the next. Lack of logical order and continuity are typical faults of a work composed by numerous authors, when anyone can add extra facts into the middle of someone else's paragraph.

2. Images

Images, and being able to enlarge them by clicking on them, should be among the advantages of an online encyclopaedia. Are there suitable and interesting illustrations here (even video or a soundtrack)? Do the images contribute to the understanding or interest of the article? Are they informatively captioned, and do the captions explain where they came from? (Note that clicking on an image will give details about it, including its provenance.) One has to make allowances for the fact that often the best images are not available to Wikipedia because of copyright.[3]

3. Quotes

Quotations, either as primary source material (that is, contemporary with the person or event being discussed) or secondary (by later commentators or historians), tend to make an article more authentic and readable. Are there any? They might be in separate boxes or just inserted in the text. On the other hand, perhaps there are too many, or they are unnecessarily long. Again, as with images, is it clear who said them and where they came from?

---

3   <http://en.wikipedia.org/wiki/Wikipedia:10_things_you_may_not_know_about_images_on_Wikipedia>.

4. Grammar and Style

Wikipedia, with its thousands of potential editors, is good at winnowing out bad grammar, but even so, mistakes frequently occur. Typical are sentences without main verbs, participles that do not agree with the subject of the sentence (for example, 'Hating to make mistakes, these articles are carefully written.'), and too few or too many commas. There might even be spelling errors in spite of all the spell checks.

Style is perhaps harder to assess, but a good indicator of the quality of the article. The important thing is clarity. There should be no sentences or phrases which you have to read several times to understand, and none whose meaning is ambiguous. An effective style is succinct, therefore mark down unnecessary long-windedness or over-elaboration. On the other hand, with reference to authorship by many hands as mentioned above, the most likely fault will probably be stylistic mediocrity and dullness. Typical of a pedestrian style are short sentences, each much like the one before. Look for some variety in sentence length, and for the sophisticated use of subordinate clauses. Also look for elegance, even wit, in the language of the article, and reward it.

5. Generalization and Neutrality

A good article will not be afraid to generalize or draw conclusions about the significance of its theme, or of sub-topics within the theme. It might also, for instance, make general comparisons with items or people outside the scope of the article, or link up two items of information which seemed before to be quite separate. Take notice of any remark which casts unexpected light on the whole subject. Definite opinions are more interesting than bland, compromise statements. Most generalizations will probably be found in the lead section or the final section, though not necessarily.

Interesting generalizations, however, often run the risk of bias. Wikipedia stresses that articles should always have a neutral point of view (NPOV), but of course this is one of the most difficult things to achieve, even when dealing with the distant past. It is also quite hard to assess, especially if one is new to the subject concerned. Look out for statements that seem to reflect a nationalist or religious (or anti-religious) or feminist (or anti-feminist) point of view. The article's discussion page may give a clue about possible bias.

6. Discrepancies, Repetition and Gaps

Discrepancies (for example, different dates given for the same event) and repetition of points made are typical faults of an article which has been constructed by several hands at different times. A gap is when you are left feeling short-changed, either because something you vaguely knew about and was expecting in the article has not come up, or because a potentially interesting or significant issue is mentioned, but not followed up. You are suddenly told, for instance, that towards the end of their life an important author or politician started taking drugs, converted to another faith or attempted suicide, but then no more is said. But why did they, and how did it affect their work?

7. Links and Internet References

One great advantage that a vast site like Wikipedia obviously has is being able to refer the reader to other parts of itself. These links are in blue, and they are usually numerous, as they can easily be made by (ro)bots. The English Wikipedia contains altogether 60 million such links, on average about 25 per article. Make sure the article has links for any names or facts which might need explaining. Links to stubs are likely to be less useful, and links in red, which are to articles yet to be written, not at all useful, except that they alert those looking to contribute that an article is needed here. Check also any footnote numbers inserted in the text which are supposed either to tell you where a particular fact came from or to provide some further explanation. Finally, check out some of the Internet references listed at the end of the article to see whether these websites are still active and are helpful.

8. References to Print Sources

Many editors of Wikipedia are likely to be more at home with the Internet than with printed material. Nevertheless, because an encyclopaedia ought to be a portal to the wider intellectual world, it is important that if possible there should also be references to recently published books or articles. In the first place, these tend to be more fixed and permanent than Internet sources, and secondly, printed sources, as opposed to websites, have usually gone through some kind of peer-review process. (Some print references may be in a 'Further reading' section.) Book references should preferably give publisher, place and date of publication, and/or ISBN number, while articles should have the name of the journal and the date and volume number.

9. Stability

Here, the suggestion is that you click on the 'History' and 'Discussion' links at the top of the article. 'History' lists recent changes, and 'Discussion' shows what parts of the article involved disagreements by different editors. Awarding the points here is a matter of fine judgement. On the one hand, perhaps the more discussion there has been, and the more editors involved in that discussion, the better for the article. But on the other hand, 'edit wars', especially if they seem to be still going on at the time of viewing, imply instability, and perhaps partiality. Edit wars might be indicated by protracted or acrimonious arguments in the article's discussion pages, or evidence in the history pages of successive versions of the article by two editors, each of whom is merely reverting the other's versions.[4]

10. Overall

You now have up to five extra points to distribute as you see fit. Consider how far you have found the article interesting, and useful for your own purposes. There may be warnings in templates at the top of the article that it does not yet conform to Wikipedia standards. They might say, for instance, that this article may not have a neutral point of view, or that it lacks references or suitable links. If so, take this into consideration. Sum up the article's good and bad points.

The article on the 'Great Fire of London' is among Wikipedia's very best. Not only is it a Featured Article, but also it is one of those chosen for the current and future release on DVD of selected articles. A brief version of this article was first created in 2002, not long after the start of Wikipedia, and since then it has been gradually improved and lengthened by dozens of editors. Consequently, its development reflects the progress of the encyclopaedia itself. There follows here three different versions of this article: from December 2002, December 2005 and December 2008. Some of the images have been removed for copyright reasons. Readers are invited to try out the above assessment scheme on these three versions for themselves before comparing their judgements with my comments and marks given at the end of the chapter.[5] Incidentally, it would be wrong to dismiss the first two versions of this article merely because they were composed some time ago; probably the majority of Wikipedia articles today resemble them more than they resemble Version 3.

---

4   In such cases, the edit summaries may merely record 'revert', 'rv' or 'rvv'.

5   It will, of course, not be possible for the reader to assess points 7 and 9 unless they access the article and its earlier versions online. If doing so, one should bear in mind that the article may well have changed since it was reproduced in this book.

[Version I]

Great Fire of London

Version as of 12 December 2002

The **Great Fire of London** commonly refers to the major fire which swept through the <u>City of London</u>[6] on <u>September 2</u>, <u>1666</u>, and resulted more or less in its destruction. (Prior to this conflagration, the fire which destroyed a large part of the city in <u>1212</u> was known by the same name.)

The fire started in a baker's shop in Pudding Lane. Most buildings in London at this time were constructed of highly combustible materials (wood, straw, etc.), and sparks which emanated from the baker's shop fell onto an adjacent building. Fanned by a strong wind, once the fire had taken hold it swiftly spread.

Some 13,200 houses and 87 churches were destroyed, among them <u>St. Paul's Cathedral</u>. Oddly enough only 9 people died in the fire.

The fire had the beneficial effect of killing many of the rats which were responsible for the spread of the <u>Great Plague</u>.
The fire had a marked and varied impact on English society. See <u>Charles II of England</u>, <u>Christopher Wren</u>, <u>Samuel Pepys</u>, <u>Ursula Southeil</u>.

The site where the fire started is today marked by a large monument. It is located near Pudding Lane near the northern end of <u>London Bridge</u>. The <u>Monument tube station</u> is named after the monument.

---

6   Words and phrases underlined refer to hyperlinks in the original.

[Version II]

Great Fire of London

Version as of 18 December 2005

The **Great Fire of London** was a major conflagration that swept through the City of London from September 2 to September 5, 1666, and resulted more or less in the destruction of the city. Before this fire, two early fires of London, in 1133/1135 and 1212, both of which destroyed a large part of the city, were known by the same name. Later, the Luftwaffe's fire-raid on the City on 29th December 1940 became known as The Second Great Fire of London.

The fire of 1666 was one of the biggest calamities in the history of London. It destroyed 13,200 houses, 87 parish churches, 6 chapels, 44 Company Halls, the Royal Exchange, the Custom House, St Paul's Cathedral, the Guildhall, the Bridewell Palace and other City prisons, the Session House, four bridges across the rivers Thames and Fleet, and three city gates, and made homeless 100,000 people, one sixth of the city's inhabitants at that time. The death toll from the fire is unknown, and is traditionally thought to have been quite small, but a recent book theorizes that thousands may have died in the flames or smoke inhalation

Contents

[hide]

Events

The fire broke out on Sunday morning, September 2, 1666. It started in Pudding Lane at the house of Thomas Farrinor, a baker to King Charles II. It is likely that the fire started because Farrinor forgot to extinguish his oven before retiring for the evening and that some time shortly after midnight, smouldering embers from the oven set alight some nearby

firewood. Farrinor managed to escape the burning building, along with his family, by climbing out through an upstairs window. The baker's housemaid failed to escape and became the fire's first victim.

Within an hour of the fire starting, the <u>Lord Mayor of London</u>, Sir <u>Thomas Bloodworth</u>, was awakened with the news. He was unimpressed however, declaring that "a woman might piss it out."

Most buildings in <u>London</u> at this time were constructed of highly <u>combustible</u> materials like <u>wood</u> and <u>straw</u>, and sparks emanating from the baker's shop fell onto an adjacent building. Fanned by a strong wind from the east, once the fire had taken hold it swiftly spread. The spread of the fire was helped by the fact that buildings were built very close together with only a narrow alley between them.

According to a contemporary source:

Then, then the city did shake indeed, and the inhabitants did tremble, and flew away in great amazement from their houses, lest the flames should devour them: *rattle, rattle, rattle*, was the noise which the fire struck upon the ear round about, as if there had been a thousand iron chariots beating upon the stones. You might see the houses *tumble, tumble, tumble*, from one end of the street to the other, with a great crash, leaving the foundations open to the view of the heavens.

The progress of the fire might have been stopped, but for the conduct of the Lord Mayor, who refused to give orders for pulling down some houses, *without the consent of the owners*. Buckets were of no use, from the confined state of the streets.

Destruction

The fire consumed a staggering 13,200 <u>houses</u> and 87 <u>churches</u>, among them the beloved <u>St. Paul's Cathedral</u>. While only 9–16 people were reported as having died in the fire, author Neil Hanson (*The Dreadful Judgement*) believes the true death toll numbered in the hundreds or the thousands. Hanson believes most of the fatalities were poor people whose bodies were <u>cremated</u> by the intense heat of the fire, and thus their remains were never found. These claims are controversial, however.

The destructive fury of this conflagration is thought never to have been exceeded in the world, by an accidental fire. *Within* the walls, it consumed almost five-sixths of the whole city; and *without* the walls it cleared a space nearly as extensive as the one-sixth part left unburnt within. Scarcely a single building that came within the range of the flames was left standing. Public buildings, churches, and dwelling-houses, were alike involved in one common fate.

In the summary account of this vast devastation, given in one of the inscriptions on the <u>Monument</u>, and which was drawn up from the reports of the surveyors appointed after the fire, it is stated, that:

The ruins of the city were 436 acres (1.8 km²), viz. 333 acres (1.3 km²) within the walls, and 63 acres (255,000 m²) in the liberties of the city; that, of the six-and-twenty wards, it utterly destroyed fifteen, and left eight others shattered and half burnt; and that it consumed 400 streets, 13,200 dwelling-houses, 89 churches [besides chapels]; 4 of the city gates, Guildhall, many public structures, hospitals, schools, libraries, and a vast number of stately edifices.

The immense property destroyed in this dreadful time cannot be estimated at less than ten millions sterling. Amid all the confusion and multiplied dangers that arose from the fire, it does not appear that more than *six* persons lost their lives. As destructive as the immediate consequences of the fire were, its *remote effects* have benefitted subsequent generations: the complete destruction of the <u>Great Plague</u>, which, only the year before, swept off 68,590 people. Most of London's public structures, the regularity and beauty of the streets, and the great salubrity and extreme cleanliness of a large part of the city of London are due to this.

The following remarks regarding the fire are recorded:

Mr. Malcom, in *"Anecdotes of the Manners and Customs of London in the Eighteenth Century,"* (vol. ii. p. 378), says:

Heaven be praised old London *was burnt*. Good reader, turn to the ancient prints, in order to see what it has been; observe those hovels convulsed; imagine the chambers within them, and wonder why the plague, the leprosy, and the sweating-sickness raged. Turn then to the prints illustrative of our present dwellings, and be happy. The misery of 1665 must have operated on the minds of the legislature and the citizens, when they rebuilt and inhabited their houses. The former enacted many salutary clauses for the preservation of health, and would have done more, had not the public rejected that which was for their benefit; those who preferred high habitations and narrow dark streets had them. It is only to be lamented that we are compelled to suffer for their folly. These errors are now frequently partially removed by the exertion of the Corporation of London; but a complete reformation is impossible. It is to the improved dwellings composed of brick, the wainscot or papered walls, the high ceilings, the boarded floors, and large windows, and cleanliness, that we are indebted for the general preservation of health since 1666. From that auspicious year the very existence of the natives of London improved; their bodies moved in a large space of pure air; and, finding every thing clean and new around them, they determined to keep them so. Previously-unknown luxuries and improvements in furniture were suggested; and a man of moderate fortune saw his house vie with, nay, superior to, the old palaces of his governors. When he paced his streets, he felt the genial western breeze pass him, rich with the perfumes of the country, instead of the stench described by Erasmus; and looking upward, he beheld the beautiful blue of the air, variegated with fleecy clouds, in place of projecting black beams and plaster, obscured by vapour and smoke. The streets of London must have been dangerously dark during the winter nights before it was burnt; lanterns with candles were very sparingly scattered, nor was light much better distributed even in the new streets previously to the 18th century. Globular lamps were introduced by Michael Cole, who obtained a patent in July, 1708.

We conclude the illustrations of this day with a singular opinion of the author just quoted. Speaking of the burning of London, he says, "This subject may be allowed to be familiar to me, and I have perhaps had more than common means of judging; and I now declare it to be my full and decided opinion, that London was *burnt by government, to annihilate the plague,* which was grafted in every crevice of the hateful old houses composing it."

Aftermath and consequences

The fire had a marked and varied impact on English society: see Charles II of England, Christopher Wren, Samuel Pepys, Ursula Southeil.

There had been much prophecy of a disaster befalling London in 1666, since in Hindu-Arabic numerals it included the number of the Beast and in Roman numerals it was a declining-order list (MDCLXVI). Walter Gostelo wrote in 1658 "If fire make not ashes of the city, and thy bones also, conclude me a liar forever!…the decree is gone out, repent, or burn, as Sodom and Gomorrah!" It seemed to many, coming after a civil war and a plague, Revelation's third horseman.

After the fire, a rumour began to circulate that the fire was part of a Catholic plot. A simple-minded French watchmaker named Robert "Lucky" Hubert, confessed (possibly under torture) to being an agent of the Pope and starting the fire in Westminster. He later changed his story to say that he had started it at the bakery in Pudding Lane. He was convicted, despite overwhelming evidence that he could not have started the fire, and was hanged at Tyburn on September 28.

Christopher Wren was put in charge of re-building the city after the fire. His original plans involved rebuilding the city in brick and stone to a grid plan with continental piazzas and avenues. But because many buildings had survived to basement level, legal disputes over ownership of land ended the grid plan idea. From 1667, Parliament raised funds for re-building London by taxing coal, and the city was eventually rebuilt to its existing street plan, but built instead out of brick and stone and with improved sanitation and access. This is the main reason why today's London is a modern city, yet with a medieval design to its streets. Christopher Wren also re-built St Paul's Cathedral 11 years after the fire.

Lessons in fire safety were learned, and when the current Globe Theatre was opened in 1997, it was the first building in London with a thatched roof since The Fire.

Cultural impact

The Monument to the Great Fire of London, known simply as The Monument, was designed by Wren and Robert Hooke. It is close to the site where the fire started[2], near the northern end of London Bridge. The corner of Giltspur Street and Cock Lane where the fire ended was known as Pye Corner, and is marked by a small gilded statue known as the Fat Boy or the Golden Boy of Pye Corner, supposedly a reference to the theory expounded by a non-conformist preacher who said:

the calamity could not have been the sin of blasphemy for in that case it would have began at Billingsgate, nor lewdness for then Drury Lane would have been first on fire nor lying for then the flames would have reached the City from Westminster Hall. No, it was occasioned by the sin of gluttony for it began at Pudding Lane and ended at Pye Corner.

John Dryden commemorated the fire in his poem of 1667, Annus Mirabilis. Dryden worked, in his poem, to counteract paranoia about the causes of the fire and proposed that the fire was part of a year of miracles, rather than a year of disasters. The fact that Charles was already planning to rebuild a glorious city atop the ashes and the fact that there were so few reported fatalities were, to Dryden, signs of divine favor, rather than curse.

This is an extract from the Diary of Samuel Pepys:

By and by Jane comes and tells me that she hears that above 300 houses have been burned down tonight by the fire we saw, and that it is now burning down all Fish Street, by London Bridge. So I made myself ready presently, and walked to the Tower; and there got up upon one of the high places, and there I did see the houses at the end of the bridge all on fire, and an infinite great fire on this and the other side of the bridge!

Further reading

- Hanson, Neil (2002). *The Dreadful Judgement: The True Story of the Great Fire of London*. ISBN 0552147893. Released in the U.S. as *The Great Fire of London: In That Apocalyptic Year, 1666*. ISBN 0471218227.
- Robinson, Bruce. Red Sky at Night. BBC's History website. —an account of the Great Fire.
- Robert Latham and William Matthews (editors). *The Diary of Samuel Pepys, a new and complete transcription*, published by Bell & Hyman, London, 1970–1983.

Footnotes

1. Farrinor's name is variously spelled Farriner, Fraynor, Farryner, or Farynor.
2. The Monument stands 61 metres (202 feet) tall, the height marking the monument's distance to the site of the king's baker Thomas Farynor's shop in Pudding Lane, where the fire began.
3. In 1986, the Baker's Company issued a public apology for the fire.
4. Categories: 1666 | City of London | Disasters in the United Kingdom | Fires | History of London

Categories: 1666 | City of London | Disasters in the United Kingdom | Fires | History of London

[Version III]

Great Fire of London

Version as of 14 December 2008

The **Great Fire of London**, a major conflagration that swept through the central parts of London from Sunday, 2 September to Wednesday, 5 September 1666, was one of the major events in the history of England.[1] The fire gutted the medieval City of London inside the old Roman City Wall. It threatened, but did not reach, the aristocratic district of Westminster (the modern West End), Charles II's Palace of Whitehall, and most of the suburban slums.[2] It consumed 13,200 houses, 87 parish churches, St. Paul's Cathedral, and most of the buildings of the City authorities. It is estimated that it destroyed the homes of 70,000 of the City's ca. 80,000 inhabitants.[3] The death toll from the fire is unknown and is traditionally thought to have been small, as only a few verified deaths were recorded. This reasoning has recently been challenged on the grounds that the deaths of poor and middle-class people were not recorded anywhere, and that the heat of the fire may have cremated many victims, leaving no recognisable remains.

The fire started at the bakery of Thomas Farriner (or Farynor) on Pudding Lane shortly after midnight on Sunday, 2 September, and it spread rapidly west across the City of London. The use of the major firefighting technique of the time, the creation of firebreaks by means of demolition, was critically delayed due to the indecisiveness of the Lord Mayor of London, Sir Thomas Bloodworth. By the time large-scale demolitions were ordered on Sunday night, the wind had already fanned the bakery fire into a firestorm which defeated such measures. The fire pushed north on Monday into the heart of the City. Order in the streets broke down as rumours arose of suspicious foreigners setting fires. The fears of the homeless focused on the French and Dutch, England's enemies in the ongoing Second Anglo-Dutch War; these substantial immigrant groups became victims of lynchings and street violence. On Tuesday, the fire spread over most of the City, destroying St. Paul's Cathedral and leaping the River Fleet to threaten Charles II's court at Whitehall, while coordinated firefighting efforts were simultaneously mobilising. The battle to quench the fire is considered to have been won by two factors: the strong east winds died down, and the Tower of London garrison used gunpowder to create effective firebreaks to halt further spread eastward.

The social and economic problems created by the disaster were overwhelming; significant scapegoating occurred for some time after the fire. Evacuation from London and resettlement elsewhere were strongly encouraged by Charles II, who feared a London rebellion amongst the dispossessed refugees. Despite numerous radical proposals, London was reconstructed on essentially the same street plan used before the fire.[4]

Contents

[hide]

London in the 1660s

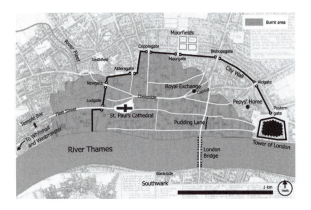

Central London in 1666, with the burnt area shown in pink

By the 1660s, London was by far the largest city in Britain, estimated at half a million inhabitants, which was more than the next fifty towns in England combined.[5] Comparing London to the Baroque magnificence of Paris, John Evelyn called it a "wooden, northern, and inartificial congestion of Houses," and expressed alarm about the fire hazard posed by the wood and the congestion.[6] By "inartificial", Evelyn meant unplanned and makeshift, the result of organic growth and unregulated urban sprawl. A Roman settlement for four centuries, London had become progressively more overcrowded inside its defensive City wall. It had also pushed outwards beyond the wall into squalid extramural slums such as Shoreditch, Holborn, and Southwark and had reached to physically incorporate the independent city of Westminster.[7]

By the late 17th century, the City proper—the area bounded by the City wall and the river Thames—was only one part of London, covering 700 acres (2.8 km²),[8] and home to about 80,000 people, or one sixth of London's inhabitants. The City was surrounded by a ring of inner suburbs, where most Londoners lived. The City was then as now the commercial heart of the capital, the largest market and busiest port in England, dominated by the trading and manufacturing classes.[9] The aristocracy shunned the City and lived either in the countryside beyond the slum suburbs, or further west in the exclusive Westminster district (the modern West End), the site of Charles II's court at Whitehall. Wealthy people preferred to live at a convenient distance from the always traffic-jammed, polluted, unhealthy City, especially after it was hit by a devastating outbreak of bubonic plague in the "Plague Year" of 1665. The relationship between the City and the Crown was very tense. During the Civil War, 1642–1651, the City of London had been a stronghold of Republicanism, and the wealthy and economically dynamic capital still had the potential to be a threat to Charles II, as had been demonstrated by several Republican uprisings in London in the early 1660s. The City magistrates were of the generation that had fought in the Civil War, and could remember how Charles I's grab for absolute power had led to that national trauma.[10] They were determined to thwart any similar tendencies from his son, and when the Great Fire threatened the City, they refused the offers Charles made of soldiers and other resources. Even in such an emergency, the idea of having the unpopular Royal troops ordered into the City was political dynamite. By the time Charles took over command from the ineffectual Lord Mayor, the fire was already out of control.

Fire hazards in the City

The City was essentially medieval in its street plan, an overcrowded warren of narrow, winding, cobbled alleys. It had experienced several major fires before 1666, the most recent in 1632. Building with wood and roofing with thatch had been prohibited for centuries, but these cheap materials continued to be used.[11] The only major stone-built area was the wealthy centre of the City, where the mansions of the merchants and brokers stood on spacious lots, surrounded by an inner ring of overcrowded poorer parishes whose every inch of building space was used to accommodate the rapidly growing population. These parishes contained workplaces, many of which were fire hazards—foundries, smithies, glaziers—which were theoretically illegal in the City, but tolerated in practice. The human habitations mixed in with these sources of heat, sparks, and pollution were crowded to bursting-point and designed with uniquely risky features. "Jetties" (projecting upper floors) were characteristic of the typical six- or seven-storey timbered London tenement houses. These buildings had a narrow footprint at ground level, but would maximise their use of a given land plot by "encroaching", as a contemporary observer put it, on the street with the gradually increasing size of their upper storeys. The fire hazard posed when the top jetties all but met across the narrow alleys was well perceived—"as it does facilitate a conflagration, so does it also hinder the remedy", wrote one observer[12]—but "the covetousness of the citizens and connivancy [that is, the corruption] of Magistrates" worked in favour of jetties. In 1661, Charles II issued a proclamation forbidding overhanging windows and jetties, but this was largely ignored by the local government. Charles' next, sharper, message in 1665 warned of the risk of fire from the narrowness of the streets and authorised both imprisonment of recalcitrant builders and demolition of dangerous buildings. It too had little impact.

The riverfront was a key area for the development of the Great Fire. The Thames offered water for the firefighting effort and hope of escape by boat, but, with stores and cellars of combustibles, the poorer districts along the riverfront presented the highest conflagration risk of any. All along the wharves, the rickety wooden tenements and tar paper shacks of the poor were shoehorned amongst "old paper buildings and the most combustible matter of Tarr, Pitch, Hemp, Rosen, and Flax which was all layd up thereabouts."[13] London was also full of black powder, especially along the riverfront. Much of it was left in the homes of private citizens from the days of the English Civil War, as the former members of Cromwell's New Model Army still retained their muskets and the powder with which to load them. Five to six hundred tons of powder were stored in the Tower of London at the north end of London Bridge. The ship chandlers along the wharves also held large stocks, stored in wooden barrels.

London Bridge, the only physical connection between the City and the south side of the river Thames, was itself covered with houses and had been noted as a deathtrap in the fire of 1632. By Sunday's dawn these houses were burning, and <u>Samuel Pepys</u>, observing the conflagration from the Tower of London, recorded great concern for friends living on the bridge.[14] There were fears that the flames would cross London Bridge to threaten the <u>borough</u> of <u>Southwark</u> on the south bank, but this danger was averted by an open space between buildings on the bridge which acted as a <u>firebreak</u>.[15]

The 18-foot (5.5 m) high Roman wall enclosing the City put the fleeing homeless at risk of being shut into the inferno. Once the riverfront was on fire and the escape route by boat cut off, the only way out was through the eight gates in the wall. During the first couple of days, few people had any notion of fleeing the burning City altogether: they would remove what they could carry of belongings to the nearest "safe house", in many cases the parish church, or the precincts of St. Paul's Cathedral, only to have to move again hours later. Some moved their belongings and themselves "four and five times" in a single day.[16] The perception of a need to get beyond the walls only took root late on the Monday, and then there were near-panic scenes at the narrow gates as distraught refugees tried to get out with their bundles, carts, horses, and wagons.

The crucial factor in frustrating firefighting efforts was the narrowness of the streets. Even under normal circumstances, the mix of carts, wagons, and pedestrians in the undersized alleys was subject to frequent traffic jams and gridlock. During the fire, the passages were additionally blocked by refugees camping in them amongst their rescued belongings, or escaping outwards, away from the centre of destruction, as demolition teams and fire engine crews struggled in vain to move in towards it.

Seventeenth-century firefighting

Advertisement for a comparatively small and manoeuvrable seventeenth-century <u>fire engine</u> on wheels: "These Engins, (which are the best) to quinch great Fire; are made by John Keeling in <u>Black Fryers</u> (after many years' Experience)."

Fires were common in the crowded wood-built city with its open fireplaces, candles, ovens, and stores of combustibles. There was no police or fire department to call, but London's local <u>militia</u>, known as the Trained Bands or <u>Train-band</u>, was at least in principle available for general emergencies, and watching for fire was one of the jobs of <u>the watch</u>, a thousand watchmen or "bellmen" who patrolled the streets at night.[17] Self-reliant community procedures for dealing with fires were in place, and were usually effective. Public-spirited citizens would be alerted to a dangerous house fire by muffled peals on the church bells, and would congregate hastily to use the available techniques, which relied on demolition and water. By law, the tower of every parish church had to hold equipment for these efforts: long ladders, leather buckets, axes, and "firehooks" for pulling down buildings (see illustration right).[18] Sometimes taller buildings were levelled to the ground quickly and effectively by means of controlled gunpowder explosions. This drastic method for creating firebreaks was increasingly used towards the end of the Great Fire, and modern historians believe it was what finally won the struggle.[19]

Demolishing the houses downwind of a dangerous fire by means of firehooks or explosives was often an effective way of containing the destruction. This time, however, demolition was fatally delayed for hours by the Lord Mayor's lack of leadership and failure to give the necessary orders.[20] By the time orders came directly from the King to "spare no houses", the fire had devoured many more houses, and the demolition workers could no longer get through the crowded streets.

The use of water to extinguish the fire was also frustrated. In principle, water was available from a system of elm pipes which supplied 30,000 houses via a high water tower at Cornhill, filled from the river at high tide, and also via a reservoir of Hertfordshire spring water in Islington.[21] It was often possible to open a pipe near a burning building and connect it to a hose to play on a fire, or fill buckets. Additionally, Pudding Lane was close to the river itself. Theoretically, all the lanes up to the bakery and adjoining buildings from the river should have been manned with double rows of firefighters passing full buckets up to the fire and empty buckets back down to the river. This did not happen, or at least was no longer happening by the time Pepys viewed the fire from the river at mid-morning on the Sunday. Pepys comments in his diary on how nobody was trying to put it out, but instead fleeing from it in fear, hurrying "to remove their goods, and leave all to the fire." The flames crept towards the riverfront with little interference from the overwhelmed community and soon torched the flammable warehouses along the wharves. The resulting conflagration not only cut off the firefighters from the immediate water supply of the river, but also set alight the water wheels under London Bridge which pumped water to the Cornhill water tower; the direct access to the river and the supply of piped water failed together.

London possessed advanced fire-fighting technology in the form of fire engines, which had been used in earlier large-scale fires. However, unlike the useful firehooks, these large pumps had rarely proved flexible or functional enough to make much difference. Only some of them had wheels, others were mounted on wheelless sleds.[22] They had to be brought a long way, tended to arrive too late, and, with spouts but no delivery hoses, had limited reach.[23] On this occasion an unknown number of fire engines were either wheeled or dragged through the streets, some from across the City. The piped water that they were designed for had already failed, but parts of the river bank could still be reached. As gangs of men tried desperately to manoeuvre the engines right up to the river to fill their reservoirs, several of the engines toppled into the Thames. The heat from the flames was by then too great for the remaining engines to get within a useful distance; they could not even get into Pudding Lane.

Development of the fire

The personal experiences of many Londoners during the fire are glimpsed in letters and memoirs. The two most famous diarists of the Restoration, Samuel Pepys (1633–1703) and John Evelyn (1620–1706), recorded the events and their own reactions day by day, and made great efforts to keep themselves informed of what was happening all over the City and beyond. For example, they both travelled out to the Moorfields park area north of the City on the Wednesday—the fourth day—to view the mighty encampment of distressed refugees there, which shocked them. Their diaries are the most important sources for all modern retellings of the disaster. The most recent books on the fire, by Tinniswood (2003) and Hanson (2001), also rely on the brief memoirs of William Taswell (1651–82), who was a fourteen-year-old schoolboy at Westminster School in 1666.

After two rainy summers in 1664 and 1665, London had lain under an exceptional drought since November 1665, and the wooden buildings were tinder-dry after the long hot summer of 1666. The bakery fire in Pudding Lane spread at first due west, fanned by an eastern gale.

Sunday

Approximate damage by the evening of Sunday, 2 September.[24]

A fire broke out at Thomas Farriner's bakery in Pudding Lane a little after midnight on Sunday, 2 September. The family was trapped upstairs, but managed to climb from an upstairs window to the house next door, except for a maidservant who was too frightened to try, and became the first victim.[25] The neighbours tried to help douse the fire; after an hour the parish constables arrived and judged that the adjoining houses had better be demolished to prevent further spread. The householders protested, and the Lord Mayor Sir Thomas Bloodworth, who alone had the authority to override their wishes, was summoned. When Bloodworth arrived, the flames were consuming the adjoining houses and creeping towards the paper warehouses and flammable stores on the riverfront. The more experienced firefighters were clamoring for demolition, but Bloodworth refused, on the argument that most premises were rented and the owners could not be found. Bloodworth is generally thought to have been appointed to the office of Lord Mayor as a yes man, rather than for any of the needful capabilities for the job; he panicked when faced with a sudden emergency.[26] Pressed, he made the often-quoted remark "Pish! A woman could piss it out", and left. After the City had been destroyed, Samuel Pepys, looking back on the events, wrote in his diary on 7 September 1666: "People do all the world over cry out of the simplicity [the stupidity] of my Lord Mayor in general; and more particularly in this business of the fire, laying it all upon him."

Around 7 a.m. on Sunday morning, Pepys, who was a significant official in the Navy Office, climbed the Tower of London to get an aerial view of the fire, and recorded in his diary that the eastern gale had turned it into a conflagration. It had burned down several churches and, he estimated, 300 houses, and reached the riverfront. The houses on London Bridge were burning. Taking a boat to inspect the destruction around Pudding Lane at close range, Pepys describes a "lamentable" fire, "everybody endeavouring to remove their goods, and flinging into the river or bringing them into lighters that layoff; poor people staying in their houses as long as till the very fire touched them, and then running into boats, or clambering from one pair of stairs by the water-side to another." Pepys continued westward on the river to the court at Whitehall, "where people come about me, and did give them an account dismayed them all, and word was carried in to the King. So I was called for, and did tell the King and Duke of Yorke what I saw, and that unless his Majesty did command houses to be pulled down nothing could stop the fire. They seemed much troubled, and the King commanded me to go to my Lord Mayor from him, and command him to spare no houses, but to pull down before the fire every way." Charles' brother James, Duke of York, offered the use of the Royal Life Guards to help fight the fire.[27]

A mile west of Pudding Lane, by Westminster Stairs, young William
Taswell, a schoolboy who had bolted from the early morning service
in Westminster Abbey, saw some refugees arrive in for-hire lighter
boats, unclothed and covered only with blankets.[28] The services of
the lightermen had suddenly become extremely expensive, and only the
luckiest refugees secured a place in a boat.

The fire spread quickly in the high wind. By mid-morning on Sunday,
people abandoned attempts at extinguishing the fire and fled; their
moving human mass and their bundles and carts made the lanes
impassable for firefighters and carriages. Pepys took a coach back into
the city from Whitehall, but only reached St. Paul's Cathedral before
he had to get out and walk. Handcarts with goods and pedestrians were
still on the move, away from the fire, heavily weighed down. The parish
churches not directly threatened were filling up with furniture and
valuables, which would soon have to be moved further afield. Pepys
found Mayor Bloodworth trying to coordinate the firefighting efforts
and near collapse, "like a fainting woman", crying out plaintively
in response to the King's message that he *was* pulling down houses.
"But the fire overtakes us faster than we can do it." Holding on to his
civic dignity, he refused James' offer of soldiers and then went home
to bed.[29] Charles sailed down from Whitehall in the Royal barge to
inspect the scene. He found that houses still were not being pulled down
in spite of Bloodworth's assurances to Pepys, and daringly overrode the
authority of Bloodworth to order wholesale demolitions west of the fire
zone.[30] The delay rendered these measures largely futile, as the fire
was already out of control.

By Sunday afternoon, 18 hours after the alarm was raised in Pudding
Lane, the fire had become a raging firestorm which created its own
weather. A tremendous uprush of hot air above the flames was driven
by the chimney effect wherever constrictions such as jettied buildings
narrowed the air current and left a vacuum at ground level. The
resulting strong inward winds did not tend to put the fire out, as might
be thought;[31] instead, they added fresh oxygen to the flames, and the
turbulence created by the uprush made the wind veer erratically both
north and south of the main, easterly, direction of the gale which was still
blowing.

In the early evening, with his wife and some friends, Pepys went again on
the river "and to the fire up and down, it still encreasing." They ordered
the boatman to go "so near the fire as we could for smoke; and all over the
Thames, with one's face in the wind, you were almost burned with a shower
of firedrops." When the "firedrops" became unbearable, the party went on to

an <u>alehouse</u> on the south bank and stayed there till darkness came and they could see the fire on London Bridge and across the river, "as only one entire arch of fire from this to the other side of the bridge, and in a bow up the hill for an arch of above a mile long: it made me weep to see it."

Monday

Approximate damage by the evening of Monday, 3 September.

By dawn on Monday, 3 September, the fire was principally expanding north and west, the turbulence of the firestorm pushing the flames both more to the south and more to the north than the day before.[32] The push to the south was in the main halted by the river itself, but had torched the houses on London Bridge, and was threatening to cross the bridge and endanger the borough of <u>Southwark</u> on the south riverbank. Southwark was preserved by a pre-existent firebreak on the bridge, a long gap between the buildings which had saved the south side of the Thames in the fire of 1632 and now did so again.[33] The corresponding push to the north drove the flames into the financial heart of the City. The houses of the bankers on <u>Lombard Street</u> began to burn on Monday afternoon, prompting a rush to get their stacks of gold coins, so crucial to the wealth of the city and the nation, to safety before they melted away. Several observers emphasise the despair and helplessness which seemed to seize the Londoners on this second day, and the lack of efforts to save the wealthy, fashionable districts which were now menaced by the flames, such as the <u>Royal Exchange</u>—combined <u>bourse</u> and shopping mall—and the opulent consumer goods shops in <u>Cheapside</u>. The Royal Exchange caught fire in the late afternoon, and was a smoking shell within a few hours. John Evelyn, courtier and diarist, wrote:

> ❝ The conflagration was so universal, and the people so astonished, that from the beginning, I know not by what despondency or fate, they hardly stirred to quench it, so that there was nothing heard or seen but crying out and lamentation, running about like distracted creatures without ❞

at all attempting to save even their goods, such a strange
consternation there was upon them.[34]

Evelyn lived four miles (6 km) outside the City, in Deptford, and so did
not see the early stages of the disaster. On Monday, joining many other
upper-class people, he went by coach to Southwark to watch the view that
Pepys had seen the day before, of the burning City across the river. The
conflagration was much larger now: "the whole City in dreadful flames
near the water-side; all the houses from the Bridge, all Thames-street,
and upwards towards Cheapside, down to the Three Cranes, were now
consumed".[35] In the evening, Evelyn reported that the river was covered
with barges and boats making their escape piled with goods. He observed
a great exodus of carts and pedestrians through the bottleneck City gates,
making for the open fields to the north and east, "which for many miles
were strewed with moveables of all sorts, and tents erecting to shelter
both people and what goods they could get away. Oh, the miserable and
calamitous spectacle!"[35]

Suspicion soon arose in the threatened city that the fire was no accident.
The swirling winds carried sparks and burning flakes long distances
to lodge on thatched roofs and in wooden gutters, causing seemingly
unrelated house fires to break out far from their source and giving rise
to rumours that fresh fires were being set on purpose. Foreigners were
immediately suspect due to the ongoing

Second Anglo-Dutch War. As fear and suspicion hardened into certainty
on the Monday, reports circulated of imminent invasion, and of foreign
undercover agents seen casting "fireballs" into houses, or caught with
hand grenades or matches.[36] There was a wave of street violence.[37]
William Taswell saw a mob loot the shop of a French painter and level
it to the ground, and watched in horror as a blacksmith walked up to
a Frenchman in the street and hit him over the head with an iron bar.
The fears of terrorism received an extra boost from the disruption of
communications and news as vital facilities were devoured by the fire.
The General Letter Office in Threadneedle Street, through which post
for the entire country passed, burned down early on Monday morning.
The London Gazette just managed to put out its Monday issue before the
printer's premises went up in flames (this issue contained mainly society
gossip, with a small note about a fire that had broken out on Sunday
morning and "which continues still with great violence"). The whole
nation depended on these communications, and the void they left filled up
with rumours. There were also religious alarms of renewed Gunpowder
Plots. As suspicions rose to panic and collective paranoia on the Monday,
both the Trained Bands and the Coldstream Guards focused less on

The *London Gazette* for 3 September–10 September, with an account of the Great Fire. Click on the image to enlarge and read.

firefighting and more on rounding up foreigners, Catholics, and any odd-looking people, arresting them, rescuing them from mobs, or both together.

The inhabitants, especially the upper class, were growing desperate to remove their belongings from the City. This provided a source of income for the able-bodied poor, who hired out as porters (sometimes simply making off with the goods), and especially for the owners of carts and boats. Hiring a cart had cost a couple of shillings on the Saturday before the fire; on the Monday it rose to as much as forty pounds, a small fortune (equivalent to over £4000 in 2005).[38] Seemingly every cart and boat owner within reach of London made their way towards the City to share in these opportunities, the carts jostling at the narrow gates with the panicked inhabitants trying to get out. The chaos at the gates was such that the magistrates ordered the gates shut on Monday afternoon, in the hope of turning the inhabitants' attention from safeguarding their own possessions to the fighting of the fire: "that, no hopes of saving any things left, they might have more desperately endeavoured the quenching of the fire."[39] This headlong and unsuccessful measure was rescinded the next day.

Even as order in the streets broke down, especially at the gates, and the fire raged unchecked, Monday marked the beginning of organised action. Bloodworth, who as Lord Mayor was responsible for coordinating the fire-fighting, had apparently left the City; his name is not mentioned in any contemporary accounts of the Monday events.[40] In this state of emergency, Charles again overrode the City authorities and put his brother James, Duke of York, in charge of operations. James set up command posts round the perimeter of the fire, press-ganging any men of the lower classes found in the streets into teams of well-paid and well-fed firefighters. Three courtiers were put in charge of each post, with authority from Charles himself to order demolitions. This visible gesture of solidarity from the Crown was intended to cut through the citizens' misgivings about being held financially responsible for pulling down houses. James and his life guards rode up and down the streets all Monday, rescuing foreigners from the mob and attempting to keep order. "The Duke of York hath won the hearts of the people with his continual and indefatigable pains day and night in helping to quench the Fire", wrote a witness in a letter on 8 September.[41]

On the Monday evening, hopes that the massive stone walls of Baynard's Castle, Blackfriars, the western counterpart of the Tower of London, would stay the course of the flames were dashed and this historic royal palace was completely consumed, burning all night.[42]

Tuesday

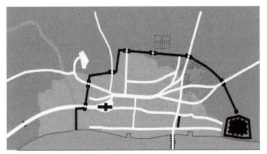

Approximate damage by the evening of Tuesday, 4 September. The fire did not spread significantly on Wednesday, 5 September.

Tuesday, 4 September, was the day of greatest destruction.[43] The Duke of York's command post at Temple Bar, at the conjunction of The Strand and Fleet Street, was supposed to stop the fire's westward advance towards the Palace of Whitehall itself. Making a stand with his firefighters from the Fleet Bridge and down to the Thames, James hoped that the River Fleet would form a natural firebreak. However, early on Tuesday morning, the flames jumped over the Fleet, driven by the unabated easterly gale, and outflanked them, forcing them to run for it. There was consternation at the palace as the fire continued implacably westward: "Oh, the confusion there was then at that court!" wrote Evelyn.

Working to a plan at last, James' firefighters had also created a large firebreak to the north of the conflagration. It contained the fire until late afternoon, when the flames leaped across and began to destroy the wide, affluent luxury shopping street of Cheapside.

Everybody had thought St. Paul's Cathedral an absolute refuge, with its thick stone walls and natural firebreak in the form of a wide, empty surrounding plaza. It had been crammed full of rescued goods and its crypt filled with the tightly packed stocks of the printers and booksellers in adjoining Paternoster Row. However, in an enormous stroke of bad luck the building was covered in wooden scaffolding, awaiting restoration by Christopher Wren. The scaffolding caught fire on Tuesday night. Leaving school, young William Taswell stood on Westminster Stairs a mile away and watched as the flames crept round the cathedral and the burning scaffolding ignited the timbered roof beams. Within half an hour, the lead roof was melting, and the books and papers in the crypt caught with a roar. "The stones of Paul's flew like grenados, the melting lead running down the streets in a stream, and the very pavements glowing with fiery redness, so as no horse, nor man, was able to tread on them", reported Evelyn in his diary. The cathedral was quickly a ruin.

During the day, the flames began to move due *east* from the neighbourhood of Pudding Lane, straight against the prevailing east wind towards Pepys' home on Seething Lane and the Tower of London with its gunpowder stores. After waiting all day for requested help from James' official firefighters, who were busy in the west, the garrison at the Tower took matters into their own hands and created firebreaks by blowing up houses in the vicinity on a large scale, halting the advance of the fire.

Wednesday

The wind dropped on Tuesday evening, allowing the firebreaks created by the garrison to finally begin to take effect on Wednesday, 5 September.[44] Pepys walked all over the smouldering city, getting his feet hot, and climbed the steeple of Barking Church, from which he viewed the destroyed City, "the saddest sight of desolation that I ever saw." There were many individual fires still burning themselves out, but the Great Fire was over. Pepys visited Moorfields, a large public park immediately north of the City, and saw a great encampment of homeless refugees, "poor wretches carrying their good there, and every body keeping his goods together by themselves", and noted that the price of bread in the environs of the park had doubled. Evelyn also went out to Moorfields, which was turning into the main point of assembly for the homeless, and was horrified at the numbers of distressed people filling it, some under tents, others in makeshift shacks: "Many [were] without a rag or any necessary utensils, bed or board.. reduced to extremest misery and poverty."[45] Evelyn was impressed by the pride of these distressed Londoners, "tho' ready to perish for hunger and destitution, yet not asking one pennie for relief."

Fears of foreign terrorists and of a French and Dutch invasion were as high as ever among the traumatised fire victims, and on Wednesday night there was an outbreak of general panic at the encampments at Parliament Hill, Moorfields and Islington. A light in the sky over Fleet Street started a story that 50,000 French and Dutch immigrants, widely rumoured to have started the fire, had risen and were marching towards Moorfields to finish what the fire had begun: to cut the men's throats, rape the women, and steal their few possessions. Surging into the streets, the frightened mob fell on any foreigners they happened to encounter, and were, according to Evelyn, only "with infinite pains and great difficulty" appeased and pushed back into the fields by the Trained Bands, troops of Life Guards, and members of the court. The mood was now so volatile that Charles feared a full-scale London rebellion against the monarchy. Food production and distribution had been disrupted to the point of non-existence, and Charles announced that supplies of bread would be brought into the City every day, and safe markets set up round the perimeter. These markets were for buying and selling; there was no question of distributing emergency aid.

Deaths and destruction

Only a few deaths from the fire are officially recorded, and actual deaths are also traditionally supposed to have been few. Porter gives the figure as eight[46] and Tinniswood as "in single figures", although he adds that some deaths must have gone unrecorded and that, besides direct deaths from burning and smoke inhalation, refugees also perished in the impromptu camps.[47] Hanson takes issue with the whole notion that there were only a few deaths, enumerating known deaths from hunger and exposure among survivors of the holocaust, "huddled in shacks or living among the ruins that had once been their homes" in the cold winter that followed, including, for instance, the dramatist James Shirley and his wife. Hanson also maintains that "it stretches credulity to believe that the only papists or foreigners being beaten to death or lynched were the ones rescued by the Duke of York", that official figures say very little about the fate of the undocumented poor, and that the heat at the heart of the firestorms, far higher than the heat of an ordinary house fire, was sufficient to fully consume bodies, or leave only a few skull fragments. The fire, fed not merely by wood, fabrics, and thatch, but also by the oil,

The Monument, London to commemorate the Great Fire of
London, designed by Sir Christopher Wren

pitch, coal, tallow, fats, sugar, alcohol, turpentine, and gunpowder stored
in the riverside district, melted the imported <u>steel</u> lying along the wharves
(<u>melting point</u> between 1,250 °C (2,300 F) and 1,480 °C (2,700 F)) and
the great <u>iron</u> chains and locks on the City gates (melting point between
1,100 °C (2,000 F) and 1,650 °C (3000 F)). Nor would anonymous bone
fragments have been of much interest to the hungry people sifting through
the tens of thousands of tons of rubble and debris after the fire, looking
for valuables, or to the workmen clearing away the rubble later for the
rebuilding. Appealing to common sense and "the experience of every
other major urban fire down the centuries", Hanson emphasises that the
fire attacked the rotting tenements of the poor with furious speed, surely
trapping at the very least "the old, the very young, the halt and the lame"
and burying the dust and ashes of their bones under the rubble of cellars;
making for a death toll not of four or eight, but of "several hundred and
quite possibly several thousand."[48]

The material destruction has been computed at 13,500 houses, 87 parish
churches, 44 <u>Company</u> Halls, the <u>Royal Exchange</u>, the <u>Custom House</u>,
St. Paul's Cathedral, the <u>Bridewell Palace</u> and other City prisons, the
<u>General Letter Office</u>, and the three western city gates, <u>Ludgate</u>, <u>Newgate</u>,
and <u>Aldersgate</u>.[49] The monetary value of the loss, first estimated
at £100,000,000 in the currency of the time, was later reduced to an

uncertain £10,000,000[50] (over £1,000,000,000 in 2005 pounds).[51] Evelyn believed that he saw as many as "200,000 people of all ranks and stations dispersed, and lying along their heaps of what they could save" in the fields towards Islington and Highgate.[50]

Aftermath

An example of the urge to identify scapegoats for the fire is the acceptance of the confession of a simple-minded French watchmaker, Robert Hubert, who claimed he was an agent of the Pope and had started the Great Fire in Westminster.[52] He later changed his story to say that he had started the fire at the bakery in Pudding Lane. Hubert was convicted, despite some misgivings about his fitness to plead, and hanged at Tyburn on 28 September 1666. After his death, it became apparent that he had not arrived in London until two days after the fire started.[53] These allegations that Catholics had started the fire were exploited as powerful political propaganda by opponents of pro-Catholic Charles II's court, mostly during the Popish Plot and the exclusion crisis later in his reign.[54]

Abroad the Great Fire of London was seen as a Divine retribution, the Lord punishing the English for Holmes's Bonfire, the burning of a Dutch town three weeks earlier during the Second Anglo-Dutch war.

In the chaos and unrest after the fire, Charles II feared another London rebellion. He encouraged the homeless to move away from London and settle elsewhere, immediately issuing a proclamation that "all Cities and Towns whatsoever shall without any contradiction receive the said distressed persons and permit them the free exercise of their manual trades." A special Fire Court was set up to deal with disputes between tenants and landlords and decide who should rebuild, based on ability to pay. The Court was in session from February 1667 to September 1672. Cases were heard and a verdict usually given within a day, and without the Fire Court, lengthy legal wrangles would have seriously delayed the rebuilding which was so necessary if London was to recover. Encouraged by Charles, radical rebuilding schemes for the gutted City poured in. If it had been rebuilt under these plans, London would have rivalled Paris in Baroque magnificence (see Evelyn's plan on the right). The Crown and the City authorities attempted to establish "to whom all the houses and ground did in truth belong" in order to negotiate with their owners about compensation for the large-scale re-modelling that these plans entailed, but that unrealistic idea had to be abandoned. Exhortations to bring workmen and measure the plots on which the houses had stood were mostly ignored by people worried about day-to-day survival, as well as by those who had left the capital; for one thing, with the shortage of labour following on the fire, it was impossible to secure workmen for the purpose. Apart from Wren and Evelyn, it is known that Robert Hooke, Valentine Knight and Richard Newcourt proposed rebuilding plans. With the complexities of ownership unresolved, none of the grand Baroque schemes for a City of piazzas and avenues could be realised; there was nobody to negotiate with, and no means of calculating how much compensation should be paid. Instead, the old street plan was re-created in the new City, with improvements in hygiene and fire safety: wider streets, open and accessible wharves along the length of the Thames, with no houses obstructing access to the river, and, most importantly, buildings constructed of brick and stone, not wood. New public buildings were created on their predecessors' sites; perhaps the most famous is St. Paul's Cathedral and its smaller cousins, Christopher Wren's fifty new churches.

On Charles' initiative, a Monument to the Great Fire of London, designed by Christopher Wren and Robert Hooke, was erected near Pudding Lane after the fire. Standing 61 metres tall and known simply as "The Monument", it is a familiar London landmark which has given its name to a tube station. In 1668 accusations against the Catholics were added to the Monument which read, in part:

> **❝** Here by permission of heaven, hell broke loose upon this Protestant city...the most dreadful Burning of this City; begun and carried on by the treachery and malice of the Popish faction..Popish frenzy which wrought such horrors, is not yet **❞** quenched..

Aside from the four years of James II's rule from 1685 to 1689, the inscription remained in place until 1830 and the passage of the Catholic Emancipation Act.[55]

Another monument, the Golden Boy of Pye Corner in Smithfield, marks the spot where the fire stopped. According to the inscription, the fact that the fire started at Pudding Lane and stopped at Pye Corner was an indication that the Fire was evidence of God's wrath on the City of London for the sin of gluttony.

The Great Plague epidemic of 1665 is believed to have killed a sixth of London's inhabitants, or 80,000 people,[56] and it is sometimes suggested, given the fact that plague epidemics did not recur in London after the fire,[57] that the Great Fire saved lives in the long run by burning down so much unsanitary housing with the accompanying rats and their fleas (which transmitted the plague). Historians disagree as to whether the fire played a part in preventing future major outbreaks. The <u>Museum of London</u> website claims that there was a connection,[58] while historian <u>Roy Porter</u> points out that the fire left the most insalubrious parts of London, the slum suburbs, untouched.[59] Alternative <u>epidemiological</u> explanations have been put forward, along with the observation that the disease disappeared from almost every other European city at the same time.[57]

Notes

1. ^ All dates are given according to the <u>Julian calendar</u>. Note that when recording British history it is usual to use the dates recorded at the time of the event. Any dates between 1 January and 25 March have their year adjusted to start on the 1 January according to the <u>New Style</u>.
2. ^ Porter, 69–80.
3. ^ Tinniswood, 4, 101.
4. ^ Reddaway, 27.
5. ^ Morgan, 293–4.
6. ^ <u>John Evelyn</u> in 1659, quoted in Tinniswood, 3. The section "London in the 1660s" is based on Tinniswood, 1–11, unless otherwise indicated.
7. ^ Porter, 80.
8. ^ 330 acres is the size of the area within the Roman wall according to standard reference works (see, for instance, Sheppard, 37), although Tinniswood gives that area as a square mile (667 acres).
9. ^ Hanson, 80.
10. ^ See Hanson, 85–88, for the Republican temper of London.
11. ^ Hanson, 77–80. The section "Fire hazards in the City" is based on Hanson 77–101 unless otherwise indicated.
12. ^ Rege Sincera (pseudonym), *Observations both Historical and Moral upon the Burning of London, September 1666*, quoted by Hanson, 80.
13. ^ Letter from an unknown correspondent to <u>Lord Conway</u>, September 1666, quoted by Tinniswood, 45–46.
14. ^ All quotes from and details involving Samuel Pepys come from his diary entry for the day referred to.
15. ^ Robinson, Bruce, <u>"London's Burning: The Great Fire"</u>
16. ^ Gough MSS London14, the <u>Bodleian Library</u>, quoted by Hanson, 123.
17. ^ Hanson, 82. The section "Fire hazards in the City" is based on Tinniswood, 46–52, and Hanson, 75–78 unless otherwise indicated.
18. ^ A firehook was a heavy pole perhaps 30 feet (9 m) long with a strong hook and ring at one end, which would be attached to the

roof trees of a threatened house and operated by means of ropes and pulleys to pull the building down. (Tinniswood, 49).

19. ^ Reddaway, 25.
20. ^ "Bludworth's failure of nerve was crucial" (Tinniswood, 52).
21. ^ See Robinson, London:Brighter Lights, Bigger City" and Tinniswood, 48–49.
22. ^ Compare Hanson, who claims they had wheels (76), and Tinniswood, who states they did not (50).
23. ^ The fire engines, for which a patent had been granted in 1625, were single-acting force pumps worked by long handles at the front and back (Tinniswood, 50).
24. ^ The information in the day-by-day maps comes from Tinniswood, 58, 77, 97.
25. ^ Tinniswood 42–43.
26. ^ Tinniswood, 44: "He didn't have the experience, the leadership skills or the natural authority to take charge of the situation."
27. ^ Pepys' diary, 2 September 1666.
28. ^ Tinniswood, 93.
29. ^ Tinniswood, 53.
30. ^ London Gazette, 3 September 1666.
31. ^ See firestorm and Hanson, 102–105.
32. ^ The section "Monday" is based on Tinniswood, 58–74, unless otherwise indicated.
33. ^ Robinson, "London's Burning: The Great Fire".
34. ^ All quotes from and details involving John Evelyn come from his diary.
35. ^ a b Evelyn, 10.
36. ^ Hanson, 139.
37. ^ Reddaway, 22, 25.
38. ^ Hanson, 156–57.
39. ^ Quoted by Hanson, 158.
40. ^ Tinnisworth, 71.
41. ^ Spelling modernised for clarity; quoted by Tinniswood, 80.
42. ^ Walter George Bell (1929) *The Story of London's Great Fire*: 109-11. John Lane: London.
43. ^ The section "Tuesday" is based on Tinniswood, 77–96.
44. ^ The section "Wednesday" is based on Tinniswood, 101–10, unless otherwise indicated.
45. ^ Quoted Tinniswood, 104.
46. ^ Porter, 87.
47. ^ Tinniswood, 131–35.
48. ^ Hanson, 326–33.
49. ^ Porter, 87–88.
50. ^ a b Reddaway, 26.

51. ∧ Purchasing Power of British Pounds from 1264 to 2005
52. ∧ The section "Aftermath" is based on Reddaway, 27 ff. and Tinniswood, 213–37, unless otherwise indicated.
53. ∧ Tinniswood, 163–68.
54. ∧ *Porter, Stephen (October 2006)*. *"The great fire of London"*. *Oxford Dictionary of National Biography*. Oxford University Press. *Retrieved on* 2006-11-28.55.   ∧ Wilde, Robert. "The Great Fire of London – 1666". About.com. Retrieved on 2006-11-28.
55. ∧ Porter, 84.
56. ∧ a b Hanson, 249–50.
57. ∧ Ask the experts, Museum of London, accessed 27 October 2006.
58. ∧ "The plague-ravaged parts—extramural settlements like Holborn, Shoreditch, Finsbury, Whitechapel and Southwark that housed the most squalid slums—were, sadly, little touched by the Fire (burning down was what they needed)" (Porter, 80).

References

- Evelyn, John *(1854)*. Diary and Correspondence of John Evelyn, F.R.S.. *London: Hursst and Blackett*. http://books.google.com/ books?vid=OCLC20137959&id=JiH6MSVCzmsC&pg=PA10&vq =fire&dq=%22John+evelyn%22+diary&as_brr=1. Retrieved on 5 November 2006.Also in text version:Evelyn, John *(1857)*. Diary and Correspondence of John Evelyn, F.R.S.. *London*. http://nils.lib.tufts. edu/cgi-bin/ptext?doc=Perseus%3Atext%3A2000.01.0023;query=pa ge%3D%2311;layout=;loc=. Retrieved on 1 January 2007.
- Hanson, Neil (2001). *The Dreadful Judgement: The True Story of the Great Fire of London. New York: Doubleday.* For a review of Hanson's work, see Lauzanne, Alain. "Revue pluridisciplinaire du monde anglophone" (in English). Cercles. Retrieved on 2006-10-12.
- Morgan (2000). *Oxford Illustrated History of Britain*. Oxford: Oxford.
- Pepys, Samuel (1995). Robert Latham and William Matthews (eds.). ed. *The Diary of Samuel Pepys, Vol. 7.* London: Harper Collins. ISBN 0-00-499027-7.First published between 1970 and 1983, by Bell & Hyman, London. Quotations from and details involving Pepys are taken from this standard, and copyright, edition. All web versions of the diaries are based on public domain 19th century editions and unfortunately contain many errors, as the shorthand in which Pepys' diaries were originally written was not accurately transcribed until the pioneering work of Latham and Matthews.
- Porter, Roy *(1994)*. *London: A Social History*. Cambridge: Harvard.

- Reddaway, T. F. (1940). *The Rebuilding of London after the Great Fire.* London: Jonathan Cape.
- Robinson, Bruce. London: Brighter Lights, Bigger City. *BBC.* http://www.bbc.co.uk/history/british/civil_war_revolution/brighter_lights_01.shtml. Retrieved on 12 August 2006.
- Sheppard, Francis (1998). *London: A History.* Oxford: Oxford.
- Tinniswood, Adrian (2003). *By Permission of Heaven: The Story of the Great Fire of London.* London: Jonathan Cape.

See also

- Great Plague of London
- Second Great Fire of London
- Great fire of Newcastle and Gateshead, 1854
- Great Chicago Fire
- Thomas Vincent - a Puritan minister's eyewitness account

External links

- BBC history site
- Museum of London answers questions
- Channel 4 animation of the spread of the fire
- Child-friendly Great Fire of London site
- Fire of London website produced by the Museum of London, The National Archives, the National Portrait Gallery, London Fire Brigade

Museum and London Metropolitan Archives for Key Stage 1 pupils (ages 5–7) and teachers

Categories: Featured articles | History of the City of London | Fires in London | 1666 disasters | 1666 in England | 17th century in London

Assessment: Version 1

1. **Length, structure:**
   Clearly very brief, yet the topics are treated in a logical order.   2/5

2. **Images:**
   None   0/5

3. **Quotes:**
   None   0/5

4. **Grammar, style:**
   A clear, lucid style with no grammatical faults.   4/5

5. **Generalizations, neutrality:**
   Mostly confined to physical facts, but 'a marked and varied impact on
   English society' is unsupported and seems unjustified.   2/5

6. **Discrepancies, repetitions, gaps:**
   Plenty of gaps, but no repetitions or discrepancies.   1/5

7. **Links, Internet references:**
   The internal hyperlink system was clearly already up and running. The
   references to Charles II and so on do not seem to produce any further
   relevant information. There are no Internet references.   1/5

8. **Print references:**
   None   0/5

9. **Stability:**
   No discussion about the article had yet been archived at this stage.

10. **Overall:**
    Considering its brevity, this article is reasonably informative and clear. It
    was written in the days before Wikipedia demanded images and references
    to sources.   2/5

    Total: 12/45 (= 13/50)

Assessment: Version 2

1. **Length, structure:**
   A reasonable structure, except that the lead section contains rather irrelevant
   material about earlier fires and the Luftwaffe. Also the Cultural impact

section is a ragbag of disparate items.   3/5

2. Images:
There are two useful images, one of which is not reproduced here for copyright reasons. There could be a map.   2/5

3. Quotes:
Deficient. The one starting 'Then, then' adds little, and the longer one starting 'Heaven be praised' is an exaggerated piece of rhetoric whose actual author is unknown. More needed from contemporary observers. 1/5

4. Grammar, style:
The pompous and old-fashioned style of parts of the article (for example, the paragraph starting 'The immense property' on p. 145) suggests they were copied from an earlier source.[7] There are several redundant adjectives such as: 'the *dreadful* time', 'a *staggering* 13200 houses'.   2/5

5. Generalizations, neutrality:
Some exaggerations: for example, 'more or less in the destruction of the city', when we are told only one sixth were made homeless (p. 143); who estimated the destruction at £10 million (p. 145), and was this in today's money?) The quoted view that the government started the fire (p. 146) is unchallenged.   2/5

6. Discrepancies, repetitions, gaps:
The number of houses destroyed is mentioned three times. The numbers of churches and gates destroyed seems to fluctuate. The explanation of 'space cleared' is difficult to follow (p. 149). There is practically nothing on the geography of the fire, or on its day-to-day progress.   1/5

7. Links, Internet references:
There is a total absence of proper references to sources. The links to Charles II, Wren, Pepys and Ursula Southeil (Mother Shipton) add nothing to 'Aftermath and consequences' (p. 146). Only one follow-up link is listed (the BBC History site).   0/5

8. Print references:
Only two books are mentioned, one of which is about the fire.   1/5

9. Stability:
No edit wars or vandalism detected.   4/5

---

7   This source turns out to be *The Mirror of Literature, Amusement, and Instruction*, London (1827): <http://www.gutenberg.org/ebooks/11401>.

10. **Overall:**

The article gives the impression of having been cobbled together from various, not particularly trustworthy, sources. 2/5

Total: 18/50

Assessment: Version 3

1. **Length and structure:**

Version 3 is extremely long, but I felt the detail was relevant throughout. Because the lead section was also lengthy (three paragraphs), there was some – perhaps unavoidable – repetition as between it and the rest of the article. As to structure, a fair balance was achieved between the earlier descriptive topics (for example, 'Seventeenth-century firefighting') and the later day-by-day narrative of the fire. One criticism is that the topic of sources and diaries of the fire really needs separate treatment, but was put under 'Development of the fire' (p. 155). Another is that the article stops rather abruptly, and could end with a summary, perhaps including a comparison with other urban disasters in history. 4/5

2. **Images:**

An excellent collection of 18 very varied images, all of them relevant. I especially liked the maps showing the development of the fire. Unfortunately, it has not been possible to reproduce most of the images here for copyright reasons. 5/5

3. **Quotes:**

Good use of quotation, especially from the three contemporary diarists, Evelyn, Pepys and William Taswell (though the latter was only cited from a secondary source). I'd have liked to know the source for the mayor's famous remark that a woman could piss out the fire (p. 156). 5/5

4. **Grammar, style:**

A clear, succinct style throughout, with no glaring grammatical faults. A few awkward repetitions, such as the two 'majors' in the first paragraph. A few nice touches, such as the houses of the poor being 'shoehorned' among the rest (p. 152). 5/5

5. **Generalizations, neutrality:**

This was not a particularly controversial topic, so preserving a neutral point of view was hardly an issue. There was useful comparison between the views of different historians on the issue of how many died in the fire (p. 163). I suppose there could have been more effort to sum up the economic, social and demographic effects of the fire.   4/5

6. **Discrepancies, repetitions, gaps:**
There were no obvious gaps. References to the unfortunate Lord Mayor involve some repetition, are scattered throughout the article, and could have been more effectively collated. There is some confusion regarding the prevailing wind, which is described in various places as 'strong east winds' (p. 149), 'an eastern gale' (p. 155), and as blowing in an 'easterly direction' (p. 157). The comparison between 'midnight on Sunday' (p. 155) and 'Sunday morning' a little further down is rather confusing. One wonders whether 'the Royal Life Guards' (p. 156), the 'Coldstream Guards' (p. 159) and 'James and his life guards' (p. 161) all refer to the same group of soldiers.   4/5

7. **Links, Internet references:**
There are a very adequate number of internal links to other Wikipedia articles, coloured blue. One of the end references to Evelyn's diary appears not to work; the other is to an 1854 edition in Google Books. It is surprising that there is no reference to the six-volume standard 1955 edition.[8] It is also surprising that the brief account of the fire on the BBC History website, dating from 2001, is referred to as a source (for example, for London's water supply: ref. 21) when more recent scholarly material is available. Why is there another reference to a journalistic website to support a long quotation (ref. 55), especially when the accompanying date given for the Catholic Emancipation Act is wrong?[9] Of course, this is not really a topic that lends itself to web citation as opposed to print.   3/5

8. **Print references:**
A useful reading list, with recent accounts of the fire (Tinniswood, Hanson) as well as diarists, and histories of London. Criticisms: no direct references to the diary of William Taswell or to the rounding up of foreigners during the fire (p. 160). The views of 'modern historians' on firebreaks (p. 154 and ref. 19) are sourced with a reference to a book published in 1940, which is hardly modern.   4/5

9. **Stability:**
No sign of edit wars in the article's recent history, but a fair amount of vandalism, due to the article's prominence. There are amicable debates on the article's discussion page about topics such as whether to describe the capital as 'London, England' or just 'London', on the appropriate use of

---

8   E.S. De Beer (1955), Oxford, 6 vols.
9   The reference is to the site About.com, owned by the *New York Times*. The date of the Act is given as 1830, and should be 1829.

the word 'conflagration', and on whether the page reproduced from The London Gazette is from an original copy or a modern facsimile.   5/5

10. **Overall:** This was an excellent article on an important historical topic. Particularly impressive were the images accompanying it. As well as the geography and day-to-day narrative of the fire, several interesting points were raised, such as the relationship between the king and the City, and the subsequent allegations against Catholics.   5/5

Total: 44/50

Chapter 16
Contributing to Wikipedia

What we share is at least as important as what we own; what we hold in common is as important as what we keep for ourselves; what we choose to give away may matter more than what we charge for. ... Much of what we most value – in culture, language, art, science and learning – comes from a kind of gift exchange, in which ideas are passed from person to person, and accumulate over long periods.

Charles Leadbeater

Anyone who has ever browsed Wikipedia for any length of time, or better still has read certain articles critically, will be aware of the possibility of numerous improvements, in style, grammar or content. It might be argued that having enjoyed the fruits of other people's labour, one has some kind of moral obligation to remove a few of these if it lies within one's power. Even the odd comma added to a sentence is a contribution to this joint world-wide project. Relevant here is the reply of Peter Murray-Rust to a conference in Oxford when asked whether he trusted Wikipedia: 'The bit of Wikipedia that I wrote is correct'.[1]

Editing most Wikipedia pages is not difficult.[2] Simply click on the 'edit this page' tab at the top of a Wikipedia page (or on the edit link accompanying each paragraph). This brings up a new page with a text box known as the 'edit window', which contains the editable text of the original page. Having suitably modified the text, one should then add an edit summary in the field provided, and also, if appropriate, tick the 'This is a minor edit' box. To view the differences between the newly edited page and the previous version, press the 'Show preview' button, and if satisfied, the 'Save page' button. The changes will immediately be visible to all Wikipedia users, and will also be recorded on the list of Recent Changes so that other editors with an interest in the article can be alerted. If the changes are likely to be at all controversial, it is also recommended to post a comment on the article's talk page explaining one's motives, which will improve the chances that one's contribution will remain. The talk page can be edited in the same way as the article page. To start a new topic, click + at the top of the page. It is also suggested that you sign your name after any discussion contribution by typing four tildes (~~~~), which will automatically record your user name and the date.

---

1 Quoted by John Naughton, *The Observer*, 5 April 2009: Peter Murray-Rust is Reader in Molecular Informatics at the University of Cambridge.

2 Much of this chapter has been adapted from two recent publications: Phoebe Ayers, Charles Matthews and Ben Yates (2008), *How Wikipedia Works*, San Francisco, CA: No Starch Press; John Broughton (2008), *Wikipedia: The Missing Manual,* Sebastopol, CA: O'Reilly Media.

Before editing, it is recommended, though not essential, that one creates an account, which merely entails pressing the 'Create account' button found at the top right-hand corner of every page, and then giving a password and the name with which one want to be known on Wikipedia. Some editors use their real names, but the vast majority adopt a pseudonym. It is probably better to register, and then to log on whenever revisiting the site, because edits carry more weight with the Wikipedia community if the editor is registered, and also because with an account you acquire a user page on which others can post messages about your edits. Those who edit without being registered are, paradoxically, less anonymous than registered users since their Internet Protocol (IP) address is recorded whenever they edit, and the IP number's owner can often be traced quite easily.

Users who have registered and have logged on can easily consider starting a new article. One way to discover what articles are still needed is to click any red link in an existing article, and another is to go to 'Category:Wikipedia missing topics', which is an umbrella category giving lists of possible missing articles. A similarly useful collection can be found at 'Category:Red list'. Yet another method is to type into the search box the name of an article one would like to write, which leads to an invitation to write one. Of course, it is crucial before starting work on a new article to make absolutely sure that no comparable article already exists, by searching for any possible variation in title. In fact, given the size of Wikipedia, it is far more likely that a poor-quality article, possibly a stub, already exists and needs expansion. Approximately 70 per cent of all Wikipedia articles are classified as stubs, meaning that they are short and, by definition, incomplete.

Having chosen a suitable subject and a title for the new article, the next stage is to compose it, probably by writing several drafts before posting it to the site. These drafts could be written offline, and the completed article then cut and pasted onto its new page. Alternatively, one might make a sub-page in one's user space by creating a red link to a new page. To do this, first 'Edit' the User Page, then type a name for the new page inside square brackets, for example, [[Draft page]], and save. Clicking on this link will produce a new blank page on which the projected article can be composed and then pasted onto its page. There is an enormous quantity of advice on Wikipedia on how to choose a topic and write a good article.[3]

Another obvious way to contribute is to improve existing articles. As the authors of *How Wikipedia Works* write:

> Please don't say you're at a loss for something to do on Wikipedia today. There is far too much that needs to be fixed for that! Wikipedia's broad concept of clean-up includes most tasks to improve articles once they have been created. Any time you need a break from writing new articles, you'll find plenty of work waiting for you on existing ones.

---

3 For instance, <http://en.wikipedia.org/wiki/Perfect_article> and <http://en.wikipedia.org/wiki/Wikipedia:Guide_to_writing_better_articles>.

'Cleanup' is the general term for improving articles. It may involve sourcing, formatting, rewriting, linking, or merely correcting points of grammar or spelling. When editors find articles that need to be cleaned up, they can immediately fix the problems themselves, or they can flag the article with a template describing the problem for other editors to tackle later. To add a template to a page, one simply encloses the name of the template in double curly brackets at the top of the page when in edit mode. These templates are small pieces of code that can be placed on pages to produce standardized messages, and there are hundreds of them. For example:[4]

> **The grammar of this article needs to be improved.**
> Please do so in accordance with Wikipedia's style guidelines.

> **To meet Wikipedia's quality standards, the use of images on this page may require cleanup, involving adjustment of image, placement, formatting, size, or other adjustments.**
> Please see our picture tutorial and image placement for further information. Image help is available.

> **This appears to have been copied and pasted from a source, possibly in violation of a copyright.**
> Please edit this article to remove any nonfree copyrighted content, attribute free content correctly, and be an original source. Follow the Guide to layout and the Manual of Style. Remove this template after editing.

Those who would like to work in collaboration with other editors can find plenty of places where collaboration is encouraged. One of these is the Community Portal, accessible from the left-hand sidebar on any page. Another is the Project Council, where possible collaborations are suggested.[5] The following is a typical example:

Etruscans

User A: I propose a taskforce to work on the articles related to the Etruscan civilization. There are quite a lot of articles, but a large amount of them are stubs, so I think coverage could be improved greatly and quickly. The taskforce could be setup under, Wikipedia:WikiProject Classical Greece and Rome or even Wikipedia:WikiProject Italy (or a combination).
Interested Wikipedians (please add your name)

1. **User A**

---

4   The codes for these three templates are: {{grammar}} {{Clean-up-images}} {{copypaste}}.

5   <http://en.wikipedia.org/wiki/Wikipedia:WikiProject_Council/Proposals>.

2. **User B**
3. **User C**
4. **User D**
5. **User E**
6. **User F**

Discussion

User B: I'd personally favor making it a task force of Wikipedia:WikiProject European history over Classical Greece and Rome, as it doesn't really deal with Classical Greece and Rome per se, but think that the subject certainly merits focused attention.

User C: European history at the top, sure, but keep some parentage from Greece and Rome too – same time period, related issues (relations with Magna Grecia, descent of the Etruscan kings, Rome seeing its ancestry in Etruria – or not …), etc.

User D: I'd favor Italy or Classical Greece and Rome. So much of it is archaeology it would rather fit European prehistory than European history but then much is in fact history told by the Greeks and Romans. Insofar as the populations assimilated to the Italics in the Roman period and Roman culture took elements from the Etruscan it is in fact an element of classics; classical history is for the most part European history. It is nearly all Italian as most of it took place on Italian soil. Why do we have to go with someone else's task force, why not our own?

PS I'm pleased to be in the company of such distinguished editors, all of whom have many more edits than I. If I start to collide with you let me know. If you have any issues at all with me or I am not following the conventions we decide on let me know. I think I will start on Etruscan cities last-first so as not to collide. Best wishes.

Finally, here are ten suggested ways in which one might make a contribution towards Wikipedia:

1. Look for stub articles which you might be interested in expanding. As an example of a possible search: go to 'Category:Stub categories'; choose History stubs; from the 22 sub-categories, choose 'European history'; from the 25 sub-categories, choose 'Danish history stubs'; from the 127 articles listed, choose 'Viking Ship Museum, Roskilde'. This article contains at present about 100 words, and could easily be expanded using Internet resources.

2. Go to 'Wikipedia:Pages needing attention'; as an example, choose 'Philosophy'; choose 'Portal:Philosophy'; choose 'Things you can do – WikiProject Philosophy task list'; choose a topic, such as 'Socratic Dialogues', said to be an article which 'could do with some tidying and

classification'.

3. Incorporate current events. Wikipedia articles constantly need to be updated to reflect recent developments and to publish background information to clarify such events. Choose a recent news story, check Wikipedia's coverage, and help expand the coverage.

4. For those with knowledge of a foreign language, compare the coverage of a particular topic in that language's Wikipedia with the English Wikipedia.[6] Choose an article to translate from one to the other.

5. Choose a book, preferably non-fiction, which you have read recently, and check whether Wikipedia has an article on it or on its author. If not, write one, if only a stub.

6. Even new users can help answer factual questions on the 'Wikipedia: Reference desk', which serves as a general information centre. Users leave questions on the reference desk, and any Wikipedia volunteer can help to find the information required. If you answer a question, remember to sign with the four tildes (~~~~).

7. Find suitable images for Wikipedia articles, either by contributing your own work or by browsing 'Wikimedia Commons', a collection of about three million files of free media.[7]

8. Those with programming skills are always needed to improve the software that runs Wikipedia. One way to help would be to go to 'Wikipedia:Bot requests', which has a link to 'How to create a bot'.

9. There are numerous ways to ask questions of the Wikipedia community. One is to type your question on your user page, followed by {{helpme}}. This will alert editors who monitor that category, and will perhaps provide an answer. Another way is to go to 'Help Desk' (shortcut: WP:HD) or to 'New contributors help page' (shortcut: WP:NCHP).

10. Donate to the Wikimedia Foundation. There is a constant need for more server capacity, bandwidth and other technical services to keep the project running, and fast enough to be useful. For more information and a video, click on 'Donate to Wikipedia' on the Main page.[8]

---

6   A list of foreign-language Wikipedias is available on the left-hand side of the Main page.

7   See   <http:commons.wikimedia.org/wiki/Commons:First_steps>   and   <http://commons.wikimedia.org/wiki/Commons:Contributing_your_own_work>.

8   Or go to: <http://wikimediafoundation.org/wiki/Donate>.

Conclusion

Information that is gathered collectively, over time, with minimal consultation and organization but with equal zeal and care by people who have never met each other, may make up large and important databases. Here we will encounter what may be the fundamental conflict of interest in scholarly publishing: that between the freedom to speak one's mind and the responsibility to produce information that is assuredly valid and reusable by others. Freedom of inquiry and speech demands a world in which we give power to people who are editors when we like them and censors when we do not. However that tension works itself out, an important but flawed or preliminary treatment of some vital subject, by the time it has been worked over, discussed, revised, enhanced, and reworked by as many hands as care to turn to the job will become the ultimate postmodern authorless creation.

James J. O'Donnell[1]

This book has been my attempt to map out and weigh up the implications of a means of knowledge dissemination, but also production, that is the most far-reaching of any in existence today. The second half of the book has focused predominantly on Wikipedia itself – approaching the latter from a variety of different angles or with different questions in mind (and with the last chapters inviting the participation of the reader in this exploration). The first part of my study, on the other hand, used history in order to compare and contrast different historical group projects with a project from the Internet era. All the groups described in those chapters can be classed as communities of practice, meaning communities in which the members come together to pursue collaboration in a shared practice. It is this joint activity towards a common goal which bonds the individuals in such a community, and not their particular characteristics or place of origin. Wikipedians form a community of practice, but so too did the encyclopedists and the founders of the Royal Society. All the historical groups described here had something in common with Wikipedia, in that all sought to produce non-linear textual systems, whether a library, an academic journal or an integrated collection of books.[2] Each also shared other particular features, such as the universalist aspirations of the Alexandrian librarians or the recruitment of volunteers by the editors of the *Oxford English Dictionary*.

---

1   James J. O'Donnell (1998), *Avatars of the Word: From Papyrus to Cyberspace*, Cambridge, MA: Harvard University Press, 63; these prescient remarks were made some time before the birth of Wikipedia.

2   For non-linear systems see p. 2.

Communities of practice, like other communities, need to be organized. Such a community might arise in response to particular circumstances, as did the Left Book Club, but if it is to survive it has to evolve its own structure and rules, and find ways of dealing with the transaction costs which will inevitably incur. Questions about aims and methods, about membership, about the community's relations with the outside world will arise and need answering. Forceful characters may appear, either to evoke trust and become leaders or to split the community into factions. For a successful and long-lived project, the danger of creeping bureaucracy is also always present, and awareness of this danger has led to the instruction 'If the rules prevent you from improving or maintaining Wikipedia, ignore them' becoming one of the project's fundamental principles.[3] All of the above issues were the subject of constant argument and debate among the various groups described here.

The question arises: what are the salient differences between virtual (Internet) communities of practice, and real ones? According to one commentator, 'an online community [is] a persistent, sustained network of individuals who share and develop an over-lapping knowledge base, set of beliefs, values, history and experiences focused on a common practice and/or mutual enterprise'.[4] Such a definition fits Wikipedia very well. The trouble is, it also seems to fit the historical communities I have chosen. Is the difference between virtual and real that virtual communities subsist in an extension in time and space beyond what we experience directly with our senses? This distinction, between on the one hand virtual communities, and on the other communities in which people actually meet one another physically seems crucial and obvious. Face-to-face communication is fundamentally different from, for instance, the written communication of Wikipedia, because it allows an exchange of both verbal and non-verbal information. Inflections, accent and tone of voice, posture, gestures, even dress, all provide meaningful clues. But on the Internet, as the dog in the famous *New Yorker* cartoon pointed out, no one knows you're a dog.

One difficulty that remains, however, is that by this definition most pre-Internet communities of practice in modern times, including the examples given here, also turn out to be largely virtual, because in many cases their members did not meet, but instead communicated through intermediaries, or by post or telephone. Several of the foreign scientists who wrote to Oldenburg never travelled to London, and many of the writers recruited by Diderot and d'Alembert no doubt never came to see their editors in Paris. The Left Book Club had a network of supporters throughout Britain who were politically active in their own neighbourhoods, but many of them probably never met Gollancz and his staff. These communities were also 'imagined', in Benedict Anderson's terminology: they existed because their

---

3   <http://en.wikipedia.org/wiki/Wikipedia:IAR>.

4   Sasha Barab, 'An Introduction to the Special Issue: Designing for Virtual Communities in the Service of Learning', *Information Society*, vol. 19, no. 3 (July–August 2003), 197–201.

members believed in them as communities, irrespective of how many times they actually encountered each other in the flesh. In fact, according to Anderson, 'all communities larger than primordial villages of face-to-face contact (and perhaps even these) are imagined. Communities are to be distinguished, not by their falsity/genuineness, but by the style in which they are imagined.'[5]

But perhaps one difference between Internet and historical communities is that for the latter, the *possibility* of face-to-face contact is always assumed, so that it would be difficult and unusual for individuals seeking to join such a community to attempt to mask their identities or present themselves as other than they really were.[6] Even if community members did not know the new recruit, they would know someone who did, and personal recommendations might carry the day, as with the Delft draper van Leeuwenhoek when he applied to join the Royal Society.[7] In the case of an Internet community such as Wikipedia, this system no longer applies, and those wishing to do so may preserve total anonymity even when operating in the heart of the community.[8] Becoming a wikipedian is analogous to the immigrant from a far-away country who arrives with only a suitcase and sets out to build a new life, acquire a new language, perhaps even a new name, in order to assist assimilation. In this second incarnation, it may also turn out to be possible to develop a new reputation, but this will depend entirely on achievements in their country of adoption, and not at all on any previous career, however noteworthy.

Another difference is surely that Wikipedia and other social sharing networks are international in a way that was probably out of the question for pre-Internet groups of any kind. In spite of the bias towards more affluent societies, and also towards English as the predominant medium of communication, Wikipedia has a truly global perspective. It has even been suggested that the growing strength of virtual communities in general will one day cause nation states to wither.[9] Be that as it may, there seems a good chance that members of such groups are likely to have an increasing awareness of global issues, an awareness which often goes hand in hand with a certain scepticism towards their own governments and towards the dominant institutions of the 'real' world. Participating in such a widespread community to further a common project surely tends to make one less parochial, less selfish in outlook. Wikipedians are in some sense citizens of the world.

---

5 Benedict Anderson (1983), *Imagined Communities*, London: Verso, 5–7.

6 Yet surely this was just what William Chester Minor, the 'surgeon of Crowthorne' did. He worked for years as a principal assistant to the editor of the *Oxford English Dictionary* while keeping secret the fact that he was an inmate of Broadmoor Criminal Asylum.

7 See p. 25.

8 One may even reinvent oneself, as did User:Esjay, a young student who claimed (on his user page) to have a theology doctorate and a university professorship. He held a trusted position on the English Wikipedia, but was unmasked in 2007, causing considerable embarrassment all round.

9 Joseph Nye (2004), *Soft Power: The Means to Success in World Politics*, Cambridge, MA: Perseus Book Group, 83.

A final difference, and the most significant of all, concerns the degree of collaboration within a group. It is true that the members of all the historical groups described here worked together to some extent, but the technology of the Internet, and specifically of the wiki software, allows a much more intensive form of collaboration than ever before in human history (except within face-to-face communities). Every article in Wikipedia, even when predominantly written by one person, has in all probability been copy-edited, peer-reviewed, argued over or had images added to it by many others. A culture of sharing and participation is the most radical feature of the entire project, and the most promising for the future of the Internet, and hence for our way of life.

Index